THE LAST GREAT GAME

GENE WOJCIECHOWSKI is the senior national columnist for ESPN.com and a contributing writer for *ESPN The Magazine*. Before joining ESPN in 1998, he worked as a sports reporter for *The Dallas Morning News*, the *Los Angeles Times*, the *Chicago Tribune*, and other publications. He has received four Associated Press Sports Editors national writing awards, and his work has been featured in the annual Best American Sports Writing series. He has authored or coauthored eight other books, including *The Bus*, the bestselling autobiography of Jerome Bettis. Wojciechowski lives in Wheaton, Illinois.

Praise for *The Last Great Game*

"Wojciechowski takes you inside the huddles and locker rooms, and inside the heads, of some of the best, most complicated, and most interesting teams, players, and coaches in college basketball history. I was there, and I learned things I didn't know from this book. It is a remarkable read."

—Jay Bilas, ESPN college basketball analyst

"A great book about a great game, but most of all, it's a compelling narrative about the people who produced the most spine-tingling moment in modern college basketball history." —Seth Davis, *Sports Illustrated* and CBS

"Recaptures the energy of one of sport's greatest moments . . . A fitting, illuminating tribute to a game that many believe was the best ever." —*Kirkus Reviews*

"You think you know all the stories? So did I. But I had not heard these."
—*Courier-Journal* (Louisville)

"[A] fascinating portrait . . . This thoroughly enjoyable book will attract college basketball fans across the country, regardless of team loyalties."
—*Booklist* (starred review)

"Excellent reporting." —*The Charlotte Observer*

"Wojciechowski offers a nice blend of past and present perspectives as he tells the story of how an unlikely classic came to be, how it played out, and how it lives on . . . [*The Last Great Game*] is both fun and thorough without getting tedious."
—*The Christian Science Monitor*

"It's Wojciechowski's eye for the people on the edges that make the account especially compelling." —*The New Yorker*

"As a native Kentuckian who has always wanted to peek inside the Big Blue fortress, I read this book with equal parts fascination and awe. I was fascinated with the Madmen world of Rick Pitino, and I was awed by how Gene Wojciechowski was somehow able to drag it out of the shadows and place it under a relentless and unforgettable light." —Bill Plaschke, *Los Angeles Times* sports columnist

ESPN BOOKS

A PLUME BOOK

DUKE 3 KY.
102 00.2 103
PERIOD
OFFICIAL TIME

The Last Great Game

DUKE VS. KENTUCKY AND THE 2.1 SECONDS

THAT CHANGED BASKETBALL

GENE WOJCIECHOWSKI

PLUME
Published by the Penguin Group
Penguin Group (USA) Inc., 375 Hudson Street, New York, New York 10014, U.S.A. •
Penguin Group (Canada), 90 Eglinton Avenue East, Suite 700, Toronto, Ontario, Canada
M4P 2Y3 (a division of Pearson Penguin Canada Inc.) • Penguin Books Ltd., 80 Strand,
London WC2R 0RL, England • Penguin Ireland, 25 St. Stephen's Green, Dublin 2, Ireland
(a division of Penguin Books Ltd.) • Penguin Group (Australia), 707 Collins Street,
Melbourne, Victoria 3008, Australia (a division of Pearson Australia Group Pty. Ltd.) •
Penguin Books India Pvt. Ltd., 11 Community Centre, Panchsheel Park, New Delhi – 110
017, India • Penguin Group (NZ), 67 Apollo Drive, Rosedale, Auckland 0632, New Zealand
(a division of Pearson New Zealand Ltd.) • Penguin Books, Rosebank Office Park, 181 Jan
Smuts Avenue, Parktown North 2193, South Africa • Penguin China, B7 Jiaming Center,
27 East Third Ring Road North, Chaoyang District, Beijing 100020, China

Penguin Books Ltd., Registered Offices: 80 Strand, London WC2R 0RL, England

Published by Plume, a member of Penguin Group (USA) Inc. Previously published in a
hardcover edition by Blue Rider Press.

First Plume Printing, February 2013
10 9 8 7 6 5 4 3 2 1

The Library of Congress has catalogued the Blue Rider Press edition as follows:

Wojciechowski, Gene.
    The last great game : Duke vs. Kentucky and the 2.1 seconds that changed basketball /
Gene Wojciechowski.
        p. cm.
    Summary: "A sports book about the greatest college basketball game ever played"—
Provided by publisher.
    ISBN 978-0-399-15857-5 (hc.)
    ISBN 978-0-452-29895-8 (pbk.)
    1. Duke Blue Devils (Basketball team)—History.   2. Kentucky Wildcats (Basketball
team)—History.   3. Duke University—Basketball—History.   4. University of Kentucky—
Basketball—History.   5. Sports rivalries—United States—History.   I. Title.
    GV885.43.D85W65 2012
    796.323'6309756563—dc23   2011046428

Printed in the United States of America
Original hardcover design by Amanda Dewey

In Memory of Gina

PROLOGUE

March 28, 1992

Dick Vitale couldn't take it anymore. Nobody could. Forget manners. Forget dinner at one of his favorite Italian joints in Sarasota, Florida. Vitale had to see how this game was going to end. Had to. Because it wasn't just a game anymore. It had become a basketball passion play, something epic. He could feel it.

So he got up from his chair and made a beeline for the TV in the restaurant bar. He wasn't alone. Almost everyone else had also left their tables to watch the end of the NCAA Tournament East Regional final in Philadelphia between No. 1–ranked Duke and underdog Kentucky. Standing room only.

It wasn't just the 103–102 score, the bolo tie–thin Kentucky lead, or the 2.1 seconds left in overtime that had led them there. It was more than that. The game had made everyone in the restaurant choose sides.

Vitale, the former college and NBA coach turned ESPN announcer, watched as Kentucky set up its defense. And that's when he noticed.

There's nobody guarding the passer! Kentucky doesn't have anybody on the ball!

Jalen Rose saw it, too. The Michigan freshman point guard sat in the

Wolverines' team hotel in Lexington, Kentucky, site of the Southeast Regional, and stared disbelievingly at the TV screen.

What the . . . ? Go find the biggest Lurch on the bench and stick him in front of Grant Hill on the baseline. Jump up and down like your feet are on fire. Doesn't anybody know that Hill is right-handed? If you force him to run left on the baseline, it's going to be harder for him to make an accurate throw.

P. J. Carlesimo, whose Seton Hall team had lost to Duke on the same Spectrum court two days earlier, watched the game from New Jersey. He was friends with both Duke's Mike Krzyzewski and Kentucky's Rick Pitino—but especially with Pitino. Still, coaches coach, even when they're watching a ball game on TV. And Carlesimo the coach knew Pitino was taking a gamble.

In the 1989 Final Four, Carlesimo's Pirates had needed to convert a long, last-second pass-and-score attempt against Michigan. Michigan coach Steve Fisher put a man on the ball and disrupted the pass attempt ever so slightly, and the Wolverines won the game.

Now Carlesimo's close friend was trying to defy history.

CBS color analyst Len Elmore was courtside at the Spectrum. He saw Hill stand at the baseline. Alone.

Why is Kentucky giving Hill a clear view on the pass?

University of Utah coach Rick Majerus sat in the sports bar of the Little America Hotel in Salt Lake City and immediately took note of Pitino's strategy. Majerus's coaching mentor, the great Al McGuire, had always said to put a guy on the ball. McGuire had a collection of tall, bench-warming stiffs at Marquette that he used for that very purpose.

Majerus could recite the reason by heart: *It's hard to make a pressure pass with pressure on the ball.*

But hey, Pitino was in the East Regional final and Majerus was sitting on a bar stool in Salt Lake, so what did he know, right? Majerus didn't have all the answers, but he knew this: If you don't put a man on the ball, then you definitely have to force Christian Laettner, Duke's star center who was positioned near the opposite end of the court, to work to catch the long inbounds pass. Put a guy in front of him and in back of him. Surely the Wildcats were going to do that against the All-American.

Not much was at stake. Only a trip to the Final Four, that's all. Kentucky and Duke measured themselves by such standards. They wore different shades of blue and represented different constituencies, but they shared an obsession with winning not just games but championships.

Kentucky, the land-grant institution whose basketball reach stretched well beyond the borders of the commonwealth, owned five NCAA championships and 37 Southeastern Conference titles, and constantly played tag with several other elite programs for most all-time victories. Duke, the prestigious private school in Durham known for its bitter and claustrophobic basketball turf war with the University of North Carolina, didn't have the same hoops muscle mass as the Wildcats. But it did have eight Final Four appearances, a coach whose last name was its own spelling bee (Krzyzewski), and a national championship won in 1991.

Now the Blue Devils—and their hopes of back-to-back titles—were 2.1 seconds away from elimination. They would need a miracle.

Everybody in America, including UNLV coach Jerry Tarkanian, was positive that Hill's pass was coming to Laettner. After all, the Vegas coach knew Duke's personnel well. His Runnin' Rebels had humiliated Duke in the 1990 Final Four championship game, only to suffer a jaw-dropping defeat to Krzyzewski's team in the 1991 national semifinals.

Tarkanian watched the official give the ball to Hill and whistle for play to begin. The ball came off Hill's hand. The CBS sideline camera followed its flight. So did Tarkanian and the rest of the country. He was shocked at what he saw next.

They don't have a guy in front of him! thought Tarkanian.

Him.

Laettner.

ONE

Summer 1967

The truth? The truth is Mike Krzyzewski liked the shape of her legs. Actually, he liked her legs, loved her miniskirt, and adored her address: Chicago—his hometown.

It was the Summer of Love. Haight-Ashbury was the capital of the hippie nation. The counterculture manifesto, as written by one of its founding fathers, Timothy Leary, exhorted America's youth to "turn on, tune in, drop out."

But love and LSD had its limits. It also was the summer of rage and riots, when cities such as Detroit and Newark burned and crackled because of the matchstick of racism, when the polarizing war in Vietnam created a deep cleft between young and old, right and left, silent majority and vocal minority.

Krzyzewski was not a hippie and definitely wasn't counterculture. He might have thought LSD was a standardized admissions test. His hair had never covered his ears, nor would it. He was a cadet at the United States Military Academy at West Point, a place where those who were deemed worthy were trained at taxpayer expense to become, if all went well, the best and the brightest of military officers. Duty. Honor.

Country. Those were their core beliefs, not the drugs, sex, and rebellion that belonged to the flower children.

Of course, being an Army man doesn't blind you to a killer pair of legs. So when Krzyzewski stepped into the Lakeview-area apartment of United Airlines stewardess Carol Marsh that summer day in '67, he couldn't help doing a subtle double take.

Marsh shared a one-bedroom apartment, located only blocks away from Wrigley Field, with another woman. Marsh's roommate happened to be the former girlfriend of one of Krzyzewski's buddies. The buddy, who was visiting Krzyzewski in Chicago, arranged to see the former girl-friend and brought Krzyzewski along as his wingman. By pure accident, Marsh was there when they arrived.

Known as "Mickie" to her family and friends, Marsh was a Southern Baptist WASP from Virginia. Krzyzewski, also nicknamed "Mick" or "Mickey" by his boyhood pals, was a Polish Catholic from the north-west side of Chicago. He was home on leave from West Point, having just completed his second year at the Academy. In West Point–speak, he was no longer a Third Classman—a "yuk" or "yearling." Instead, he was transitioning to junior status—a Second Classman or "cow," as they were called.

It didn't take long for Krzyzewski, in his nasally Chicago accent, to ask Marsh out. For their first date, he took her to a Martha Reeves and the Vandellas concert. Marsh loved the Motown group and its conga line of rousing hits such as "Heat Wave," "Dancing in the Street," and "Jimmy Mack." There was no question the cadet had scored major style points with the attractive Marsh.

His leave complete, Krzyzewski reported back to West Point, the achingly beautiful campus located along the Hudson River about 50 miles north of New York City. He later wrote a letter to Marsh, inviting her to a Chicago Bears game at Soldier Field when he returned home that fall. She accepted.

It was at Soldier Field that Krzyzewski mentioned, almost as an afterthought and with little regard for the collateral ego damage, that Marsh had been his third choice for the Bears game. She was livid. Her pride was bruised to the bone, but beyond that her sense of competitiveness was challenged by this socially clumsy yet intriguing cadet. That clumsiness was partly the result of having attended an all-boys high school and the then all-male West Point. He simply didn't know any better.

Krzyzewski was not handsome in a traditional frat-boy way. His nose dominated his face, and you wouldn't use the word *stylish* to describe his civvies wardrobe. He wasn't a guy who'd wear a tennis sweater tied jauntily around his neck. Chances are he didn't own a tennis sweater.

But he had a confidence and an almost naïve sense of right and wrong about him that attracted Marsh. "His blatant honesty was part of it," she says. "He would say things that people shouldn't say."

Romance developed. Marsh eventually transferred to New York to be closer to Krzyzewski. Not long after visiting him at West Point, she received nine yellow roses from him. Nine? Not twelve? Not red? The odd number and color choice stuck with Marsh. Months later, she asked her boyfriend why he had sent nine yellow roses.

"To make you think about it," Krzyzewski said. "Any guy can send you a dozen."

Krzyzewski wasn't any guy. He was born, raised, and hardened in Chicago. His parents were Old Country Poland, as was much of the Wicker Park neighborhood where they lived. His father, William, was an elevator operator for much of his working life at the 38-story Willoughby Tower on tony Michigan Avenue in the Loop. His mother, Emily, was a cleaning woman at the Chicago Athletic Club. He had an older brother, Bill.

Krzyzewski's father, like most of the fathers in the neighborhood, worked all the time. Not just at the Willoughby Tower, but also at the restaurant he would later own (where Mike worked mopping floors, hating every second of it). Each day was a repeat of the previous day:

work, sleep, work. The old man wasn't a drinker, but nearly every night at 7:30 you could find him walking wearily down the street to his favorite place for a cup of coffee.

The relationship between the younger son and his father was occasionally sparse and trying. Krzyzewski loved his father and the father loved his son, but the truth is, they had little in common.

"[Mike] didn't spend a whole lot of time with his dad," says Dennis "Mo" Mlynski, who was (and still is) Krzyzewski's best friend. "There wasn't a lot to share with Mick."

It wasn't a nuanced family, which helps explain Krzyzewski's unfiltered honesty. You worked. You prayed (in sixth grade, Krzyzewski decided he wanted to become a priest). You endured without complaint. There was no misunderstanding about what was expected of you. You would excel, even if that excellence was defined by the way you scrubbed a tile office floor or wore your uniform in the cramped, dreary confines of an Otis elevator.

Order, discipline, respect, religion, and, yes, love were all interwoven in the Krzyzewski family DNA. So was a sense of toughness. Even the Krzyzewski name, with all those concrete hard-sounding consonants, projected a certain no-nonsense ruggedness.

Krzyzewski was always a leader, beginning with his school-yard friends known as "the Columbos." Mick was the one who organized the seventh- and eighth-grade basketball league. Mick was the one who organized everything. He didn't seem older than his friends, just more assertive.

He became a star athlete and star student at Weber High School, an all-boys Catholic school run by the priests and brothers of the Resurrectionist Order in the city's predominantly Polish and Italian neighborhoods on the near Northwest Side. His résumé was impressive: National Honor Society member, senior class vice president, and captain of the Red Horde basketball team. Krzyzewski wasn't necessarily one of the most popular students (football players were first on the Weber food chain), but his classmates and teachers were aware of his potential.

"There were high expectations for him," says Mike Siemplenski, who was the team manager during Krzyzewski's sophomore and junior seasons. "People were demanding of him to perform at his highest level."

This wasn't uncommon at Weber. Students with solid B averages in a subject would occasionally be flunked for a six-week grading period if the teacher thought they were capable of A-level work. Nor did you dare challenge the traditions and conventions of the school. White shirts and ties were mandatory. Students were required each day to load all of their textbooks in a satchel, bring them home, and return with them the next morning. You couldn't study, reasoned the priests, if your books were in your locker.

Corporal punishment was administered regularly, swiftly, and without bias. One priest carried a miniature Louisville Slugger bat with him as he patrolled the hallways. If he saw a student with his hands in his pockets, the priest would crack the bat against the student's shoulder and say, "What are you doing, taking inventory? You've only got two."

One of the priests, a former wrestler who taught Latin, once called two students up to the front of his classroom after he had caught them not paying attention to his lecture. He grabbed each of them by the collar and hung them on hooks attached to the blackboard. They dangled there for several minutes until the priest sent them back to their seats.

Krzyzewski didn't mind Weber's strictness or discipline. He liked order and a system in which effort was rewarded. He had embraced basketball after a failed tryout for the Weber football team. It was the first time as an athlete he had ever been told he wasn't good enough. Krzyzewski loathed failure. He despised losing and had a legendary bad temper to prove it.

So he turned to basketball, a sport that he could practice by himself and constantly invent scenarios in which he'd make the game-winning jump shot or the game-winning free throw (and if he missed the free throw, he'd imagine a lane violation on the opposing team, giving him a second chance). "It was much more than a game to me, and always has been," he said.

His parents understood little about sports. But they understood that their youngest son thrived in a culture that emphasized work ethic, competition, will, and structure—and they approved. It didn't matter that Bill and Emily were unfamiliar with or even uninterested in this distinctly American game. They supported their sons as they always had. If that meant Emily would tend to the house during the day and then clean offices at night—so her boys could afford to go to Catholic schools—then so be it. Meanwhile, for years, no more than two dresses would ever hang in her closet. Always, family first.

Krzyzewski was good but not great at basketball. He became the team's starting point guard and the Chicago Catholic League's leading scorer as a junior and senior, but, says Siemplenski, he was "a little bit slow on defense." He was consumed by the game and took defeat personally, as if somehow it was his fault whenever Weber lost. He was always a high-effort player, but no matter the ferocity or outcome of the game, he was also the first player to seek out his opponent for a postgame handshake. But Krzyzewski was often his own harshest critic.

"Coach would be screaming at him from the sidelines, and Mike would be beside himself because he felt he didn't execute," says Siemplenski.

As his high school career was nearing its end, Krzyzewski faced the always important decision about where to go to college. His ultimate choice would have lifelong ramifications, since it brought him into the orbit of a hyperintense 25-year-old coach named Bob Knight.

Compared to the absurd fawning and attention showered on today's high school prospects, Knight's recruitment of Krzyzewski was almost skeletal. They sat in the Weber cafeteria, ate sandwiches, and discussed Krzyzewski's future. Later that night, the young Army coach visited Bill and Emily at the apartment on West Cortez Street. Knight wanted players who were committed, tough, and mentally nimble. He needed them to be able to translate his basketball theory and language to the court. Krzyzewski could do that.

But West Point wasn't his first choice. Or second. Or third. He wanted to stay closer to home and play for a school in the Big Ten Conference. Creighton, the Jesuit university located in Omaha, Nebraska, was also on Krzyzewski's short list. So he told Knight no.

It was an astounding decision, mostly because Krzyzewski had few options. Exactly zero Big Ten programs were actively recruiting him (or would). Creighton also took a pass. A coach from the University of Detroit Mercy was interested in signing him, and asked Krzyzewski to meet him on the South Side of the city, all the way down at 95th and Western. Krzyzewski, insulted that the coach wasn't willing to visit him or his family, immediately ended the recruitment.

But his dismissal of the West Point opportunity confounded his parents the most. This nice, young Coach Knight had traveled all the way from New York to offer their son a chance to attend the *United States Military Academy*—just think, a Krzyzewski at West Point!—and he hadn't jumped at the chance? How could their son be such a bright boy and yet so foolish? Didn't he understand that his own parents had no high school diplomas, that a Polish surname was considered a liability?

(Krzyzewski's father was so sensitive about his immigrant status and the stigma of being categorized as a "DP," for Displaced Person—or "Dumb Polack," as they were derisively called—that he often used Bill "Kross" as an alias. Neither of the two Krzyzewski boys was taught or encouraged to speak Polish in the house, for fear that they would develop Polish accents.)

One of the finest educational institutions in the country, perhaps the world, wanted him to join its elite club, and he didn't want in? This wasn't merely an opportunity; it was a social advantage—a rarity if you were a Krzyzewski.

Dennis Mlynski's family lived a block and a half away on Leavitt Street. One day, as they sat on the fence outside Mlynski's apartment building, Krzyzewski mentioned that his parents were pressuring him to attend West Point.

"West Point?" said Mlynski. "Where's that? Isn't that the school where all the presidents went to?"

Krzyzewski heard his parents' conversations around the kitchen table, where they would sit each morning and discuss the topic of the day. These days it was impossible not to hear them chattering away in Polish and then, for their son's benefit, lapsing briefly into English and saying, "Stupid, Mike!"—just so there wasn't any confusion about the thrust of the conversation and their stance on the issue.

After two weeks of listening to his parents' unsubtle urging, Krzyzewski relented. He couldn't disappoint Bill and Emily, especially Emily. Family first.

"I'll go to West Point," he told them. "I'll do it."

The U.S. Military Academy can be a place of profound loneliness, pressure, and incalculable stress. And it was all those for Krzyzewski. He went to West Point, but he almost didn't stay. Several times during his first year he considered quitting and returning to Chicago. He missed his family and friends, but he especially missed his freedom. When Mlynski and another friend visited him during his plebe year, Krzyzewski was waiting for them at the gate in his cadet uniform, tears somersaulting down his cheeks. "He was so happy to see a friend," Mlynski says.

Krzyzewski was accustomed to discipline. His family and a Catholic education had made sure of that. He understood the need for boundaries and rules, but what he didn't understand—and what he would come to resent, even hate at West Point—were rules written without involving those who would have to abide by them. He didn't see the logic of it.

He survived his first year, and as time passed his occasional urge to quit and go home faded. Basketball helped.

During his three varsity seasons at Army, Krzyzewski was never among the team's leading scorers (averaging 5.3 points as a sophomore, 6.4 as a junior, 6.7 as a senior). He wasn't the Black Knights' best player, but he might have been their most dependable. He was consistent but not flashy. He was controlled and efficient, but there was nothing that suggested basketball artistry. He was an extension of Knight, which is to say he was a mouse on a treadmill, always chasing after perfection and never letting up. In Krzyzewski, Knight found someone who shared his craving for excellence. It was hard to say which drove them most: the longing for victory or the dread and ache of defeat.

Krzyzewski, more than any other player on the Army roster, could handle Knight's furnace blasts of criticism and anger. He knew Knight was using him as a conduit to the rest of the team, accepted his role as the designated yellee, and separated the message from the messenger like slag from iron ore.

In the 1967, '68, and '69 Army team photos, there is no hint of a smile on Krzyzewski's black-and-white face. He wore Chuck Taylors and a look of determination. In his junior year, Army recorded its first-ever 20-win regular season and earned a berth in the National Invitation Tournament, when the NIT still meant something. The next season, with Krzyzewski as senior captain, the Black Knights won 18 games, including a 54–52 win against Bradley at the Kentucky Invitational Tournament on December 20. Krzyzewski hit two late free throws, despite an injured eye, to clinch the victory. The next evening, after a 15-point loss to Kentucky in the championship game, Knight kicked a locker in anger and spat on the second-place trophy in disgust. Happy holidays.

Army again was selected for the NIT and reached the semifinals— no small feat for a service academy. It remains the second-best ever postseason showing for Army. At least as important: Army beat Navy, as it had during each of Krzyzewski's three seasons on the varsity.

After that victory against the Midshipmen, on Saturday, March 1, 1969, Krzyzewski was presented with the game ball. Later that same day, a phone call came from Chicago: his father had suffered a cerebral hemorrhage. William Krzyzewski was dead by the time Mike could get home.

Bob Knight, who preached loyalty to his players, now practiced it. He left the team and followed his senior captain back to the Chicago apartment where he had recruited Krzyzewski, or more accurately, Krzyzewski's parents. Knight stayed for three days. He sat with the grieving Emily for hours at a time in the family kitchen. "It was as if nothing else mattered to him right then other than helping my mom and me," Krzyzewski told author John Feinstein years later.

Bill's death rocked the family, but Knight's presence was a godsend—and something Krzyzewski would never forget. Knight had been unbearably hard on Krzyzewski, but that was basketball. When it truly mattered, Knight was there for him and his family.

On the afternoon of June 4, 1969, Bill Krzyzewski's younger son, the one who had been reluctant to even consider West Point, received his bachelor of science degree, his Second Lieutenant bars, and his wedding ring. Graduation ceremony at noon; marriage ceremony at the West Point Chapel at five.

His brother Bill Jr. was the best man, and Mlynski was in the wedding party (Krzyzewski presented Mlynski with a miniature bust of a West Point cadet as a present). Emily watched proudly as the newly commissioned officer and his wife, Mickie, exited the chapel, walking under an arch of shined silver sabers to begin their lives together.

Krzyzewski served in the U.S. Army for five years and resigned as a captain in 1974. He liked the Army, but he loved basketball more. He then enlisted as a graduate assistant on Knight's Indiana University coaching staff for the '75 season. He was 26, married with a young daughter. It was the beginning of a coaching odyssey.

"What I recognized that year was how all-consuming the job is," says Mickie, who slowly sanded down some of the jagged edges of Krzyzewski's personality. "The family can be put on the back burner forever and ever and you end up not being together. I told him that if this was going to be his career, I was going to be part of it. He agreed, but this was a time when women didn't get to be part of that."

At West Point, coach Dan Dougherty was putting the finishing touches on a 3–22 season (wins only against Scranton, Iona, and Pitt-Johnstown) that would cost him his job. Thanks to both power broker Knight's recommendation and Krzyzewski's convincing interview, Army hired one of its own.

Krzyzewski's 1976 Army team finished 11–14; the program he had just left, Indiana, went undefeated and won the national championship. In 1977, Krzyzewski's Black Knights won 20 games and followed it up with 19 victories and an NIT appearance in 1978. He was a coach on the rise. And then he wasn't.

Army won 14 games in 1979, but then dropped to 9–17 in 1980. Krzyzewski's coaching career was beginning to track the wrong way.

Not long after the regular season ended, the phone rang at the Krzyzewski house. Mickie answered.

"This is Tom Butters," said the caller in a booming, authoritative voice. "I have the awesome responsibility of hiring the next basketball coach for Duke University."

A shocked Mickie said, "And you're talking to me?"

Duke had reached the national championship game two years earlier (losing to Kentucky), and was again on an NCAA Tournament run. But Bill Foster, the popular coach who took the Blue Devils to the title game in 1978, had already accepted a job to coach South Carolina, effective at season's end. His decision prompted instant predictions of doom for Duke.

"If he leaves, Duke has nothing left," Art Chansky, *Durham Morning Herald* sports editor, told the *Washington Post*. "Its whole athletic program is down the tubes. He's the only winner they have over there."

Butters had recently hired a former Duke basketball player named Steve Vacendak to join the athletic department staff. A captain on Vic Bubas's Final Four team in 1966 (the Blue Devils lost to Kentucky in the national semifinal game), Vacendak was not yet officially on the university payroll. That didn't stop Butters from asking him to assist in the coaching search.

"What are you looking for?" said Vacendak.

"I'm looking for someone who is the best defensive coach in the country," Butters said. "Because I believe you win most games on defense. If we can be successful against the team eight miles down the road [Dean Smith's mighty North Carolina program], then we are a national power. That's all we have to do."

Butters wanted Vacendak's help, but Butters was essentially a one-man search committee. The decision was going to be all his, which is how he wanted it. A former Pittsburgh Pirates pitcher, Butters came to Duke in 1967 as director of special events, was named AD in 1977, and had earned a reputation for being decisive, independent, fearless, and soaked in integrity.

He initially considered contacting the legendary Jack Hartman about the Duke opening. Hartman, then a 55-year-old coach at Kansas State, would eventually retire as one of the best coaches never to have won an NCAA title. He was everything Butters admired: ethical, loyal, a man of high character. His teams played unselfishly, they defended, and they won.

"I was really fascinated by him," says Butters. "To this day he doesn't know that, because I never talked to him."

Instead, Butters put together a list of possible candidates that included Mississippi's Bob Weltlich, Duke assistant Bob Wenzel, Old Dominion's Paul Webb, and one other name: Mike Krzyzewski.

Vacendak lobbied hard for Krzyzewski, telling Butters, "I think he's one of the best young defensive coaches in America."

But the best young defensive coach in America was coming off a horrible 9-win season at Army. How was Butters going to sell that to his alums, to his big-money donors, to his school president, and to any prominent recruits? The Duke AD called Bob Knight, whom he had long valued for his bullshit-free opinions. Knight could be dictatorial, rude, and crude. But he was also a brilliant basketball tactician and strategist, bright, loyal to a fault, and, when so moved, charming. When asked about coaching candidates, Knight often campaigned for his own coaching protégés. This time he began selling some of his favorites to Butters: Weltlich, Tennessee's Don DeVoe, and Oklahoma's Dave Bliss.

"What about Mike Krzyzewski?" Butters said.

Butters knew that Knight wouldn't mislead him. If Butters was seriously going to consider an Army coach coming off a 9–17 season, he wanted to hear Knight's unvarnished truth. Knight was many things, but he wasn't a liar.

"Butters, you have always liked my style of coaching," said Knight. "This is a man who has all my good qualities and none of my bad ones."

Knight actually was concerned about one of his boys taking the Duke coaching job. He knew Butters was an honorable athletic director, that academics was a priority at Duke, and that Krzyzewski was ready to take the next step in his career. But he thought Krzyzewski was better suited for the opening at Iowa State, which had just dismissed Lynn Nance. The pressure to win there wouldn't be as immediate and as intense as it would be at Duke, where Blue Devils fans had been spoiled by Foster. But Butters asked for his opinion, so Knight gave it to him.

The recommendation prompted Butters to make that first surprising phone call to the Krzyzewski house in New York. They arranged to meet in West Lafayette, Indiana, where Duke won its second-round NCAA Tournament game against Pennsylvania. Krzyzewski and Butters spoke for several hours, but the Duke AD sent him back to West Point without an offer.

Meanwhile, Duke advanced to the Mideast Regional in Lexington, Kentucky, where it would play (and win) its regional semifinal game against Kentucky. While there, Butters called Krzyzewski and asked him to come to the tournament site for another interview.

"We got 13 inches of snow, but I'll figure out a way to get there," Krzyzewski said.

This time Butters and Krzyzewski spoke for nearly five hours before the interview ended again without a hint of an offer. Butters couldn't get that dreadful 9–17 record out of his head, but he also couldn't bring himself to cross Krzyzewski's name off the short list. If anything, the 33-year-old Krzyzewski was moving *up* the list. "Aside from his record," says Butters, "he had all of the qualities I was looking for."

Duke lost to Purdue in the regional final, and Butters returned home and brought in his finalists: Weltlich, Wenzel, Webb, and Krzyzewski. He had asked Krzyzewski to bring Mickie on the trip to Durham (after all, he told Krzyzewski, Duke was hiring not a man but a family) and arranged for the Army coach to be the last candidate to speak to the Duke athletic council: Butters, school senior vice president Chuck Huestis, and chancellor Ken Pye.

The interviews were held at Huestis's home. The Krzyzewskis spoke to the council, answered a barrage of questions, and then were taken to the airport. Afterward, the three council members and Vacendak sat at Huestis's kitchen table, and Pye and Huestis gave Butters the go-ahead to hire any of the four candidates.

Butters didn't hesitate. He turned to Vacendak and told him, "Get to the airport. Don't let [Krzyzewski] get on that plane."

"My god, you're not going to interview him again."

"No, I'm going to hire him."

Krzyzewski and Mickie were scheduled to take separate flights: Mickie to Washington, D.C., to see her parents and retrieve her children; Krzyzewski to New York and West Point. After arriving at her parents' home, Mickie called the house at West Point (this was the pre-cell-phone age). No answer. She called again. And again. And again. Worried, she called the airline and was assured that the flight to New York had landed safely.

Mickie was nervous. This was unlike her husband not to call and check in. It wasn't until midnight that the phone rang. It was Krzyzewski.

"You okay?" Mickie said.

"Yes, I'm fine," Krzyzewski said. "Just before I got on the plane I was paged. The people from Duke wanted to ask me one more question."

Mickie had a meltdown. Another question? You've got to be kidding. How many questions did these people need to ask? Why didn't they ask their precious question during one of the *three* interviews they had already done? Seriously, the nerve of these people.

Krzyzewski let her vent. Then he told her the question.

"They wanted to ask me if I would take the job."

Krzyzewski had returned to Huestis's home, been offered the coaching position, and had accepted the offer.

"How much are you going to get paid?" said Mickie.

Silence.

"Mike? How much are you going to get paid?"

More silence and then finally, "I don't know. I didn't ask."

Krzyzewski had taken the job without bothering to discuss the salary. There were no agents involved. He had taken a leap of faith, but so had Butters and Duke.

On March 18, 1980, Butters cleared his throat, stepped to the front of a room at the on-campus Alumni House, and introduced the new Blue Devils basketball coach to the local media.

"He is my first choice," said Butters, almost defiantly.

The coach's name was Krzyzewski, which was confusing enough. Or as a local sports anchor said as he fumbled through the pronunciation on the evening broadcast, "Mike Prishevski."

Prishevski's first-year salary: $40,000.

The hiring was met with disbelief by ACC observers and many Duke followers. If the obscure Krzyzewski was Butters's first choice, they said, who was number two—the Coast Guard Academy coach? The *New*

York Times was so impressed that it devoted 14 words to the announcement. Even the Duke student newspaper, *The Chronicle*, mocked the hiring. Read the front page headline: *Krzyzewski: this is not a typo.*

North Carolina, only eight miles away, had the great Dean Smith. North Carolina State had just hired a human caffeine pill named Jim Valvano. Smith and Valvano were NCAA Tournament regulars. Meanwhile, Krzyzewski was fresh off that 9-win season at Army, with more than half of those victories coming against programs even more obscure than Krzyzewski: Manhattanville, Lycoming, Merchant Marine Academy, Rensselaer Polytechnic Institute, and Rochester.

In one day's time Krzyzewski had gone from the flyweight division to the heavyweight, from the west bank of the Hudson River to fabled Tobacco Road and the cutthroat ACC.

"First of all," said the new coach to the media, "it's K-R-Z-Y-Z-E-W-S-K-I. If you think that's bad, it was a lot worse before I changed it."

Kenny Dennard, a carefree 6'8" junior forward for Duke, was on spring break and drinking a mai tai at the Pier House Resort bar in Key West, Florida, when he glanced at the TV screen and saw that he had a new coach. The new coach was the same guy who had tried to recruit him to Army.

Dennard knew he wasn't a West Point kind of guy. Now, through nothing other than blind fate, Dennard would play for Krzyzewski.

Krzyzewski wasn't quite Knight Jr., but he had a military edge to him and a biting sarcasm; he was familiar with all the four-letter words and used them often. "This was the late '70s, early '80s," says Dennard. "Nobody had this open, Oprah, investigate-your-feelings thing going. It was Robby Benson's coach in *One on One*.... [Krzyzewski] wasn't Oprah-like at all."

With seniors Dennard and All-American Gene Banks, Duke finished 17–13 in Krzyzewski's first season, but missed the NCAA Tournament and was left to accept a berth in the lesser-regarded NIT.

While the Blue Devils settled for the NIT, Smith's North Carolina team, which lost to Duke in its final regular-season contest, went on to reach the NCAA championship game, where it played Indiana. Krzyzewski was not unhappy when his mentor Knight and the Hoosiers defeated the Tar Heels.

In 1982, Duke staggered to a 10–17 record. Krzyzewski's emotions poured out when he cried in the locker-room shower after a 17-point loss at Princeton that dropped Duke to 1–4. Meanwhile, in Chapel Hill, a baby-faced freshman assassin named Michael Jordan helped give Smith his first NCAA championship.

There was pandemonium and joy on Franklin Street, the celebration area of choice for Carolina students and followers. At Duke there was embarrassment, shame, and growing dissatisfaction with Krzyzewski.

The situation did not improve the following season, when Carolina tied for first in the ACC and reached the Elite Eight of the NCAA Tournament, while Valvano led N.C. State to an improbable national title.

Duke finished 11–17 overall and 3–11 in the conference, losing by 21 and 24 points to Carolina and by a mind-numbing 43 points to Virginia in the ACC tournament. After the Virginia defeat, Mickie Krzyzewski accidentally wandered into the Duke hospitality suite at the team hotel. It was there that she realized that a group of "concerned" Iron Dukes—the fund-raising and booster arm of the athletic program—had convened an impromptu meeting. The first and only item on the agenda: Fire Krzyzewski.

Three years in Durham had brought zero NCAA Tournament appearances, a single-season record for losses, and a 1–6 mark against North Carolina. Some opposing coaches were telling Duke recruits that Krzyzewski could be dismissed any day. Krzyzewski's oldest daughter, Debbie, was even taunted at school. She called home in tears, asking Daddy to pick her up, but found no sympathy; Krzyzewski said he would give her a Duke T-shirt to wear to school the next day. "A Krzyzewski," he told her, "doesn't back away from something like that."

Meanwhile, Butters's office was flooded with phone calls and letters demanding that he take immediate action. One prominent Blue Devils booster wrote, "Why don't you hire an American coach?"

In short, says Butters, "Everybody wants his ass and my ass out of Durham, North Carolina."

Butters wasn't going to quit. "You can't succeed while running scared," he says. And Krzyzewski wasn't going to quit. To do so would be a betrayal of everything he had learned from his parents, at Weber High, and at West Point, from Knight, and from his own family. He had signed a handful of high school recruits—Johnny Dawkins, Jay Bilas, Mark Alarie, David Henderson, and Bill Jackman—whom he was convinced would give his program a much needed infusion of blue-chip talent. And he was right.

In 1984, Duke won its first 8 games and 15 of its first 16, including a payback victory against Virginia. But then came four consecutive ACC losses, and the anti-Krzyzewski drumbeat grew deafening again.

Butters summoned Krzyzewski to his office. When Krzyzewski arrived, Butters immediately noticed what poker players call a "tell," a gesture or facial expression that tips a player's hand. Krzyzewski's tell was his mouth. It was small to begin with, and Butters had noticed that when Krzyzewski was especially angry about a situation, it would get even smaller and more tightly pursed. As Krzyzewski sat down in Butters's office, the Duke AD realized that "you couldn't have driven a tenpenny nail between his lips."

Said Butters: "Mike, we got a problem."

Krzyzewski said nothing.

Butters continued. "The problem is we've got a public that doesn't know how good you are. We've got a press that's too damn dumb to tell them how good you are. But my greatest problem is that I've got a coach who I'm not sure knows how good he is."

And with that, Butters handed Krzyzewski a new five-year contract.

Krzyzewski stared at the contract in disbelief. Tears began streaming down his face.

"Tom, you don't have to do this," said Krzyzewski.

"Coach, on the contrary, I not only need to do it, I need to do it right now."

Butters received death threats after the contract extension was made public. But Krzyzewski and those freshmen-turned-sophomores finished 24–10 that season and reached the NCAA Tournament. Two seasons later they would play for the national championship.

"And the rest is history," says Butters. "I've been credited with that decision for 25 years, but it was a no-brainer. When you looked [at those freshmen] . . . the handwriting was on the wall for anyone who knew anything about basketball. I would love to take credit for making a brilliant move, but I made the move that anyone sitting in my seat would have made."

But not even Butters could have envisioned what would come next. He knew he had brought in a great coach, but he hardly suspected he had hired a dynasty maker.

TWO

December 31, 1988

A s C. M. Newton steered his Pontiac sedan onto Interstate 65 North, there was little about the two-hour drive from Nashville, Tennessee, to Elizabethtown, Kentucky, that excited the Vanderbilt basketball coach. If anything, he found himself second-guessing his decision to make the trip.

A few days earlier Newton had received a phone call from Dr. David Roselle, president of the University of Kentucky. Roselle was deep in the middle of a growing crisis. UK's famed basketball program, the pride of the commonwealth, was under siege by the NCAA for alleged rules violations and academic fraud. Ultrapopular but ineffective athletic director Cliff Hagan had been forced to resign two months earlier after a 13-year reign; Roselle had exerted much of the force. The Wildcats were in the process of setting a record for most losses in a single UK season, and coach Eddie Sutton's grip on his job was as thin as one of the permed hairs on his head.

Reports of rules abuses had been bubbling to the surface for years. The *Lexington Herald-Leader* had uncovered widespread cheating in 1985, earning the newspaper a Pulitzer Prize and the scorn of many

Kentucky fans. It also earned a bullet hole through one of the newspaper's office windows.

Some fans thought the allegations were the convenient work of rival SEC schools jealous of Kentucky's 5 NCAA championships, its record 32 NCAA Tournament appearances, its status as a member of basketball's holy trinity (along with Kansas and North Carolina), its 33 All-Americans, its 36 SEC titles, its massive Rupp Arena, and its luxurious player dorm, Wildcat Lodge.

There *was* jealousy among coaches in the conference and around the country. But there was also indignation and a feeling that Kentucky, because of its stature, had gotten away with more than most programs. Boosters, players, and coaches had gotten sloppy and arrogant—or had simply thought they were immune to detection and punishment. Now it was payback time.

By 1989, NCAA investigators had uncovered multiple major violations. It wasn't merely a whiff of scandal, it was a stench. A Kentucky assistant coach named Dwane Casey stood accused of sending $1,000 in an Emery Worldwide package to the father of Wildcats recruit Chris Mills. Eric Manuel, a blue-chip recruit who would later play as a UK freshman, was accused of cheating on a standardized entrance test. Those were the biggies. In all, the NCAA said Kentucky was guilty of 18 rules infractions.

Roselle needed more than a new athletic director. He needed someone with strong Kentucky ties, an impeccable reputation, unquestioned credibility within the college basketball community, and the willingness to don a haz-mat suit and rid the UK hoops program of all its radioactive cargo. He needed Charles Martin Newton.

Newton wasn't interested. First of all, he didn't know David Roselle from Pete Rozelle, but he did know Cliff Hagan. Hagan and Newton had played on the Adolph Rupp–coached Kentucky team that won the 1951 NCAA championship. In the official team photo, Newton is seated in the second row next to Hagan, who is next to the great Rupp.

Hagan was a star, an All-American whose UK jersey was later retired. Newton was a self-described role player—meaning, he liked to joke, that he was the guy who rolled out the balls at the beginning of practice. He had no desire to become a full-time administrator, especially one hired to replace a friend he had known for four decades. Newton thought Hagan had been made something of a scapegoat. The problem at Kentucky wasn't Hagan, thought Newton, it was the coaching staff.

Plus, Newton was happy and comfortable at Vanderbilt, where he was associate athletic director as well as basketball coach. He was 58 years old and content to end his career at a place that valued wins but also valued academics and rule books. NCAA investigators probably couldn't tell you where Vanderbilt's Nashville campus was. In Lexington, they practically needed apartment leases.

Newton told Roselle all these things on the phone, and the UK president listened politely before playing his trump card. "I'm in a difficult situation," Roselle said to him. "You're an alum. I think you owe me a sit-down."

So out of obligation and perhaps a little bit of guilt, Newton drove north that late December day in his Vanderbilt-issued car. Roselle, who was driving from Lexington, had made all the arrangements for the secret meeting, including a call to the president of Elizabethtown Community and Technical College (at the time, Roselle also oversaw the state's 15 community college campuses). His instructions to the ECTC president were simple: Leave your office door unlocked, make sure nobody is there, and then make yourself scarce. Roselle didn't say why he needed the office. He wanted no leaks to the media, so only four people (Newton; Newton's wife, Evelyn; Roselle; and Southeastern Conference commissioner Roy Kramer) knew about the rendezvous.

The first 30 minutes of the meeting did not go well. Roselle's sales pitch was compelling, but it wasn't convincing. He could feel his chances slipping away.

But the longer the two men talked, the more Roselle kept pounding home a central theme: There was a difference between being wanted and being needed. Kentucky needed one of its own to clean up its basketball mess. Hagan had been a fine representative of the school, but he was from the Paleozoic Era of athletic directors, when the extent of their duties were handing out plaques, telling remember-when stories to boosters, and tinkering with game schedules. "[Hagan] didn't get it that he was running a big organization," says Roselle.

Roselle told Newton he would be given the keys to the athletic department and freedom to do whatever he thought necessary. So much was at stake: a program's legacy, a school's reputation, nothing less than the future of Kentucky basketball. Newton, Roselle said, could be the difference between UK's ruin or its redemption.

Newton walked into that community college office thinking no, but he walked out of it saying yes. There would be a more formal meeting in early January with UK committee members, but for all intents and purposes the job was Newton's. Roselle had appealed to Newton's sense of Kentucky loyalty but also to his ego: In the end, Newton was seduced by the monumental challenge of repairing college basketball's most dysfunctional machine.

On January 24, 1989, Roselle announced that Newton would become Kentucky's new athletic director, effective the first of April. Newton had his own season to finish at Vanderbilt, and Roselle had some additional work to do before the start date. High on Roselle's list was squeezing out Sutton, whom he considered a liability and at least an accomplice in Kentucky's basketball woes. Roselle wanted Newton to arrive in Lexington without having to fire a coach he had just faced during the regular season.

Sutton was enough of a pragmatist to understand his dilemma. He still had friends in high places, but Hagan was gone and it was obvious that Roselle wasn't an ally. "The new president I don't think was as enthusiastic about basketball as he should have been," says Sutton.

Newton signed a five-year deal worth a little more than $500,000, and his hiring was hailed statewide and nationwide. The winner of more than 500 games at Transylvania (located in Lexington), Alabama, and Vanderbilt, Newton had many friends in the coaching profession. He was a Southern gentleman whose word was as solid as reinforced concrete. His calm, honest demeanor was exactly what a panicked and jittery Big Blue Nation needed.

Kentucky's season ended March 10 at the SEC tournament in Knoxville, Tennessee, with a 14-point loss to Vanderbilt and its SEC Coach of the Year and imminent UK AD, Newton. Afterward, Chris Mills stood in the Kentucky locker room and apologized to his teammates for being the centerpiece of the season-long controversy and investigation.

Newton's Commodores advanced to the NCAA Tournament, while 13–19 Kentucky suffered its first losing record in 62 seasons and advanced to the NCAA Committee on Infractions. Nine days later, much to the displeasure of Kentucky governor Wallace Wilkinson (one of the coach's friends in high places), Roselle forced Sutton to resign.

"Who knew if Kentucky would ever be Kentucky again?" says *Herald-Leader* sportswriter Jerry Tipton, who began covering the team in 1981.

Roselle knew Kentucky's program was a candidate for the NCAA's so-called death penalty, a one- or two-year forced closure of a program guilty of repeated major violations. He had ordered an internal investigation of the program a year earlier, telling its lead man, former Kentucky Court of Appeals judge Jim Parks, "If it's out there, find it."

Parks found it. Lots of it. The evidence was so overpowering that Newton began preparing the Kentucky faithful for the worst. He told the Lexington Rotary Club in late April, "If we are found guilty of a major violation, there will be serious penalties. In my opinion, there will be some findings of major violations. . . . We need your support through some tough times, and believe me, there are going to be some tough times."

Newton had seen such a scandal before. In 1952, the year he earned his bachelor's degree from Kentucky, the NCAA shuttered UK basketball for a full season because of points-shaving allegations and payments to players. He also witnessed the recuperative powers of the program; the next year, UK finished the regular season ranked No. 1 in the country, and in 1958 it won its fourth national championship.

Newton was selling reality to Kentucky fans. But he also was selling optimism. The program would recover if—and only if—he hired the right coach. But if he screwed this up, Kentucky could suffer the same fate UCLA did in the post–John Wooden era. Wooden led the Bruins to 10 national titles, including 7 consecutive championships in the late 1960s and early 1970s. His final championship came in 1975, the year he retired. It would take 20 years and six different coaches before the Bruins won another national title.

Newton's mandate was simple but also imposing: *Don't screw it up*. Roselle had done his part and disposed of Sutton. Now it was up to Newton to find a successor. The right one.

His first choice was New York Knicks coach Rick Pitino, an ultra-demanding 36-year-old Long Islander with an accent as thick as rush-hour traffic. He had been recommended to Newton by Dave Gavitt, the Big East Conference commissioner and former Providence College coach. Gavitt's endorsement carried weight and gravitas. It also made sense.

Pitino was born on September 18, 1952, and grew up in Oyster Bay, New York. He was a "Dom's Guy"—a graduate of St. Dominic High School. It was a close-knit community, and word traveled fast when it came to basketball. And the word was that this kid Pitino, a little guard with a shoot-first mentality, was worth watching play at Oyster Bay's Roosevelt Park. (There was no AAU stranglehold back then; kids actually played in public parks and liked it.)

Pitino would become a regular at a newly formed basketball camp in Honesdale, Pennsylvania, called Five-Star, co-owned and run by a gravelly voiced, cigarette-smoking New Yorker named Howard Garfinkel—"Garf" to everyone who knew him. Garf, who had made his bones as a basketball talent evaluator, liked the Italian kid from out on the Island. He even invited Pitino back as a "graduate" camper after high school.

Pitino had enough skills to get a full ride at the University of Massachusetts, where he averaged 5.2 points and 6.5 assists as a senior. But when the Minutemen lost to Jacksonville in the National Invitation Tournament at Madison Square Garden in March 1974, Pitino's college career was finished. The NBA wasn't an option, so Pitino planned to play pro ball in Italy.

After the loss, Pitino and Garfinkel met at a hotel across the street from the Garden. Pitino told Garfinkel about his plans to play overseas.

"Don't do that," said Garfinkel. "You were born to coach."

Pitino, though a devout student of the game, wasn't convinced. For starters, he didn't have any coaching job prospects.

At that exact moment, Garfinkel recognized a familiar face in the same hotel: University of Hawaii coach Bruce O'Neil, whose team also was playing in the NIT. O'Neil was finishing his first year at Hawaii.

"Rick, sit here a minute," said Garfinkel. "I'll be right back."

Garfinkel approached O'Neil.

"You wouldn't happen to have a job open, would you?"

"I do," said O'Neil. "I need a grad assistant."

"You got him," said Garfinkel, who introduced Pitino to the Hawaii coach.

Arrivederci, Italy. *Aloha*, Honolulu.

Pitino moved steadily up the coaching food chain: two years as an assistant at Hawaii; two years as an assistant at Syracuse; five years as head coach at Boston University, where he inherited an 0–15 team and won 17 games the next season, and later took his team to the NCAA Tournament; two years as an assistant coach for Hubie Brown and the Knicks; two years as a head coach at Providence, where he led the Friars to the Final Four in 1987. After the turnaround at Providence, the

Knicks offered him their head coaching job. It was perfect—a New York kid coaching the New York Knicks.

Pitino's 1988 Knicks team won 38 games, a 14-victory improvement from a season earlier. His 1989 team, featuring Patrick Ewing, Charles Oakley, and Mark Jackson, was on its way to a 52-win season, the franchise's first division title since 1971, and an NBA playoff appearance. Newton called in early April: Would Pitino mind if Newton came to New York and discussed the Kentucky opening with him?

If it were any other athletic director and any other school, Pitino would have said no. It wasn't that he wanted the job—he didn't—but out of respect to Newton (and, okay, a bit of curiosity on his part), Pitino invited the Kentucky AD to his home in Bedford, New York, located about 45 minutes from Manhattan.

Newton had never been to Bedford. When he thought of New York, he thought skyscrapers, Madison Square Garden, the subway. He didn't think of the bucolic, moneyed charm of upper Westchester County. Part of his sales pitch was built around wowing Pitino with the appeal of living in Lexington. But as Newton made his way to Bedford, past the mansions and estates of Pitino's neighborhood, it was apparent that Lexington had some serious competition. Bedford was gorgeous. So was Pitino's home.

Pitino had already briefed his wife, Joanne, about the visit. Newton, he said, was going to drench them with Southern charm. He was going to blow them away with the many reasons why Kentucky was the Roman Empire of college basketball and why Pitino should be its Julius Caesar. He was going to be irresistible. Pitino told Joanne not to show any emotion during the hard sell. A nod of the head, a smile, an excited look would only encourage Newton.

This would not be a problem, since Joanne had no intention of moving her family (again), and certainly not to Kentucky. The only thing she knew about the Mason-Dixon Line was that she wanted to be on the north side of it. She had made it clear that if Pitino wanted to coach college ball, he should have stayed at Providence.

Newton arrived at the house. As he walked toward the front door, he made a decision that would alter the basketball future of Kentucky: He decided to try to talk Pitino *out* of taking the job.

Pitino, Joanne, and Newton sat down. Newton looked around the finely appointed home and said in that soft drawl of his, "I don't know what I'm doing here. You've got a Mercedes out there. You've got this beautiful house. You're the coach of the Knicks. To be honest with you, after driving through this neighborhood, I don't know why the head coach of the Knicks would ever want to come coach at Kentucky."

Pitino laughed. "Well, C.M., then why are you here?"

"Well," said Newton, "Dave Gavitt told me to take a shot to see if you'd be interested. But we've got these problems with the NCAA and it's going to be pretty serious. We've got no players. Your players would be guys I was trying to recruit at Vanderbilt, and they're marginal at best. And the expectations of the fans are not going to change. You've got it going right now with the Knicks, so it's not a very attractive situation."

Joanne stood up. She had heard enough.

"Coach Newton, it's really an honor meeting you," she said. "My husband has told me so many great things about you. I've got to go run some errands and I'm sure you want to talk to Rick alone."

Then she turned to her husband. "Uh, Rick, can you walk me out?"

Once at the front door—and out of Newton's earshot—Joanne said, "I just had to leave because I was *so* blown away with that program. Boy, he sure wowed us. So if you don't mind, I'm going shopping."

Pitino knew his wife's sense of humor. He smiled. There was no way they were going to Lexington.

Pitino returned to the room. It was time to put Newton out of his misery.

"C.M., you kind of paint a bleak picture of the place."

"Rick, it is bleak. The media is very negative and we're taking a lot of hits. We need a shot of adrenaline."

Pitino knew he was supposed to be the adrenaline. But it wasn't going to happen.

Newton continued. "Rick, I have one problem with you."

"What's that?" said Pitino.

"I've got to know now."

Truth time.

"C.M.," said Pitino, "I'm the wrong person for the job. I believe we have a legitimate chance of winning the NBA championship. I think we have a chance to go far in the playoffs."

"I can't wait that long," said Newton. "I've got to know now."

"I'm sorry, C.M."

Newton had taken a chance and failed. Pitino wouldn't budge. It was time to move to Plan B.

"So tell me what you think of P. J. Carlesimo."

Pitino brightened. He was a close friend of the Seton Hall coach. Carlesimo, 39, had just led the Pirates to the NCAA championship game, where they lost to Michigan in overtime. He was single, a Fordham grad who had spent most of his life in the Northeast and specifically in the New York area. He was also a helluva basketball coach.

"He'd be awesome for you," said Pitino.

"How would he like living in Lexington after being in the city for so long?" said Newton, who had served on several USA Basketball committees with Carlesimo.

"He'll be great anywhere," Pitino assured him.

"Okay," said Newton. "That's what I'm going to do."

The two men shook hands and Newton left. That night Joanne and Pitino had dinner together and laughed about the bizarre meeting. Newton had been so refreshingly honest about the state of Kentucky's program that for a moment, just a moment, Pitino had let his mind consider the challenge of UK. Pitino loved challenges and appreciated the basketball history of a place like Kentucky. But no, the circumstances weren't right. Instead, their friend Carlesimo would earn every penny of whatever Newton was going to pay him.

Newton made Carlesimo a priority, but he had also contacted Arizona coach Lute Olson, Los Angeles Lakers coach (and former Kentucky star) Pat Riley, and Duke's Krzyzewski. (Krzyzewski had thought enough of the job opening to discuss the pros and cons of a move with his family. His daughter Debbie wore a Kentucky T-shirt to high school the next day, and a photo of her and the shirt made its way into the local newspaper.) The three men were flattered, but not enough to agree to a campus visit.

As it turns out, neither was Carlesimo, at least at first. He felt loyal to Seton Hall, which had stuck by him as he had rebuilt the program in the early 1980s. In 1988 Carlesimo led the Pirates to their first-ever NCAA Tournament appearance, and he followed it up with the Final Four run in '89. Recruiting was going well. The program was getting stronger. And anyway, Carlesimo was a big-city type of guy.

"You need to come and look at this thing," Newton told him. "The worst thing that could happen is that you come look at it and maybe make some more money off this."

Carlesimo said no and kept saying no until his father, Peter Carlesimo, a longtime college coach and later NIT executive director, told him he was foolish not to at least consider the job. Gavitt and Bob Knight (both friends of Newton's) told Carlesimo the same thing. Even Seton Hall athletic director Larry Keating offered his blessings. After all, they said, it was Newton and Kentucky. So Carlesimo reluctantly flew to Lexington.

Once there, he had to admit that Kentucky's basketball tradition was something to behold. And with Newton as athletic director, Carlesimo knew he had someone who understood exactly what it would take to rebuild and restore the program's luster. It wouldn't be easy to scrape the shame off Kentucky's reputation, but it could be done with enough elbow grease, patience, and talent.

Carlesimo spent most of his two-day April visit with Newton, Kentucky associate athletic director Gene DeFilippo, and college athletics power broker and marketer Jim Host of the Lexington-based Host Communications. There was also an interview with the school president. At one point, Carlesimo asked, "Dr. Roselle, if you had another coach who cheated, would you fire him, too?"

"No," said Roselle, "I'd shoot him."

Carlesimo liked that answer. But something still didn't feel right to him. He was interested in the *idea* of the Kentucky job, but not in the job itself.

"It was just strange, to be honest with you," he says. "I should have not gone down there."

Meanwhile, the local media was in a frenzy. Carlesimo's visit was no secret: an 80-year-old woman had recognized him in the airport and began talking Big Blue hoops. There were rumors that an official announcement could come at any minute. The Associated Press reported that an agreement had been reached between Carlesimo and UK. Even the school's Sports Information Department began preparing for a news conference.

"We thought P.J. was a done deal," says former assistant athletic director Chris Cameron, who oversaw the school's sports communication department.

Suddenly a strange furor arose in the commonwealth over, of all things, Carlesimo's thick beard. It was bad enough, said some Kentucky fans, that UK wanted to hire a Yankee from New York who wore sweaters while coaching and had an overall losing record, but couldn't they at least hire a clean-cut one?

There were even newspaper stories about Carlesimo's whiskers. A *Herald-Leader* columnist floated the idea that Carlesimo should carry a photo of the Kentucky-born Abraham Lincoln, just to reassure UK's suspicious fans that beards were okay.

With the countdown to an official announcement supposedly under way, Cameron wrote a note to Carlesimo and dropped it off at the front desk of the Radisson Hotel, where Carlesimo was staying in Lexington. In the note he suggested that when Carlesimo appeared at his introductory news conference the next day, he do so without the beard. The gesture would immediately endear him to Kentucky fans and, given the recent circumstances, provide a lighthearted moment.

But the next day there was no shaved beard and no news conference. That's because there was no Carlesimo. Carlesimo had left Lexington without an official offer or even a negotiating session. He had flown to Washington, D.C., to fulfill a speaking commitment at Georgetown with Hoyas coach John Thompson—and he wasn't coming back.

"It was not a good time for me," says Carlesimo. "I really had no intention of leaving Seton Hall. . . . I made the mistake of going down there and muddied everything up for a couple of days."

On May 1, Carlesimo officially announced what Newton already knew: He was staying at Seton Hall. As Carlesimo's candidacy evaporated, Newton was forced to reexamine his options. He knocked around the idea of hiring former UK star Kyle Macy, with Newton serving as an assistant coach and AD. Virginia's Terry Holland emerged as a possibility, but Newton and Holland agreed that a younger man was needed for the job. If all else failed, Newton decided he would coach the team for the 1989–90 season while continuing the search.

Pitino was still his first choice, but Pitino wouldn't commit. Then again, he hadn't exactly said no, had he? Newton had recruited enough players and charmed enough parents in their kitchens and living rooms to know the difference between a hard no and a soft no. Pitino was interested; Newton could feel it in his bones. But how interested? And would he truly be able to escape the gravitational pull of his native New York? Having nothing to lose, Newton called.

"Look, I'll wait for you to win the championship," Newton told Pitino.

"Are you sure, C.M.?" said Pitino. "Because I can't guarantee you I'd take the job, because my wife's never been there. And I've only been there one time to do a clinic."

Newton didn't care. "I'm going to wait for you."

Shortly thereafter, Pitino and Joanne had dinner with Carlesimo at one of their favorite restaurants, Bravo Gianni on the Upper East Side. Carlesimo explained that he had gotten to Kentucky and instantly realized it wasn't the right fit.

"But if I had a family, I'd take it in a second," said Carlesimo.

That was exactly what Pitino was hoping he'd say. The question was, Is Joanne listening?

The Knicks completed a 3–0 playoff sweep of the Philadelphia 76ers on May 2. Immediately after the first-round series, Pitino informed New York general manager Al Bianchi that Kentucky officials had called again. In a telling response, Bianchi told Pitino to listen to Kentucky's offer and keep all of his options open.

Pitino and Bianchi were a bad match from the start, hired separately by the Knicks' ownership just five days apart in July 1987. Such forced marriages, where the general manager has no say in the selection of the coach, rarely work, and this one didn't. They clashed over issues of power as well as basketball philosophy.

The Knicks were eliminated from the playoffs by the Chicago Bulls on May 19. That same day, the NCAA took a very large sledgehammer to Kentucky's basketball program.

While avoiding the death penalty, Newton and Roselle got the kind of punishment they had expected and feared: no postseason play for the 1989–90 and 1990–91 seasons; no television appearances for 1989–90; a reduction in scholarships for 1989–90 and 1990–91; three years' probation; the forfeiture of 1988 NCAA Tournament money and two NCAA Tournament victories.

The Committee on Infractions had gutted the program. It wasn't technically dead, but the priest had been spotted clearing his throat. According to the report, the committee had "seriously considered" suspending UK basketball for as many as two seasons.

Recruiting was already suffering because of the long investigation and Sutton's shaky job status. But now, what elite high school prospect would want to sign with UK after its ban from postseason play and TV? And it wasn't a question of whether Wildcat players would transfer to other programs, but how many.

Kentucky fans were in shock, and many of them turned their anger on the university president. Roselle had been *too* helpful to the NCAA, some UK followers said, and hadn't fought hard enough for the program. One letter arrived on Roselle's desk saying that he ought to be taken deep into the Kentucky mountains and taught "the Kentucky way."

It was true that Roselle had done nothing to camouflage Kentucky's wrongdoing. When he first appeared in front of the NCAA committee (the hearing took place in Charleston, South Carolina, at, ironically, the Mills House hotel), Roselle told its members, "What your investigation showed and what you've accused us of—and there are few nuances—we did those. We're guilty. But our investigation showed a hell of a lot worse than what we're accused of. And we did those, too."

Still, the fans' outrage was misguided. Had Roselle taken any other approach, UK basketball would have likely been shut down for a season, maybe two. Far from betraying the program, he and Newton had saved it from almost certain banishment.

Sutton had also appeared in front of the committee. He was never specifically cited for any wrongdoing.

"Coach Casey, I think, just fell in line perhaps with what they had been doing for years [at Kentucky]," says Sutton. "I wasn't aware of it. I was the person in charge of the program. I should have been more alert in what was going on."

There are those with intimate knowledge of the investigation who contend that Casey was no more at fault than others within, or affiliated with, the UK program, and that Sutton knew—or should have known—the extent of the improprieties.

More than anyone, Roselle understood how the scandal, investigation, and sanctions would traumatize the university and its followers. But he also recognized who the real victims of the scandal would be. So during the darkest days of the controversy, Roselle visited the UK locker room and spoke to the remaining Wildcat players.

"I know it's very, very tough on you right now," he told them. "The public is on you. I think, I hope, and I believe there will be a day you'll be able to say to yourself, 'I am glad I accepted a scholarship to be a basketball player and student at the University of Kentucky.' I think you'll see that day."

Given Kentucky's NCAA transgressions, just having a season was no small feat. And Newton soon informed Roselle that Pitino had agreed to visit Kentucky. There was still hope.

The owners of the Knicks had other ideas. Despite Bianchi's tepid response, some in Knicks management didn't want Pitino to talk to Kentucky. Pitino was summoned by representatives of Gulf + Western, parent company of the Knicks (and New York Rangers and Madison Square Garden) and told not to take the interview. And then, says Pitino, "the most interesting thing happened."

Pitino's next-door neighbor in Bedford—a bit of a misnomer, given that you sometimes couldn't actually *see* your neighbor's house through the heavily wooded acreage—was Stanley Jaffe, famed Hollywood producer of such films as *Kramer vs. Kramer*, *Fatal Attraction*, and *The Bad News Bears*. Pitino knew Jaffe very well. And Jaffe was a huge Knicks fan.

Shortly before Pitino was scheduled to leave for Kentucky, Jaffe pulled up in his Mercedes.

"Rick, I don't want you to leave," Jaffe said. "I want you to stay with the Knicks. You gotta trust me on this."

"Stanley, you're a producer of movies. What do you mean, trust you?"

"I can't go into any further detail. You need to trust me. I don't want you to leave."

"Stanley, I'm gonna go there. If I like it, I'm gonna go. I think it's in my best interests."

"Rick, can you just trust me?"

"I do trust you, but you're a producer."

"Gulf and Western buys all my movies." (Paramount Pictures was another of Gulf + Western's holdings.)

"Stanley, I appreciate it." Pitino shrugged off the odd conversation and went back to his preparations.

On Monday, May 22, Pitino flew to Lexington. While at dinner at the city's well-known Coach House, he was approached by Jerry Tipton of the *Herald-Leader*. Would Pitino care to comment on a 1977 NCAA report implicating him in eight of 64 rules violations that led to two years of probation for the University of Hawaii?

Uh, oh.

At 10 o'clock that night, Newton knocked on the door of the condominium where Kentucky officials had hidden Pitino for the trip (no more Radisson hotels for candidates). He had heard about the incident at the restaurant and was aware of the Hawaii/NCAA story that would appear in the next day's *Herald-Leader*. He was there to cut his losses.

"We're in so much trouble here, we can't have the slightest thing go wrong," Newton said. "I'll have a plane take you back [to New York] in the morning. I really want to apologize for everything."

Pitino was furious, but also relieved. He could return to the Knicks and try to outlast Bianchi. He wouldn't have to battle Joanne over a move to Kentucky. He wouldn't have to deal with the reconstruction of a gutted program.

At 6:30 Tuesday morning, Newton called Roselle. "Have you read the paper yet?"

Roselle had not, so Newton gave him the broad strokes of the Hawaii infractions story. He told Roselle he was putting Pitino back on an airplane.

"Well, I'd like to meet him," said Roselle, who had spoken with Pitino on the phone several times in recent weeks. "Don't send him away."

At 8 a.m., as Pitino was packing his bags, there was another knock on the condo door. It was Newton again.

"David Roselle wants to meet with you," said a beleaguered Newton. "Would you do me one favor and just meet with him?"

"C.M., I don't know . . ."

"Look, I just need a favor, Rick. We'll take you home right afterward."

Pitino and Newton drove to Roselle's office later that day, unsure how the situation would play out. Newton believed in Pitino, but was convinced that the Hawaii story had ended the courtship. Roselle had other ideas.

Roselle was surprised by the Hawaii report, mostly because UK had contacted the NCAA during its background check of Pitino. He was concerned about the *Herald-Leader* story, but it wasn't a deal-breaker. He liked Pitino. More important, he trusted Pitino and trusted Newton, the man who had made him Kentucky's first choice. If Pitino had made some mistakes as a low-level assistant more than 10 years earlier, Roselle could live with that. He was certain Pitino was the coach Kentucky needed.

Preliminary negotiations began, with Roselle insisting he would deal only directly with Pitino. He was hiring Pitino, not Pitino's agent, so why complicate the discussions with a third party in the room?

Roselle asked Pitino what would be an acceptable contract length. Pitino said five years was the standard. Roselle said he would give him a seven-year deal.

"Two of the first years should be on us, not on you," said Roselle, referring to the NCAA's two-year ban on postseason play.

Newton was thrilled by the meeting and the job offer. But Pitino still had to convince Joanne. There was also the matter of calming the media storm regarding the Hawaii story. In an earlier news conference, Pitino had told reporters, "One thing you won't have to worry about is cheating with Rick Pitino. It didn't happen in Hawaii as far as I'm concerned." Newton had added, "I have absolutely no questions about Coach Pitino's integrity or compliance, or so on, as head coach throughout his entire head coaching career."

As it turned out, Joanne had been listening to Carlesimo that night at Bravo Gianni. She had heard their friend rave about Lexington and the people at UK. She still didn't want to leave New York, but she had no objections about Lexington.

What she couldn't understand is why Pitino would walk away from the Knicks. It was his dream job. He had the players. And he had turned them into title contenders. But Pitino explained that it would only be a matter of time before the Bianchi–Pitino combination unraveled.

"Look, Joanne, you've got to trust me on this one," he told his wife. "It's not a question of if I go or the GM goes. It's a question of longevity in this business—and I'm not going to have that longevity with the Knicks."

(Nearly two years later, Pitino got a phone call alerting him to a news story about to appear that he would find interesting. As would be reported in the next day's New York papers, there was a major shakeup at Madison Square Garden, and among other changes Bianchi was ousted and replaced by Dave Checketts. The prime mover behind the changes was soon introduced as the president and chief operating officer of the Garden's corporate parent. The new president's name? Stanley Jaffe. "I couldn't believe that he didn't tell me, because obviously things would have probably changed if he did tell me," says Pitino. "I would have stayed [in New York]. I just didn't put two and two together that a movie producer and my next-door neighbor was going to be the head of Paramount.")

Pitino returned to New York, met with Knicks management, and told them he was taking the Kentucky job. Newton then sent DeFilippo and his wife, Anne, to pick up the Pitinos on the school's private plane. On June 2, he was introduced as Kentucky's 19th head basketball coach. Pitino was a Yankee, but he was now *their* Yankee.

"You know how it is in Kentucky," says Oscar Combs, founder of the widely read *Cats' Pause* and cohost of the UK pregame radio show. "You're only a Yankee down here if you're losing."

Pitino's arrival in Lexington was considered a major coup by most fans. It came about a week after an issue of *Sports Illustrated* hit the newsstands with a cover photo that was provocative and memorable in its jarring simplicity. It featured a basketball player, his back to the reader, with his head bowed down and a ball held against his right hip. On the back of his blue jersey, where a player's name usually would be stitched, was the word *Kentucky*. The headline hanging over the player's head was "Kentucky's Shame." Inside was a damning and poignant analysis of the program's sins and the penalties it would have to pay for absolution. Wrote *SI*'s Curry Kirkpatrick: "Proud, elegant Kentucky stood threadbare, stripped of its medals and conceits, dispossessed of image and reputation, exposed as a common NCAA felon."

"One thing I promise," said Pitino during his introductory news conference, which was telecast live statewide. "You'll see us on the cover of *Sports Illustrated* again. And we will be cutting down certain nets. It won't be for what you saw last week. That's yesterday's news."

Tiny flecks of spit flew from Pitino's mouth as he spoke. Cameron, who was standing nearby, could see them silhouetted against the TV lights. He also could see the faces in the crowd, spellbound and astounded by Pitino's audaciousness. The new coach warned UK fans to do whatever was necessary to buy season tickets, because "they're going to be the most precious things in life sometime."

It was a halftime speech to the commonwealth, a one-man pep rally. His words resonated with those who lived and died with Big Blue. For at least one day, Kentucky was Kentucky again.

THREE

August 1988

Christian Laettner stood alone in his empty dorm room, his bags still packed, his college life only minutes old. A day earlier his dad had pulled the Plymouth Voyager loaded with Laettners and luggage out of the driveway of their rural home in Angola, New York, and begun the 12-hour drive to Durham, North Carolina. About 700 miles later they were in another world: on the campus of prestigious Duke University.

He would miss his family. The Laettners, especially his mother, Bonnie, weren't afraid to show their emotion. The farewell had been emotional, full of long hugs, handshakes, and misty eyes. But they were gone now, leaving Laettner to wrap his long, thin arms around the reality of his new situation. His first thought: *Damn, I don't know anyone here.*

Scared wasn't the right description. Laettner was nervous, anxious, excited about his first day at Duke, but not scared. He didn't even like the word.

For him there was only one thing to do. Now that his parents had left, Laettner would connect with his new family: Duke basketball. He walked from his West Campus dorm to Cameron Indoor Stadium, the quaint, iconic little gym tucked in the corner of that same side of campus. The Blue Devils' basketball offices were located on the first floor of Cameron.

Nobody was there. No Krzyzewski. No assistant coaches. No players. Laettner was about to give up and return to his dorm when he saw Danny Ferry, the 6'10" consensus All-American forward. Ferry would begin his senior season as one of the favorites to earn national player-of-the-year honors.

Laettner was just happy to see a familiar face, and even happier when Ferry said, "You want to play some one-on-one?"

"Of course," said Laettner.

This will be fun, thought Laettner. After all, Laettner and Ferry had hit it off during Laettner's official recruiting visit. Now the famous upperclassman was reaching out to the hours-old freshman.

Laettner and Ferry had the Cameron Indoor court all to themselves. Laettner tossed the ball to Ferry, who was standing at the top of the key. Game on.

Ferry drove to his right, but Laettner cut him off. So Ferry spun toward the lane, but with his right elbow raised like a battering ram. He popped Laettner flush in the mouth, the newcomer's head snapping back, and kept driving toward the basket. No apology followed.

This wasn't an accident; it was a message. Sure, Ferry, the other Blue Devil players, Krzyzewski, and the assistant coaches had smothered Laettner with Duke love during the recruiting process. That's how it worked. But now it was time to learn about the real Duke basketball world. The Blue Devils had reached the Final Four twice in the last three years. What was Laettner going to do to make it three out of four? Because if he couldn't help them win games and championships, then Ferry and the other Duke veterans had no use for him. That's why he got the elbow and the message.

Welcome to Duke.

What Ferry didn't know was that Laettner had taken elbows to the mouth for years. And every time, he'd just spit out the blood and keep playing. It was a Laettner family tradition.

His father, George, was a 6'5" blue-collar grinder. He didn't own a college degree, but he had earned his union journeyman's card as a printer for the *Buffalo News* in 1966. Bonnie, thin and tall at 5'10", was a grade school teacher. They were married in 1964 and started a family in 1965: first Christopher, followed a year later by Leanne, followed three more years later by Christian (August 17, 1969, to be exact), and then, in 1980, by Katherine.

Bonnie named him Christian partly in honor of their Catholic faith, but mostly because she had a soft spot for Marlon Brando and the characters he had played in two movies: Lieutenant Christian Diestl in the 1958 war film *The Young Lions*, and First Lieutenant Fletcher Christian in *Mutiny on the Bounty*. Bonnie was so sure that her neighbors and friends would visit her perfectly behaved newborn that she changed his outfit multiple times during the day.

Laettner grew up in Angola, which sits against Lake Erie about 30 minutes south of Buffalo. The family house could be found off a long country road, among the farms that dominated the landscape. They lived within their means, which is to say George and Bonnie didn't have disposable income. They paid their bills; they fed and clothed their children—they got by, barely. By any financial measurement they were the lowest of lower middle class, if that. George used to dock boats on Lake Erie to earn a little extra money after his *News* shift. Savings account? What was that?

For years the Laettners took part in a Catholic-sponsored foreign student exchange program. They were at the then Greater Buffalo International Airport one day (their exchange student from El Salvador was returning home) when four-year-old Christian recognized Buffalo Bills star running back O. J. Simpson and yelled, "O.J.! Go, O.J.!" Simpson stopped, picked up the young Laettner, and posed for a photo. Years later, Laettner would choose 32 as his jersey number. Just like O.J.

By the time he was five, Laettner could swim underwater down and back the length of his family's aboveground pool. Why? Because Chris had done the same thing. It was no surprise when Laettner's preschool teacher wrote on his progress report: "Too much self-confidence."

He was a carefree, bubbly child. He would hug anyone and everyone. It seemed he always had a smile on his face.

Chris was tough on his four-years-younger brother. Everything was a competition, and if Laettner lost, Chris would let him know it with a slap to the back of the head. If Laettner cried or complained, Chris would wrestle him to the ground, place a knee on his brother's chest, and slap him around some more. They fought constantly, with Chris telling his brother how stupid it was for him to take the beatings. But Laettner would never back down. If it wasn't Chris roughing up Laettner, it was their mutual best friend from down the street, Mike Taylor.

"A lot of kids say he was too intense," says Chris, "but that was on me. They should blame me. He got that from me."

They played baseball and used the flat top of a milk bottle as their ball. It might have been Laettner's best sport. He was a pitcher, as well as a first baseman and third baseman, and it wasn't unusual for him to record double-digit strikeouts in a Little League game. It also wasn't unusual for opposing coaches to question Laettner's age. At 12, he was already 6'2" and blessed with coordination and a blazing fastball. Bonnie carried a copy of his birth certificate to show anyone who doubted his birth date. (The doubters included coaches, Angola barbers giving free haircuts to anyone 12 or under, and restaurant owners with kids-eat-free buffet specials.)

They also played football, street hockey, and pond hockey in their boots (complete with make-believe play-by-play of Chris, Christian, and Taylor as the Buffalo Sabres' famed French Connection line—*Perreault to Martin, Martin to Robert, Robert back to Perreault . . .*). As Laettner got older, they played basketball together. His old man coached Chris's and later Christian's teams at the parochial elementary school, Most

Precious Blood. There were only 30 students in Laettner's eighth-grade class and only nine players on the team; to make it an even ten for scrimmages, George would play opposite his son in the post, where he would purposely foul his youngest son and battle him hard for rebounds. Christian would show up at Chris's practices and even do some of the drills. On occasion, George would play in some after-work pickup games and bring his youngest son to watch.

By the time he had reached eighth grade, it was apparent that Laettner was a gifted athlete. It wasn't just his size (6'4"). It was his gracefulness and his toughness. Nothing intimidated him.

He was beginning to love basketball, and basketball was beginning to love him back. He loved it because he was good at it, but also because of the pace of the game. Baseball was fun, but basketball was fast. Laettner liked fast.

Bonnie wanted Laettner to attend high school at the Nichols School, a tony and pricey prep academy founded in 1892 and located in north Buffalo. With its stately redbrick buildings, its vast manicured lawn, its clock steeple and gated entrances, Nichols's campus was impressive. So was the tuition for the area's most exclusive prep school. Bonnie and George Laettner didn't have that kind of money.

They were a blue-collar family that valued every nickel earned or saved. In the summers—and with the wink-wink blessings of the people who manned the ticket booths at the main gate—the Laettner children would run through a thick, grassy area called Mosquito Field and sneak through a back entrance of the Grandview Drive-In. That's where they'd meet up with Bonnie and George, who had just avoided buying four tickets. Anything to save a few precious dollars.

It wasn't uncommon for the Laettner boys to work as field laborers on a nearby farm. Fill a bushel with about 30 pounds of green beans, get 50 cents. Fill it with about 48 pounds of cucumbers, get 50 cents. It was long, backbreaking work, but that was the only way Laettner could supplement his meager weekly allowance.

Laettner's entrance exam scores were okay, but not high enough to guarantee him acceptance at Nichols's Upper School (its high school). However, given his mid-August birth date, which would make him one of the younger students in an incoming freshman class, Nichols administrators offered to let him repeat eighth grade at their middle school and then, if all went well, enroll at the high school the following year. So Laettner transferred to Nichols and became an eighth-grader again.

Laettner loved eighth grade at Nichols. It took him 40 minutes and three different rides to get him there, but for the first time in his life he enjoyed reading books, a fact not lost on his mother, the teacher. So Bonnie and George enrolled him in the Nichols Upper School, took a big gulp, and arranged for a monthly payment coupon book. They would scrape together the minimum and pay the remainder over time. Laettner received a financial aid package that helped pay part of the tuition, but in return he had to spend parts of his summers at Nichols doing janitorial work at the school: washing floors, painting, installing carpet, mowing the grass. He was, in all probability, the poorest student at the school and almost certainly the only one whose parents ordered his clothes from the Sears catalog, which was the one place they could find pants that fit his growing frame.

He was a basketball player with promise by then. He was 6'7" as a freshman and earned a starting position on the varsity team. On the first play of his first game at Nichols, he got elbowed in the nose. Laettner didn't flinch. In his dad's pickup games, the men from the *News'* printing press room would bang and bump Laettner on the low post, testing him with a hard foul or an elbow to the ribs or jaw. Laettner never backed down.

Midway through his freshman season he received his first recruiting letter—from St. Bonaventure University, located about 90 minutes from Angola. He was thrilled. But it would be only the beginning of the letters. After attending Howard Garfinkel's Five-Star basketball camp—the must-see skills camp on the college recruiting tours—Laettner found his name on the mailing lists of dozens of Division I programs.

During his sophomore season, now 6'9" and 210 pounds, Laettner began to establish himself as a national recruit. Anybody who thought of him as just a white stiff from a prep school in Buffalo knew better after they saw him play.

He was clearly the best player on the Nichols team, but he often made sure to involve his teammates in the scoring. After a game in which he had 14 points, 14 rebounds, and 14 assists, his father asked him why he hadn't scored more.

"Well," explained Laettner, "they have to be good, too."

As Laettner's skills and reputation grew—Nichols won state titles in 1985 and 1986 and reached the state semifinals in 1987—so did the recruiting efforts. The excitement over a letter from St. Bonaventure was a distant memory. Now nearly every major program in the country wrote him: Indiana, North Carolina, Syracuse, Virginia, Kentucky, Notre Dame, Pittsburgh, and Duke, among others. One time the phone rang and Chris answered the call.

"Hi," said the voice, "this is Robert Knight from Indiana University."

Chris laughed and hung up the phone. He thought it was a neighbor playing a practical joke. It wasn't.

The phone rang again. This time George answered.

"Sorry, Coach Knight, that was my idiot son."

A phone ban was later instituted: no coaches were allowed to call the Laettner home. Instead, Jim Kramer, the Nichols coach, would become the clearinghouse for such calls. Eventually Laettner whittled his short list to 11 candidates.

Bonnie, who had never heard of Duke until Laettner first mentioned it to her, wanted him to sign with Notre Dame. So did Chris, who went on a trip with his brother to the South Bend campus. The Irish were playing No. 1 North Carolina that day. Digger Phelps's team upset the Tar Heels as the two Laettners watched from seats directly behind the

ND bench. Afterward, an awestruck Chris told his brother, "Christian, you've *got* to go to Notre Dame."

But Laettner, despite his mother's wishes and the family's Catholic background, wasn't interested in playing for the Fighting Irish. And as much as he respected Knight, he wasn't interested in the Hoosiers, either. The reason was simple: Laettner considered himself a basketball purist, and the finest, most elegant form of college hoops, he decided, was played in the Atlantic Coast Conference (ACC). He would make official visits to only three campuses: Virginia, Carolina, and Duke.

Laettner attended Five-Star camp for three years beginning in 1985. He found himself spellbound by the basketball teachings of such visiting hoops dignitaries as Knight, the legendary Hubie Brown (who had coached at the first Five-Star camp in 1966), and future NBA coaching fixture Brendan Malone.

There was one other coach who made a lasting impression on Laettner. He was young, intense, and absolutely committed to his basketball beliefs. He would play against campers in one-on-one games and won regularly. His lectures and demonstrations on ball-handling technique, on offensive theory, on the fundamentals of passing, dribbling, and shooting captivated Laettner. Laettner practiced and perfected those teachings until they became second nature. And he never forgot the young coach's name.

Rick Pitino.

In the spring of 1986 he began paying close attention to the Final Four, and he saw a Duke team that featured Johnny Dawkins, Mark Alarie, Jay Bilas, Tommy Amaker, David Henderson, and Danny Ferry. Laettner liked the vibe of that team. When he watched them on TV he was struck by their body language (upbeat), their up-and-coming coach (Krzyzewski), their uniforms (Laettner loved blue and white), their status (Cinderellas), their style of play (intense), even their shoes (Adidas). Duke would lose to Louisville in the championship game, but Laettner started following the Blue Devils and the ACC on a regular basis. ACC teams—at least, the ones coached by Krzyzewski at Duke, Smith at North Carolina, and Terry Holland at Virginia—played the way he had been taught at Five-Star. Indiana won the national title in 1987, his junior year at Nichols, but Laettner didn't care for the Big Ten style of play. Nor was he a fan of the Big East's emphasis on physical play. Laettner wasn't afraid to mix it up, but he wasn't built like Alonzo Mourning, considered the number-one high school prospect at the time. His game relied less on power and more on nuance.

Krzyzewski had first seen Laettner as a Nichols junior, when he attended the pregame warm-ups of the state tournament at Glens Falls, New York. Duke was preparing for its own NCAA Tournament game, so Krzyzewski had to be back in Durham that night. He was at the Civic Center for less than 15 minutes, but he was instantly impressed with Laettner's athleticism. Krzyzewski watched Laettner handle the ball during warm-up drills; he was fluid, not mechanical like some big men whose coordination had yet to catch up with their height. And his eyes—my god, thought Krzyzewski, the kid looked like he was counting the nanoseconds until tip-off. Krzyzewski wanted players who craved the moment, whose own basketball egos wouldn't suffer from stage fright. Laettner, he decided quickly, wouldn't have that problem.

He also watched to see how Laettner interacted with his coach, his teammates, the game officials. Was he respectful of authority? Did he work within the framework of a team? Did he look like he loved the game? Laettner passed each test.

Even before he took his official recruiting visits, Laettner had decided on Duke. Those visits came in late October and early November. First was Virginia. It was very nice, but it wasn't Duke. North Carolina (his mom's favorite of the three) was next, and suddenly Laettner found himself wavering on the Blue Devils. The campus, the program, the coach, the school, and the vibe were all outstanding. Laettner wasn't sure how Duke could top his Carolina experience.

He later returned to Tobacco Road and Duke. It was a football weekend, so the Duke players, assistants, and recruits met at Krzyzewski's house to eat lunch and watch games. Laettner's arrival did not go unnoticed by Mickie Krzyzewski and her oldest daughter, Debbie, who was a junior in high school.

"Coldly beautiful," says Mickie. "No girls had any interest in what he had to say." Translation: They were too busy staring.

Krzyzewski was interested in what his family thought about his team and the recruits. After all, his wife and his three daughters were around the program so much—at games, at team functions, on the team bus on occasion—that they sometimes noticed things that Krzyzewski didn't. Through osmosis they had come to learn basketball from their husband and father, and through them he had come to learn something about Duke's players.

Laettner was unlike any recruit who had ever stepped into their home. "Dad, he's really cute," said Debbie. "He's incredibly confident. How can you be *that* confident?"

Laettner's personality reminded Mickie of a certain West Point cadet she had met years earlier in Chicago, the one who had told her she was his third choice for a Bears football date.

"I thought he was blatantly honest the way Mike had been blatantly honest back in the day—before he gained some social graces," Mickie says. "I was intrigued by what came out of [Laettner's] mouth. 'Did the kid really say that?' Then I realized he wasn't being sarcastic or mean, but he was just blatant in what he said. . . . He never tried to be charming. He never tried to flatter a person or charm a person. He just always was him."

The last visit to Duke convinced Laettner he had found his basketball home. He liked everything about Smith and Carolina, but he loved the idea of helping the Blue Devils make history. Krzyzewski and Duke had never won an NCAA national championship; Smith and North Carolina had.

"I didn't want to go to the already established team," he says. "I wanted to go to the team that was looking like they were heading there, but just needed a little more help. I didn't know that I would be that help, but I knew I wanted to be part of the process."

On the November 1987 night he made his decision, Laettner stayed at his coach's house and called Holland, Smith, and Krzyzewski each with the news. He wanted to make the calls himself, rather than have his father or Kramer deliver the decision. Then he called his mother. She burst into tears.

"Why are you crying?" said Laettner, baffled by his mother's reaction. This was supposed to be one of the best moments of his life—he was going to Duke on a full scholarship . . . Duke!—and his mother was inconsolable.

"Because I love Dean Smith," she whimpered.

Laettner's seven-year-old sister, Katherine, also cried when she heard the news. Her frustration wasn't with Laettner's choice of school but with the coach's name. She could spell Smith and Holland, but not Krzyzewski.

The family would meet Krzyzewski in early December. He had been to Buffalo and the Nichols gym before, but never to Angola and the Laettner house.

Krzyzewski's visit was part White House State Dinner, part *Seinfeld* episode, and part Salute to Poland. Though George Laettner's last name was German, his family was Polish. His grandparents had spoken and argued in Polish. George had attended a Polish-American school.

The dinner theme would be pure Polska: fresh Polish sausage, just-baked Polish rye bread, horseradish and butter, smoked sausage, handmade pierogies. Laettner's sister Leanne had made cabbage rolls the night before, but George deemed them too salty. They were tossed outside, where the raccoons gobbled them up.

George left work early that afternoon to pick up Krzyzewski at the airport. They drove the 30 miles back to Angola, where Krzyzewski was greeted by Bonnie and Leanne. The Laettners couldn't afford a proper dining room table, so Bonnie covered a Ping-Pong table with a table-cloth. A trouble light, like the kind used by auto mechanics while working under the hood of a car or by plumbers under a sink, hung from the ceiling. Krzyzewski saw it, smiled, and said, "Oh, a Polish chandelier."

Bonnie had warned Krzyzewski that a fellow teacher at her elementary school might stop by the house. "She's a big fan," said Bonnie.

The big fan was a 50-year-old gym teacher with a Polish last name and, as it turned out, a few drinks in her. She pawed at Krzyzewski as if he were a dancer at Chippendales. So attentive was the woman that the Laettners were worried that she'd try to kiss Krzyzewski. Fortunately for the coach, he had to leave to watch Laettner's game at Nichols.

Laettner was considered one of the better recruits in the country—Dick Vitale rated him the seventh-best big-man prospect—but he wasn't ranked among the elite of the elite of the 1988 signing class. He was very good, but not necessarily considered the best Duke signee. Crawford Palmer, a 6'9" center from Arlington, Virginia, was thought by some on the Duke coaching staff to be more ACC-ready than Laettner.

Krzyzewski and his assistants were excited about the arrival of Palmer and Laettner for the 1988–89 season. They were less sure about the other signee of the class, 6'6" Brian Davis from Bladensburg, Maryland.

Davis was born in Atlantic City, New Jersey, and his family moved to the Washington, D.C., area when he was 11. He dreamed of playing in the ACC and for Maryland, where his basketball idol, the great Len Bias, was a star. Davis liked Michael Jordan, too (who didn't?), and had met the young Chicago Bulls guard at a local barbershop. A mutual friend even presented Davis with a pair of Air Jordans and a poster of His Airness.

But with all due respect to M.J., Jordan wasn't Bias. When Bias walked into the Landover Mall shoe store where Davis worked as a salesman, the high schooler couldn't help himself. He told Bias, "I'm going to go to Maryland and win championships."

On June 19, 1986, just two days after being selected by the Boston

Celtics with the second overall pick in the NBA draft, Bias died of cocaine-induced cardiac arrest. His death had a profound effect on Davis, who knew and had played against Bias's younger brother Jay. Davis became even more determined to earn a basketball scholarship at Maryland.

It was a storybook plotline, but without a storybook ending. Maryland didn't want Davis. Lefty Driesell, who knew of Davis and liked his game, was forced to resign in the aftermath of Bias's death. His successor, Bob Wade, wasn't all that interested in a 6'6" prospect who played center at Bladensburg High School. Nor was Duke at first.

By chance, nothing more, Krzyzewski had noticed an issue of *Eastern Basketball* in the car while returning from a scrimmage. As he thumbed through the pages, he noticed a ranking of the top 50 players in the region. Davis was tied for 50th.

"What about this guy?" he said, handing the magazine over the backseat to his young assistant, Mike Brey.

Brey, 28, had played at powerhouse DeMatha High School in Hyattsville, Maryland, and later at George Washington University before returning to DeMatha as a history teacher and assistant coach for the legendary Morgan Wooten. Wooten wasn't fond of the recruiting wars and had asked Brey to be the liaison between college coaches and DeMatha's players. One of those players was Danny Ferry. Several years later, when Krzyzewski needed to fill a coaching opening, he took an educated flier on the high school assistant.

Even with his many D.C. and Maryland high school connections, Brey didn't know much about Davis, but he knew Davis's coach, Bob Patterson, and called him the next day. Patterson said Davis had missed much of his senior season with injuries, but that he was worth a look.

Davis had never liked Duke—he rooted against the Blue Devils when Bias played them. But he was running out of ACC options. Other non-ACC programs were recruiting him, but Davis had vowed that he would somehow squeeze his way into the conference.

Brey brought Krzyzewski to a hoops event at Capitol Heights, on the border of D.C. and Maryland. Davis did well enough, but it was obvious he wasn't a polished player. He couldn't dribble the ball more than once with his left hand. His shooting stroke needed work. He had averaged 16.5 points during his senior season in a motion offense similar to Duke's, but it was his 10.0 rebound average that caught their attention—that and Davis's willingness to work hard on defense. It meant Davis was an effort guy—at 185 pounds he had to be. Duke was always looking for effort guys with an upside.

Krzyzewski was interested, but not enough to offer a scholarship. He was honest about it: Duke wanted the more heralded Bryant Stith and wouldn't commit to another swing player until Stith made up his mind. Virginia, also in hot pursuit of Stith, told Davis the same thing. Meanwhile, North Carolina offered a scholarship to Davis—Hubert, not Brian. If Hubert Davis accepted (and he eventually did), Brian was out of luck.

"I was the ultimate fallback," says Davis. "It was humbling. It pissed me off. I still take it personally."

He might have been humiliated and angry about the circumstances, but Davis was also desperate. He called Brey almost every night asking different versions of essentially the same question: "Are you going to take me?"

Once Maryland learned of Duke's interest in Davis, the Terrapins peeled back and tried to get involved in his recruiting. But with Stith finally committing to Virginia, Krzyzewski was now in position to offer Davis a scholarship. He still had his reservations about Davis and said so during his home visit; he told Davis it would be a struggle to earn playing time and that his skills translated into that of a complementary player, not a starter or sixth man.

"That's ridiculous," Davis told Krzyzewski. "I'm better than all those guys."

Ridiculous or not, there wasn't any debate about whether to accept the scholarship offer. Davis's stepfather, who had fought in the Vietnam

War, was a Krzyzewski guy because of the coach's West Point background and Army service. Davis's mother also gushed about Krzyzewski. Davis couldn't wait to play for Krzyzewski—or, more correctly, couldn't wait to prove Krzyzewski wrong. How dare anyone question whether he could succeed at Duke. In Davis's mind, Duke was lucky to have *him*, not the other way around.

"I didn't go there with a chip on my shoulder; I went there with a boulder on it," says Davis. "I didn't care about points. I wanted to be a winner. I knew they had a reputation of being suckers, of not winning Final Fours. Me and Laett wanted to change that."

Davis already knew Palmer. They often had played with and against each other in D.C. gyms and rec centers. But Davis knew little about Laettner, other than he was a McDonald's All-American from western New York. Phone numbers were exchanged, and Davis began calling Laettner on a regular basis. They later played in the same Capital Classic game that summer.

There was something about Laettner that Davis liked. He had an edge to him, a swagger. They talked about making a difference in the program. They didn't want to spend their first season as glorified cheerleaders. They were going to compete, and if the upperclassmen didn't like it, tough.

"Laett and I were really hungry," says Davis. "Laett grew up modest. He wasn't no country-clubber. He might have looked like one, but he wasn't. And me? Nobody gave me anything."

Davis was motivated by the memory of Bias, by the humbling recruiting process, by being the first person in his family to attend college. He would not allow himself to fail.

Laettner's motivation was simpler: He wanted to win and he wanted to play. And in case he needed more incentive, word trickled back to Laettner about a comment Krzyzewski had made during an exhibition tour of Spain and Greece that summer—the three incoming freshmen weren't allowed to join the Blue Devils on the three-week trip.

The comment was the product of Krzyzewski's growing frustration at not winning Final Fours. Krzyzewski had come close in 1986 and 1988, and now he had a team, led by seniors Ferry and guard Quin Snyder, capable of making another deep tournament run. But after watching the Blue Devils struggle against the national teams of Italy, Yugoslavia, Spain, Czechoslovakia, Greece, and the USSR, an angry Krzyzewski issued a warning to his veteran big men during a walk-through practice in Greece. Never mind that it was June and that these were meaningless exhibition games against pro players preparing for the Olympic qualifying tournament. Krzyzewski wanted their attention—and got it.

"I'll tell you what, big guys," he said. "We've got this freshman big guy coming in and he's going to knock you all on your asses."

The players knew Krzyzewski was referring to Palmer, the supposed crown jewel of the recruiting class. When Laettner found out, he seethed.

Krzyzewski believed in a basketball meritocracy, where performance and excellence were rewarded with playing time and starting positions. Seniority mattered if all things were equal, but things were rarely equal. Either you produced or you didn't. The film, the box score, and the scoreboard didn't lie.

Most Duke observers envisioned a 1988–89 starting five of Ferry and Robert Brickey at forward, Phil Henderson and Snyder at guard, and Alaa Abdelnaby at center, with sophomore Clay Buckley and the freshman Palmer the most likely to work their way into the rotation behind Abdelnaby. But the observers weren't at Cameron Indoor to see Laettner just play harder after Ferry crushed him in the mouth with that elbow. And they weren't at a basketball clinic at Cameron a few days later, when nearly 600 high school coaches, as well as members of the Duke staff, saw Laettner run drills and then play in a full-court game.

Brey and fellow assistant Bob Bender had served as referees in the game. Afterward, about 25 different high school coaches approached the Duke assistants.

"That Laettner kid," said one coach, "did you know he was that good?"

"Oh, yeah," said Bender, who had been the point man during Laettner's recruitment.

"Yeah, we really did," said Brey, who had also helped recruit Laettner.

At clinic's end, Brey and Bender returned to their offices for a staff meeting. They looked at each other and said, almost simultaneously, "Holy shit!" They had no idea Laettner was that good.

Laettner was now 6'10", but he could walk on his hands the length of a basketball court. His hand-eye coordination was off the charts. He played tennis and Ping-Pong and was nearly unbeatable. "He was a 5'11" guy in the body of a 7-foot guy," says Brey. "He had a unique psyche that was fearless and different. I've been in it 30 years and I've never been around a psyche similar to that."

The photograph next to his player biography in the 1988–89 Duke Basketball Yearbook/Media Guide should have given some indication of Laettner's single-mindedness. Rather than use just a simple mug shot in the yearbook bios, the guide editors asked Duke's players to wear a coat and tie for their individual photo shoots, which would take place at campus locations of their choice. Seniors got first pick of the prime locations, followed by the juniors, sophomores, and finally the freshmen. Ferry posed at the world-famous Duke Gardens. Abdelnaby, his suit coat flung casually over his right shoulder, was pictured in front of the Duke Chapel. Brickey stood in front of the Fuqua School of Business.

Laettner stood happily and defiantly in front of a bush.

Laettner and Davis tried to fit in and stand out at the same time. They wanted to be respectful but also aggressive. They called themselves "The Young Guns" because, says Davis, "we came in there firing."

Practices were heated. Ferry vs. Laettner. Abdelnaby vs. Laettner. Buckley vs. Laettner. Palmer vs. Laettner. Davis against anybody who tried to get in his way. "We had some nice juicy fights at Duke," says Davis.

Scrimmages usually featured the starters on the White team and reserves on the Blue team. Laettner and Davis played on the Blue team, and when they won, which happened more than a few times, Laettner would chirp and celebrate in front of the starters. They didn't like it, but to Laettner they were taking it the wrong way. He was there to earn minutes, but also to make the White team better.

There was no question in Laettner's mind that he would be a factor. He hadn't come to Duke to be an accessory. While walking off the court after practice one day, he turned to student manager Mark Williams and said, "If you don't think I'm going to start by the end of the year, you're crazy."

Williams did a double take. A freshman was saying this?

Laettner made his official Duke playing debut November 19, 1988, at the Tipoff Classic in Springfield, Massachusetts. The opponent: Kentucky. By then, NCAA investigators had already begun digging into the muck of the UK program. For one of the few times in his Duke career, Laettner was nervous. He came off the bench and scored 2 points and had 1 assist in about a half dozen minutes of play. Duke won, 80–55.

It wasn't long before Laettner moved ahead of Palmer and Buckley in the substitution rotation. He eventually replaced Abdelnaby and joined the starting lineup in the Blue Devils' eighth game of the season, scoring 20 points against Cornell. He was in a daze of sorts, amazed by his good fortune. Laettner loved his school, his coaches, his teammates, the wins, his classes, the parties, the coeds. He was exhilarated by the newness of everything.

Duke won its first 13 games, but then lost four of its next five as Laettner struggled early in the ACC schedule. The Blue Devils recovered and had a seven-game win streak heading into its February 26 made-for-TV matchup against No. 2–ranked Arizona at the Meadowlands in East Rutherford, New Jersey. Krzyzewski liked playing against quality nonconference opponents late in the regular season as a way to prepare the Blue Devils for the NCAA Tournament.

Laettner scored 12 points and had 10 rebounds against the Wild-cats, but in the final second he missed the front end of a one-and-one free throw opportunity that could have forced overtime. Instead, ninth-ranked Duke lost, 77–75. Afterward, Laettner was approached in the locker room by an old man wearing a suit and a Duke hat. The man had asked school officials if he could speak with the freshman.

"I know you feel badly, young man," said former president Richard Nixon, Duke Law School—Class of 1937. "But everything will be just fine. I've won and lost a few myself."

His teammates noticed a slightly different, more mature Laettner after the Arizona loss. He had always been intense, but now he had scar tissue from a missed free throw that cost him and his team. It was as if he had decided it wouldn't happen again.

The Blue Devils were a No. 2 seed in the NCAA Tournament and advanced to the East Regional final, where they played top-seeded Georgetown in the same Meadowlands Arena where Laettner had failed at the free throw line. This time he would face Alonzo Mourning, who had dominated college basketball as a freshman, averaging 13 points, 7 rebounds, and 5 blocks per game. At stake was a place in the Final Four.

Laettner was, as the *Washington Post*'s Tony Kornheiser would write in his March 27 column, "a revelation to the crowd, and possibly even to Mourning." Laettner made 9 of 10 shots, scored a career-high 24 points, added 9 rebounds, and forced Mourning to the bench with foul trouble. Mourning finished with 11 points and 5 rebounds in 26 minutes of play as Duke won, 85–77.

The Georgetown fans tried to rattle Laettner by yelling "Zona!" and "One second!" as he shot a pair of free throws late in the first half. He sank both shots.

At game's end, the same Ferry who had greeted Laettner to Duke with an elbow to the molars now wanted to exchange high-five fist bumps. Ferry knew that without Laettner, the Blue Devils wouldn't have reached the Final Four.

Ferry still had his fun with the freshmen. He and Snyder had told them at the beginning of the season that it was a Duke "tradition" that the freshmen carry the seniors' bags on road trips. What was supposed to be a one-game gag turned into a season-long lie.

Laettner didn't complain. He considered himself a grunt. Grunts carried bags.

This would be the first Final Four for Laettner, but the third—and last—for Ferry, Snyder, and Smith. The finality of it all caused Krzyzewski's seven-year-old daughter, Jamie, to burst into tears.

"What's wrong?" said Krzyzewski to his youngest daughter.

"We're not going to have Quin and Danny and John anymore," she said.

Five years earlier, as a senior at Mercer Island High School, Snyder had half-kiddingly told friends that his final college game would be played at the Kingdome in Seattle, site of the 1989 Final Four. The stadium was no more than a 10-minute drive from his house.

And four years earlier, while riding together in a car as freshmen at Duke, Snyder and Ferry had promised each other they'd win a national championship as Blue Devils. This would be their last chance to make good on the deal.

Krzyzewski, too, was beginning to feel the heat about an NCAA title. The questions were polite and respectful during his third visit to the Final Four, but the theme was unmistakable: Are you ever going to win one of these things?

"That's not the one thing I want more than anything else," Krzyzewski said. "I'd have to have my head examined to think that's the one thing I want more than anything else, a national championship. . . . I mean, I hope we win. Don't get me wrong. I'll compete out there. But I'm not going to let it possess me."

Krzyzewski and the Blue Devils received an all-expenses-paid trip to Seattle; Bonnie and George Laettner did not. But they weren't going to miss their son's Final Four debut. So instead of paying the mortgage that month, they bought plane tickets. (Their bank later imposed a late fee. When Bonnie returned home, she pleaded with the bank president to waive the fee. Every dollar mattered to the Laettners. The president relented when he learned of the circumstances.)

As it turned out, the Laettners traveled a long way to see a monumental collapse. In the semifinal game against P. J. Carlesimo's Seton Hall team, Duke led by 18 points, 26–8, with 8:45 remaining in the first half. It lost by 17, 95–78. The rumblings that Krzyzewski couldn't win the big one grew louder, especially when Michigan, led by a 44-year-old interim coach named Steve Fisher, beat Seton Hall in the title game.

Ferry scored 34 points against the Pirates, but Snyder, Henderson, and Smith were a combined 8 for 30 from the floor. Brickey was injured two minutes into the game.

"I couldn't have picked too many teams to lose an 18-point lead," Ferry told reporters. "But we did."

Laettner, who fouled out after scoring 13 points in 21 minutes, was disappointed by the loss, but not devastated. He was much like Ferry had been three years earlier as a freshman on the 1986 Duke Final Four team. He didn't understand how truly difficult it was to reach a Final Four. Nor did he face the reality that Ferry, Snyder, and Smith now faced: They had played their last game for Duke.

It wasn't until afterward, when Laettner walked from the main locker room to the back area where the bathroom stalls were located, that he realized how precious these championship opportunities were. Laettner heard someone crying. He peeked around a corner. It was Snyder. Ferry, his eyes red with tears, was also there.

That's when it hit him. These were Laettner's teammates, his guys. He made a promise to himself in that Kingdome locker room.

"I never want this to happen again."

FOUR

August 1989

Not that Pitino had time to notice, but the political world was in the midst of extraordinary change. George H. W. Bush was the new U.S. president (Okay, Pitino noticed that one), taking the oath of office about five months before Pitino left the Knicks for Kentucky. Communism in the Eastern Bloc nations was facing extinction. The Solidarity Party was winning its stare-down with the Soviet-backed Communist government in Poland, and East Germany's Communist regime was under siege by pro-democracy protesters. It was only a matter of time before those protesters would stand in triumph atop the growing concrete rubble of the Berlin Wall.

In China, a student protester defiantly blocked the path of a column of Type 59 tanks in Beijing's Tiananmen Square—and by doing so, became an international hero. Martial law would be declared, and in June, military forces opened fire and massacred demonstrators in the square.

Iran's Ayatollah Khomeini was dead. So were vast numbers of fish and wildlife after a ship pilot ran the *Exxon Valdez* aground in Alaska, spilling 10.8 million gallons of crude oil into Prince William Sound.

Pete Rose was banished from baseball for life after an investigation detailed his gambling on the sport. *Driving Miss Daisy* won the Academy Award for Best Picture. *Batman, Bill & Ted's Excellent Adventure, Road House,* and *Do the Right Thing* were all released in 1989. A TV show about nothing—*Seinfeld*—also made its debut.

Meanwhile, the Roman Empire of hoops, as Pitino once referred to it, lay in ruins. Its rise and rule had lasted the better part of five decades, but its fall had come swiftly and with devastating results. Kentucky followers mourned not only what the program had become (instantly irrelevant), but what it could have been. Had those twenty $50 bills never spilled out of the Emery package . . . had Eric Manuel's entrance exam scores never been questioned . . . had the NCAA investigators never been able to find any major wrongdoing, Kentucky could have entered the 1989–90 season with a roster befitting a basketball superpower.

The electrifying Manuel wouldn't have been banished to junior college ball. Center LeRon Ellis wouldn't have transferred to Syracuse. Chris Mills might have appealed his ineligibility at Kentucky instead of transferring to Arizona. Sean Sutton, Eddie's son, might have stuck around rather than go first to Purdue, then a local junior college, and then Oklahoma State when his dad was hired there in 1990. Eddie Sutton would have almost certainly remained as UK's coach. A national championship—the program's first since beating Duke in the 1978 NCAA title game—might have been theirs.

The expectations of Kentucky basketball fans were unrelenting and often suffocating. Blame the Baron, Adolph Rupp, who spoiled the UK faithful with his 876 victories and 4 national championships. His last NCAA title came in 1958, and it would be 20 more years before Kentucky won another one, this time under former Rupp assistant Joe B. Hall. In Hall's third season, he took a freshman-led team all the way to the national title game, where it lost to UCLA in John Wooden's last season. Over the next three years, the pressures and demands grew steadily, and when the now seniors won the 1978 championship, Hall looked far more relieved than happy. The next year, the defending national champions failed to reach the NCAA Tournament and were eliminated in the first round of the NIT.

Pitino's team would have no such burden because nobody expected them to win a thing. Instead, there were widespread predictions of long-term doom. Ole Miss coach Ed Murphy told reporters, "It will take years for them to recover from [the sanctions], even with the emphasis and resources that they have." Chimed in Mississippi State coach Richard Williams: "I really feel bad for the people at the University of Kentucky. It's not good for them and it's certainly not good for our league."

Kentucky's best players were gone, and Pitino was left with the mutts, the basketball orphans. Two months earlier he had coached Patrick Ewing in the Eastern Conference semifinals against Michael Jordan's Chicago Bulls. Now he oversaw a UK team—or what was left of it—with just seven scholarship players. None of them remotely resembled a Ewing or a Jordan.

The program's relationship with the local and state media had become adversarial at best. But even more of a concern to Pitino was its attachment to certain boosters. Rumors and reports of hundred-dollar handshakes and wink-wink discounts/freebies from area merchants had already made their way to Pitino's desk. If his new regime was to have any chance at success, the boosters would have to be removed like ticks from skin.

There was nothing diplomatic about Pitino's methods. He visited the owners of every local restaurant or store suspected in the past of giving players free or discounted food or goods. He told them those days were done. Most, but not all, of the owners fell in line. Several restaurant owners told Pitino that if they wanted to take 5 or 10 percent off a player's bill, then by god, they were going to do it. They were private businesses and could charge whatever they damn well pleased.

"Fine," Pitino told the holdouts. "If word ever gets back to me that you've done that—and it will get back to me—I will immediately take it to the *Herald-Leader* and have them print it."

The freebies stopped. No restaurant owner wanted to risk becoming a page-one story and a reason for the NCAA to swoop in again. It was bad for business.

On the day he was hired, Pitino told the team during a 40-minute meeting, "We'll win right away." Of course, Pitino said that to *all* the teams he addressed for the first time. It had come true at Boston U, at Providence, and even with the Knicks. But Kentucky was different. Kentucky wasn't just a shadow of itself, it was a shadow of the shadow.

When Pitino looked into the faces of his remaining players, he saw uncertainty and nervousness. They had been orphaned by Sutton's forced departure and punished by the NCAA for crimes they hadn't committed. They were undersized—nobody was taller than 6'7"—and underconditioned. Pitino had never heard of any of them.

Had this been a typical Kentucky team—or a typical top 25 team anywhere—Pitino would have tried running most of them out of the program. One by one he would have called the fringe players into his office and told them, as compassionately as possible, that they would never see a minute of playing time. They might not even make it to the pregame layup line. And then he'd offer to help place them in a more, uh, appropriate program for their talent level. It happened all the time when a new coach arrived.

But there was nothing typical about this situation. Pitino needed players, even bad ones.

So he had lied (but in a good way) about winning early. His players needed to hear it. So did Kentucky's fans. But nobody really *expected* him to win. Roselle didn't. Newton didn't. The legendary Cawood Ledford didn't. Ledford was not only the UK radio network's longtime "Voice of the Wildcats," but also the UK voice of reason. He told anybody who would listen—and everyone listened to Ledford—that fans shouldn't expect more than five victories in Pitino's first season. There simply wasn't the talent and depth to survive the schedule.

Not surprisingly, the players' self-esteem had flatlined and they had no sense of brotherhood. When Pitino later asked how many of them thought they could reach the NBA, not one of the players raised his hand. When he asked them for details about their teammates' families, the Wildcats were reduced to guessing. When he asked how many had visited a teammate during the season or holidays, the answer was zero.

The team was fractured. The players wanted to trust and believe in one another, but they didn't know how. The NCAA investigation and penalties and the *Sports Illustrated* cover had tainted them. After all, weren't they part of Kentucky's shame?

Pitino's first job wasn't so much to coach basketball as to apply some mental Neosporin to his players' psyches. They needed to heal. They needed to feel wanted, useful, and important. So Pitino kept telling his players: *You have the opportunity to change the reality and perception of this program. Are you willing to do whatever it takes?*

They said yes because players always say yes. They didn't know any better. They didn't know the particular brand of hell Pitino was about to unleash on them. They said yes out of ignorance but also out of desperation.

There were two upperclassmen who chose to stay in Lexington even though NCAA rules would have allowed them to transfer without sitting out a season: guard Derrick Miller, a senior-to-be, and center/forward Reggie Hanson, entering his junior year. Besides these two, the Wildcats consisted of Sean Woods, a highly touted guard from Indianapolis who sat out the 1988–89 season for Proposition 48 reasons (he hadn't met the NCAA's mininum requirement for academic eligibility as a freshman); three Kentucky boys—forward Deron Feldhaus of Maysville, guard/forward John Pelphrey of Paintsville, and guard Richie Farmer from Manchester; and forward Johnathan Davis of Pensacola, Florida.

None of these players except Woods had the basketball chops to play for Kentucky under normal circumstances. They stayed because they either had no place else to go or didn't want to go anyplace else. UK basketball was in their cultural DNA. They had grown up listening to the beloved Ledford. He was their Vin Scully, and they could recite his favorite sayings by heart. They, like the rest of the state, had lived and died with each win and loss.

Basketball wasn't simply a sport to Kentuckians, it was part of their identity. The annual state high school tournament, where every school competes for the same championship regardless of enrollment size, was more anticipated than Christmas. Reputations were made for life in that tournament.

There were no NBA teams in Kentucky, so UK attracted most of the loyalties in the commonwealth, especially in the bluegrass region surrounding Lexington and the coal-mining and mountain towns of eastern Kentucky. (Coal-mining money from the so-called Mountain Mafia had helped build the Wildcat Lodge, where the UK players lived.) But 71 miles away was Louisville, home of the despised University of Louisville Cardinals, who had won national titles in 1980 and 1986. To eastern Kentuckians, Louisville was the big city and its own nation-state. It was more sophisticated and polished than Lexington, more racially diverse, more liberal, supposedly more sinful and less obsessed, slightly, with basketball. Lexington was the kind of place where a local radio station auctioned off dirt from the construction site where Pitino's new home was being built. Even after the house was completed, UK fans from as far away as Hazard and Pikeville would slowly drive around the cul-de-sac where the Pitinos lived.

"I didn't understand the adulation for basketball," says Pitino of his early days at Kentucky. "New York Knicks fans, because we were winning, were very passionate, and we sold out the Garden every night. But when the game was over, you go on with your lives. But when the game is over in Kentucky, they don't go on with their lives."

It was a basketball continuum. You were born a Wildcat. You died a Wildcat. In between, you talked all things Wildcat.

Farmer, from the Appalachian foothills town of Manchester in Clay County, had been born and raised in that continuum. His first-grade teacher had asked each student in the class what they wanted to be when they grew up. The answers were predictable enough: doctor, astronaut, teacher . . . the usual. Farmer said he wanted to be a Kentucky Wildcat.

His father, who worked for a coal company, rose early in the morning. Farmer, starting when he was only five years old, rose with him. Little Richie would ask his mother to make him a bologna sandwich, and then he would go outside and begin shooting basketballs at 6:30, stop briefly to eat lunch, and return to the outdoor hoop for the remainder of the day.

As he got older, he and his brother pretended to be UK stars Jack Givens, Rick Robey, Kevin Grevey, Jay Shidler, or, the universal favorite, Kyle Macy. Every kid in Kentucky wanted to be Macy, the All-American, Converse-high-tops-wearing guard imported from Peru, Indiana. Hundreds, thousands of times Farmer had hit a winning free throw or jump shot as he channeled his inner Macy. He listened to Ledford on the radio and dreamed of playing for Kentucky, dreamed of having Ledford describe a Richie Farmer game-winning shot for the Wildcats.

By the time Farmer was a high school senior, he was a basketball legend. He was ambidextrous (he pitched, bowled, and golfed left-handed, ate and dribbled with either hand), and he never lost a game in sixth, seventh, or eighth grade. Farmer played in the Sweet 16 of the state high school tournament as an eighth grader, reached the championship game three out of four years while at Clay County High, won it in 1987, and became the leading scorer in the tournament's Sweet 16 history. In one of the great state title games of all time, in 1988, Farmer scored a record 51 points in a losing effort to Allan Houston's Louisville Ballard team—and did it in the same pair of Nike tennis shoes he had worn during his entire high school career. He ended his prep career as the 1988 Mr. Basketball in the hoops-crazed state.

"He really was nothing short of a cult hero," says Herb Sendek, a UK assistant coach on Pitino's staff. "There were people who thought he walked on water. He truly was a commonwealth hero. You can talk about Elvis all you want, but Richie was the guy."

Eddie Sutton didn't think he could walk on water. He wasn't even convinced Farmer was worth a scholarship. The Wildcats already had Eric Manuel, as well as the coach's son, Sean. Farmer could score, but Sutton, who valued defense, wasn't sure Farmer could guard anyone.

LSU's Dale Brown saw things differently. He made the trip to Manchester, navigated the sometimes dangerous gravel roads, and tried to stop Farmer from bleeding Big Blue. He told Farmer that LSU had already signed Chris Jackson, a dynamic guard from Gulfport, Mississippi, and that he had commitments from two star big men: Stanley Roberts out of South Carolina and a raw but frighteningly athletic 7-footer named Shaquille O'Neal.

"I really want to put you and Chris out there and let you guys play," said the often charming and persuasive Brown, who could sell steak to a vegan. "I think we can have a lot of success."

Farmer was flattered by the offer but told Brown that it had been his lifelong dream to play for Kentucky. If UK offered him a scholarship, said Farmer, that's where he was going to play.

Brown asked if UK had extended such an offer.

"No, sir," said Farmer.

In fact, UK hadn't shown any interest in him at all. But dreams die hard. "It was a situation where anything less than the University of Kentucky would have almost been like a failure to me," says Farmer.

Vanderbilt, still coached by Newton at the time, was next. Newton had had success signing players whom UK had let slip through the cracks. The fact that some of those homegrown players helped lead Vandy to wins against the Wildcats was a point of irritation and embarrassment to Kentucky fans. Hoping to cherry-pick Farmer for his own program, Newton offered a full ride. Farmer gave him the same speech he had given LSU's Brown.

Newton sighed and then offered some advice.

"Let me tell you how to get a scholarship there," he said. "You just mention that I have offered you a scholarship at Vanderbilt."

Word made its way back to Sutton and his staff, who were already being pressured to sign the state basketball hero. It wasn't long before a helicopter landed in a field near the Farmer house. Out popped Sutton and two UK assistants. Farmer had his precious scholarship.

Pelphrey, too, grew up idolizing the Wildcats. He imitated the great Macy at the free throw line: grab the socks, three dribbles, deep crouch, shoot. He could recite every detail of UK's 1978 national championship win against Duke—Macy's baseline jumpers, Goose Givens's 41 points, the Blue Devils' late run. Time would stop in the Pelphrey house (as throughout Kentucky) when the Wildcats played. The living room TV went on with the volume turned down and the radio up so they could listen to Ledford.

Pelphrey's mother, Jennie, spent her Saturday afternoons and Monday nights as a kid in rural eastern Kentucky listening to UK games. She even kept a scorebook: X was a made field goal, O was a made free throw. Pelphrey's father, Jack, was no less devoted to Kentucky basketball. During the 1971–72 season, Rupp's last as UK's head coach, Jack and Jennie somehow got tickets for a game. Afterward, Jack made his way down to the Memorial Coliseum floor to shake hands with Rupp.

Jack and Jennie were addicted to hoops. They named John after Boston Celtics star John Havlicek. (His younger brother, Jerry, was named for West Virginia and LA Lakers star Jerry West.) When Pelphrey's parents sent out John's birth announcement in July 1968, it featured a baby with a basketball and netted rim. John was only 14 when a Lexington television reporter asked him where he wanted to play basketball. The skinny redhead, as if possessed, blurted out, "Kentucky."

Pelphrey went to bed each night determined to one day become Mr. Basketball and attract the attention of UK. He wrote down his goals: play at UK and in the Olympics. He got up each morning at 6:30 and ran alone on a nearby track, always thinking of Kentucky. Nobody was going to outwork him for a UK scholarship.

Paintsville, like Manchester, is located in the Appalachian foothills and dependent on the coal industry. It is home to about 4,500 residents and the annual Kentucky Apple Festival. Former San Francisco Giant Johnnie "Peanut" LeMaster lived in small-town Paintsville.

Pelphrey attended Paintsville High School (Jennie taught two of his classes) and led the Tigers to three regional titles and an appearance in the semifinals of the state tournament as a senior. He had a plan for everything. On game days he'd eat right after school, take a brief nap, and then get dressed. He had already laid out his blue-and-white uniform (the same colors as UK) just so.

You could almost always find him in the Paintsville gym. He had an understanding with the school janitor, Billy Fraley: He'd shoot by himself until Fraley was done cleaning for the night.

At the time of his graduation, 32 of the 55 students in his class of 1987 had received some sort of college athletic scholarship. Pelphrey, nicknamed "Dirt" by his teammates (Jerry was "Little Dirt"), wanted to be No. 33.

But Kentucky didn't have the newly named Mr. Basketball on its short list. Or its long list. Sutton hadn't offered him a scholarship during the early recruiting period, a time when about 90 percent of the commitments are made. It was a crushing blow to Pelphrey, who then waited for a late offer. Instead, UK coaches made it clear they had targeted three other players, all high-profile blue-chippers. If they struck out, they said, they'd circle back to Pelphrey.

Kentucky took the recruiting 0-fer, but continued to ignore Pelphrey. The coaches saw him as their worst-case scenario: a scholarship wasted on a mountain kid who couldn't compete at that level.

A devastated and panicked Pelphrey had no Plan B. He met with Louisville's Denny Crum at the coach's house, but Pelphrey's heart wasn't in it. Vanderbilt's Newton had long pursued Pelphrey and was now looking like the recruiting leader. Indiana's Knight contacted the Paintsville star and encouraged him to sign with his good friend Newton.

But Pelphrey clung to the possibility of a UK offer. During Newton's home visit, Jack asked the Vandy coach, "What would you do if Kentucky came and made a last-minute pitch?"

"Let's just hope it doesn't come to that," said Newton.

But Newton was nervous. Pelphrey was Kentucky born and raised. He was a Mr. Basketball. He was being pursued by Vandy. Even Louisville had shown some interest. Plus, UK had failed to sign its preferred blue-chippers. At some point, Sutton would realize he had to sign the kid from Paintsville, right?

One night the lone phone in the Pelphrey house rang. Sure enough, it was UK: Could John come to Lexington to meet with Sutton?

Father and son made the 100-mile drive to UK. When they got there, Sutton invited them into his office and offered Pelphrey the scholarship he had always dreamed of.

Pelphrey's stunning answer: "We'll have to think about it."

Later, on the ride back to Paintsville, Pelphrey, now second-guessing himself, turned to his father and said, "How did we get out of there without signing that scholarship?"

"Just drive, son. Just drive."

Rumors swirled in Big Blue Nation that Pelphrey's father was upset that Sutton had taken so long to offer a scholarship. In truth, it was Pelphrey's mother who was upset with Sutton and UK. Meanwhile, Pelphrey took a couple of days to consider his future. He could sign with Vandy and Newton, where he was wanted and needed. Or he could sign with UK, where he was considered a spare part, the product of an indifferent recruitment. It was as if Sutton's staff was more concerned with keeping Pelphrey from Vandy and Louisville than adding him to Kentucky's roster. In the business it's called "defensive recruiting."

Pelphrey met his dad and mom at a local restaurant for a Saturday morning breakfast.

"What do you want to do?" said Jack.

"I want to go to the University of Kentucky," said Pelphrey. "If I fail, I want to fail at the best."

Poor Newton had been scheduled to speak at the Paintsville athletic banquet. A motel room had been reserved. Announcements had been printed. But the appearance was quickly canceled after Pelphrey informed the Vanderbilt coach of his school choice.

Pelphrey was the seventh player signed in a seven-man UK recruiting class. Even in Paintsville, where they loved him, there were those who said he'd never leave the end of the UK bench. There were simply too many talented players in front of him.

Woods was more talented, though there were questions about his academic staying power. He was from Indiana, but his mother and grandmother were from Lexington. In fact, that entire side of the family was from the commonwealth. "I was like a Kentucky kid not being from Kentucky," says Woods.

He had always told his grandmother that if he ever got a chance to sign with UK, he'd do it. When the offer came, Woods didn't hesitate. The only downer: He was labeled a Prop 48, meaning he couldn't play as a freshman and would lose a year of eligibility.

Feldhaus's recruitment didn't feature the last-minute dramatics of Farmer and Pelphrey or the academic uncertainty of Woods. Feldhaus's father, Allen, had played for Rupp in the early 1960s at Kentucky. Yes, Feldhaus and the Pelphreys had visited Vanderbilt together. Yes, Newton had recruited him hard from Day One. (Was there a Kentucky kid Newton *wasn't* recruiting?) Yes, Tennessee was making a late run. None of it mattered.

"That was my lifelong dream, to play at UK," says Feldhaus. "Once I got the offer to go there, there was no other." (When Newton became the Wildcats' athletic director in 1989, the reserved but dry-witted Feldhaus told him, "Hard to say no to Kentucky, isn't it, Coach?")

Its roster loaded with talent, Sutton's 1988 team won 27 games, won the SEC regular season and SEC tournament championships, and reached the Sweet 16 of the NCAA Tournament. Pelphrey, Feldhaus, and Davis watched as redshirts. It was just as well.

"That team right there, probably the best team by far," says Feldhaus of his ranking it among the five best UK teams he saw during his time in Lexington. "That team was loaded."

Kentucky was in its rightful, familiar place: on top of the SEC standings, near the top of recruiting rankings, and poised to build on the success of the 1988 season.

And then it wasn't.

The March 30, 1988, discovery by Emery Air Freight employees of an opened package containing a videotape and $1,000 sent from the UK basketball offices to the father of Chris Mills triggered the downfall. Conspiracy theories followed.

"Just think about it," says Pelphrey. "Have you ever gotten one of those packages in those white Teflon envelopes, the kind they sent videotapes in, and had it open up by itself? You need a crowbar [to open it]. You need a chain saw. They're not just popping open. . . . We believe someone set us up intentionally."

The program began to crumble from within. Gone were the five leading scorers from '88. The Wildcats had talent—Ellis and Mills in particular—but the almost daily revelations of alleged wrongdoing slowly suffocated the program. A crisis of confidence developed as UK lost its season opener (to Duke by 25 points) as well as three of its next five games, including the supposed gimme-win home opener to Northwestern State.

"You kind of start feeling sorry for yourself," says Feldhaus. "You finally make it to what your dream was and then pretty much the roof caved in. Players were leaving. We had the probation. 'Why now?' is what you're asking."

Says Pelphrey: "The next thing you know we're down to seven players. . . . You really find out what you believe in. I couldn't go anywhere. Go where? There's no place to go. No way. That would have been like deserting my country. That wasn't happening. I wasn't turning my back on my school."

But what about the teammates who transferred? "They weren't from Kentucky," says Pelphrey. "It wasn't their home."

Woods, even with his family's Kentucky roots, wanted to leave UK. Sutton was gone. The NCAA sanctions had arrived with hurricane force. Newton hadn't hired a new coach. UK's best players were already plotting their exit. "I thought I was out of there," says Woods, who was considering a move to Purdue or Indiana. "With those penalties? C'mon. I'm not staying there."

Woods's mother reminded her son that this was the first time he had dealt with real adversity. What was he going to do—run away when the going got tough? But it was Marta McMackin, a longtime administrative assistant in the UK basketball office, who ultimately convinced Woods to stay. The two talked for nearly an hour one day. The gist of her argument: If Newton hires the Yankee from New York—Pitino—you'd be silly to leave.

The Yankee got hired. Woods stayed.

Pitino's staff was an interesting collection of assistant coaches. Sendek had come to UK in early June from Providence College. Pitino first hired him as a graduate assistant there in 1985 and then promoted the 23-year-old to full-time assistant in 1986. Pitino respected Sendek's work ethic and intellect—and with good reason. Sendek had graduated summa cum laude at Carnegie Mellon University. "He was so organized," says Roselle. "He was the only guy I know whose schedule included time for making schedules."

Graduate assistant Billy Donovan and assistant coach Tubby Smith were the next hires. Donovan had played his final two seasons at Providence for Pitino. Before Pitino, Donovan averaged about 3 points a game. With Pitino, he became a 20-point scorer, led Providence to the 1987 Final Four, and was later inducted into the school's hall of fame. He played one year of pro basketball (44 games on Pitino's Knicks team) before calling it quits, passing his Series 7 securities exam, and joining a New York investment firm. About four months later he wanted out of Wall Street.

"I was cold-calling guys . . . selling stocks, whatever they were pushing," says Donovan. "I'm thinking, *There's no way I can do this the rest of my life.*"

He called Pitino in late April 1989 and requested a meeting. The Knicks had just started their playoff series against Philadelphia.

"I want to get into coaching," Donovan told Pitino when they met.

"Billy, don't get into coaching. You're doing well on Wall Street."

"I hate it. I can't do it anymore."

Donovan asked for suggestions. Pitino told him they'd talk after the season. When he took the Kentucky job, he called Donovan with an entry-level grad assistant gig. The 24-year-old Donovan jumped at it.

Tubby Smith had come to UK from South Carolina and was considered an up-and-comer in the business. Newton recommended Smith to Pitino; in 1997, Newton would hire Smith to follow Pitino as UK's head coach.

In late July, Pitino's longtime friend, fellow St. Dominic alum, and Knicks assistant Ralph Willard also agreed to come to UK. Willard, seven years older than Pitino, shared the same ballbusting New York sensibilities as his boss. They had similar personalities and similar competitive streaks.

Pitino had surrounded himself with mostly familiar faces and young type A achievers. Donovan and Sendek were only a few years older than the players. But the hiring with the biggest impact was that of Ray "Rock" Oliver, a little-known strength and conditioning coach from the University of Pittsburgh. To this day, the very mention of Rock to those UK players causes them to momentarily clench in fear.

Oliver was type double-A. He was a football guy (he had played defensive back at Ohio State before transferring to Cincinnati) and looked the part. Body fat was allergic to him. His neck and shoulders were as thick as a concrete wall. You didn't want to mess with Rock Oliver.

Oliver wasn't sure he wanted the Kentucky job. But a young Pitt assistant basketball coach convinced Oliver to take the Pitino plunge. "If you take the job," John Calipari told him, "it will help your career."

There was no wiggle room in Pitino's instructions to Oliver. If Pitino's system of pressing, shooting threes, and constantly playing up-tempo was going to work at UK, the Wildcats would have to be the best-conditioned players in the country. Anything less and UK would have no chance to succeed, especially with its thin scholarship roster and thinner talent level.

"I was just a guy doing what I was told," says Oliver, only 26 at the time. "I was afraid of Rick Pitino. Anybody on that staff who says he wasn't is lying to you. Because your job was day-to-day."

If Oliver was going to live in fear, then so were the players. During his first meeting with the team, Oliver pulled a photo of his wife and daughter out of his wallet and held it up for the Wildcats to see.

"If you make me choose between you or them, I'm going to choose them," said Oliver.

It wasn't a threat but a promise. Oliver had less than four and a half months before the first official practice. That meant he had to accelerate and intensify the off-season conditioning program. The Wildcats had no conception of how their lives were about to change.

"I was the Antichrist to those guys," says Oliver. "All they had was each other."

The facilities at Memorial Coliseum were outdated and primitive. The weight room was partly enclosed with chicken coop wire—not that Oliver cared. His methods and equipment were equally primitive.

Oliver believed in pain, in sweat, in garbage cans for vomiting, in running until you dropped, and in his own original sadistic training device called "Coach Buddy."

In an earlier life, Coach Buddy had been a manual push reel lawn mower, the kind used in the 1940s and 1950s, before everyone started buying Briggs & Stratton mowers. The faster you pushed the heavy, two-wheeled mower, the faster the cutting blades spun.

Oliver attached a disc brake to one of the wheels and wired it so he could vary the amount of resistance. The more resistance, the harder it was to push.

Woods was one of the first players to spend a training session with Coach Buddy. It wasn't so much that Woods had done anything wrong, it was his reputation that did him in. Oliver had been told that Woods was the team's best athlete, but also a sweet talker, a schmoozer, and a bit too confident for his own good. The description reminded Oliver of someone he used to know: the younger version of Oliver, always playing the angles, always trying to outsmart the other guy.

They first met at Memorial Coliseum. Woods had come directly from the airport, only a day removed from playing in the Olympic Festival that summer in Oklahoma City. He stopped by the UK basketball offices wearing street clothes.

"Sean, how you doing?" said Oliver innocently enough. "Hey, how about you and I go out there and do a quick workout."

"But I don't have my gear," said Woods.

"We'll get you some gear."

Oliver introduced him to Coach Buddy. Woods snickered and looked at the mower suspiciously. *What does this crazy man want me to do with this thing?*

"About six minutes later his lung was hanging out of his mouth," says Oliver. "I said, 'Let's get you a greasy pork chop on a dirty ashtray.' He threw up."

The volume of vomit spewed by UK players that summer and early fall would have qualified for the *Guinness World Records*. They met at five o'clock nearly every morning at the UK track, which was several miles from Memorial Coliseum. Equipment manager Bill Keightley, who had been with the basketball program since 1962 and was known as "Mr. Wildcat," initially arranged for a van to take the players to the track. Oliver bolted out of Memorial just as the Wildcats settled into their bench seats.

"What the hell is going on?" yelled Oliver. "Get out of that fucking van. Are you nuts? You better get out of that van and you better beat me to the track."

Scared and shocked, like first-day Marine recruits at Parris Island, the players made it to the track before Oliver. Once there, Oliver put them through athletic torture. Sprints. Middle-distance runs. Long-distance runs. A 6-minute mile was required—or else.

Hanson threw up almost every morning. "I can't do this," he'd mutter under his breath.

Farmer spent so much time with his head in a trash can that teammates joked they didn't remember what his face looked like.

The gentle Keightley, thinking he was doing Feldhaus a favor, had bragged to Oliver that the redshirt freshman was "the toughest guy you'll ever meet."

"We'll see about that," said Oliver, who began pushing Feldhaus harder than the other players.

As Feldhaus staggered through a workout, Oliver mockingly said, "I can't believe someone thought you were the toughest guy out here."

Feldhaus, head down, kept running. When he was out of earshot of Oliver, he turned to a teammate and said, "I want to find out who the *hell* told him that."

Pelphrey would lay in bed each night, his body in revolt, and wish something bad would happen to Oliver. Pelphrey had run so many miles he wasn't sure if he had a basketball scholarship or a track scholarship.

"Mom and Dad, he's killing us," Pelphrey told his parents about Pitino's conditioning edicts. "There's no way we can do what this man says."

Oliver was trying to separate the wheat from the chaff. What was it Vince Lombardi had said? *Fatigue makes cowards of us all.* Oliver wanted to see what fatigue did to his Kentucky players. Who fought through it? Who succumbed to it? His goal wasn't to run the weak ones out of the program, but to identify the players Pitino could depend on.

Of course, if a player did want to call it quits, Oliver would happily help him pack his bags.

This was Bear Bryant and the Junction Boys—but without the attrition. The dreaded track work at 5 a.m. Then weight-lifting sessions in the chicken coop. The post-workout pickup games. Then another workout at the track at 3 p.m. Then Coach Buddy. And this was just the preseason conditioning program. Once school began it was worse: early-morning conditioning, practice, classes, individual instruction, classes, another practice. A player could leave his room before dawn and not see it again until close to midnight. Pitino worked them like mountain mules.

Psychological profile exams, the same ones Pitino had used with the Knicks, were given to each player. The results showed that Hanson, more than any other Wildcat, was the best equipped to handle criticism, to project strength, and to keep an even disposition.

"I was in his grille, man," says Oliver. "And he never complained. He was the guy who kept the ship running. Hardest worker I had."

Farmer, the basketball prodigy and Kentucky high school player of the decade, was not the hardest worker. In many ways—and it wasn't necessarily his fault—he had been pampered, even spoiled, as a high school star. He had enjoyed the attention and adulation that came with peppering the high school record books with his name. But UK wasn't the Clay County Tigers. He wasn't in Manchester anymore.

Pitino instructed Oliver to toughen up the prodigy. He also wanted Farmer to lose at least 25 pounds. Oliver did what he was told. "If I was going to keep my job," says Oliver, "his ass was going to be in shape."

Farmer led the team in vomiting. He led it in unfinished conditioning drills. He led it in falling behind his teammates on the track. He thought the world was against him. He was convinced Oliver and Pitino had it in for him.

"Richie, at the beginning, was considered a prima donna," says Woods. "He was a down-home country boy, came from a great family, was just an A-1 guy. I used to feel sorry for Richie because what they were asking him to do, his body couldn't do it. Rock Oliver would just kill him."

For weeks, Farmer reported to Memorial in the early-morning darkness for a *pre-conditioning* conditioning session—under the unrelenting eye of Oliver. Farmer would run on the treadmill. Or he'd be ordered to start pounding the steps on the StairMaster. He did it in the morning. In the afternoon. In the evening. His teammates would get some occasional R&R time—to go "courtin'," as Farmer put it. But Farmer spent his days and nights sweating away the weight.

There would be no sympathy from Oliver. When Farmer glanced down at the workout machine's video monitor, it read: *Richie Farmer . . . Your days are limited as a Wildcat.* Oliver had programmed it that way.

Farmer had never been treated like this. How could he be revered in the commonwealth but reviled by this SOB of a strength and conditioning coach and the little Yankee from New York? All he ever heard was, "Richie, I'm going to send your ass back to eastern Kentucky."

Didn't they understand that he was a basketball player? That he was a winner? Helloooooo? Didn't anybody remember what he'd done against Ballard? Or even against Ole Miss on Senior Night last season? Ol' Richie Farmer the true freshman had won the game at the buzzer with a three-pointer from the top of the key. It meant Mike Scott, a scholarship senior on the team, got a win on his final night at Rupp. It meant that no matter what happened in their final regular-season game or in the SEC Tournament, the Wildcats wouldn't lose 20 games. It meant that Sutton's final victory at Kentucky was made possible by a player he hadn't wanted to sign. Didn't that count for something to these people?

"We get a new coach and we think he's like the exorcist," says Farmer. "I kept waiting for his head to spin around. He was unlike any guy we had ever seen—and I say that lovingly."

Farmer was trying to make sense of his new world. He was a good student, but his life was basketball—Kentucky basketball. He wasn't complicated. He liked to hunt and fish. He liked to dip. His nickname was "Vern," in honor of the redneck humor shtick done by Lexington-born Jim Varney's "Ernest P. Worrell." Farmer could imitate Ernest doing his "Hey, Vern" commercials. Of course, half the time the non-Southern members of the team couldn't understand a word he was saying. In a later UK media guide, each thumbnail bio would include the fill-in-the-blank statement, "Before a basketball game I . . . ." Farmer's answer: "Think about the game."

Still, Farmer was reaching his breaking point. Woods found him sitting on his bed one day listening to some Hank Williams Jr.

"You all right?" said Woods.

"Woody," said Farmer, "by god I am going to take my ass back to eastern Kentucky if this shit keeps up."

"Richie, look around," said Woods. "He's *got* to play us. There's only eight of us." (Jeff Brassow, a freshman guard from Houston, had joined the team.)

"You got a point there. But I don't know if my body can take it."

A few days later, as Farmer was grinding away during another pre-dawn workout on the StairMaster, the despair hit critical mass. It could have been Oliver's cursing that did it. Or the loneliness of those early morning solo conditioning sessions. Or that he simply wanted someone to acknowledge that he was trying to get better. Whatever it was, Farmer had had enough.

Farmer hit the Stop button on the StairMaster, stepped off the machine, looked at Oliver, and said, "That's it."

He was quitting. Farmer had never quit anything in his life—especially basketball—but this isn't what he'd signed up for. He walked into the locker room and began to cry. He was walking away from the game and the school he loved. He couldn't believe he wouldn't fulfill his dream of playing four years for Big Blue.

"You need to go tell Coach what you've done," said Oliver.

Farmer didn't change out of his workout clothes. He wadded his street clothes together, tucked them under his arm, and walked upstairs to the basketball office. On any other day there would have been some-one there by now. But Pitino was out recruiting and none of the other assistants were in their offices. So Farmer walked out to his truck, dumped his stuff on the seat, and started crying again. He couldn't drive to Manchester in this condition. Instead, he drove across campus, woke up a buddy, and asked him to take him home.

"Why?" said the friend.

"'Cause I quit. I quit the team."

"What? You can't quit."

When Farmer arrived in Manchester, his mother, father, brother, and sister were waiting for him in the living room. Farmer vented.

"I can't take it anymore," he said. "I'm doing everything that they've asked me to. I'm working out three times a day and nobody else is doing that. I'm trying to do everything right and it's not working. I don't think they want me there. So I don't want to play if they don't want me."

By the time Pitino returned from his recruiting trip, the Farmers had driven back to Lexington and to Pitino's house. Joanne Pitino briefed her husband after he pulled into the driveway.

"Mr. and Mrs. Farmer are in the kitchen and Richie is downstairs crying his eyes out," she said. "His parents say he's quitting basketball."

Pitino walked into the house, and the mood was decidedly somber. Richard and Virginia Farmer looked as if someone had died. They said their son was leaving UK and that he wasn't changing his mind.

"But we haven't even started practice yet," said Pitino.

Pitino met Farmer downstairs.

"What's going on, Rich?"

"Coach, basketball's not fun anymore. I'm not having fun."

"Well, let me get this straight. Rock is putting you through hell in the weight room trying to get you in shape. You're running up and down the track. Rich, you think that's fun? Fun is when you step on the court and you compete in front of 24,000 people. This is the pain you've got to go through to make it someday."

"Coach, I don't want to stay with it. I want to quit."

"You know what, Rich? I want to quit, too. I just came off a long recruiting trip. It wasn't fun. I'm tired of battling guys who turn me down. That's not fun. I'm tired of trying to make you quick. I'm tired of the whole thing, and I'm going to quit, too. We're going to have a joint press conference, and we're going to quit together."

Pitino's sarcasm was as thick as cookie dough. But Farmer wasn't sure at first.

"Aw, come on, Coach. You can't quit."

"No, Rich, we're going to quit together. Let's go upstairs, have a press conference, and we're going to make national news."

Farmer finally got it. He laughed.

"Coach, I just want you to know that I would give anything in the world to play here and be part of what you're doing. I love this university more than anything in the world. I love you and I love being part of this, but I just feel like you don't want me."

"I'm trying to make you better," said Pitino. "You've been doing great, and part of it is my fault. You needed a pat on the back, and you weren't getting it. I want you to be part of this team. Rich, you've got to go through this another three or four weeks, and then it will be fun for you."

"Well, Coach, that's all you had to say. All I needed to know is that you wanted me to be part of this team."

An understanding was reached, but Pitino and Oliver's conditioning methods remained draconian. One morning Oliver worked the players so long and hard that Feldhaus fell asleep at the UK training table, his face plopping down into a bowl of cornflakes. Skim milk and cornflakes, by the way—Feldhaus was under orders to lose weight, too. He was weighed every day, and his lunches and dinners were almost always low-cal turkey. "If I eat one more piece of turkey, I'm going to start gobbling," Feldhaus groused.

But nobody was under a stricter calorie limit than Farmer.

"Richie Farmer—I wouldn't blame him if he weighed 900 pounds now," says Oliver. "We had him eating fucking Tic Tacs. When they say to other players, 'You guys couldn't do what we did,' well, they ain't lying. Nowadays you can't do the things we did to those kids. It's a different young person these days. . . . I'm here to tell you, those guys became the best-conditioned team that ever played basketball."

Everyone worked—no one more than Pitino. When he was in town, his mornings almost always began with a 5:30 pickup game at Memorial Coliseum. Assistant coaches, selected staff members, and team managers were expected to be there if they were in town.

"He's kidding, right?" said Smith to Willard.

"Tubby, understand that these games are going to be bloodbaths. And whatever you do, don't be late."

Smith, scared stiff by the warning, went to bed that night wearing a jockstrap and shorts with his sneakers positioned at the foot of the bed.

The full-court games *were* bloodbaths. Oliver, the former defensive back, broke two of Smith's ribs and nearly did in Newton's son, Martin. Sendek blew out a knee. The ultracompetitive Pitino would battle Donovan. Donovan, no dummy, knew what to say whenever Pitino called a foul in a tight ball game.

"Yeah, Coach, you're right," said Donovan, the lowly grad assistant.

Not surprisingly, Pitino's teams won a lot.

"Rick was pretty good," says Oliver. "He was even better at counting."

As October 14 bled into October 15, about 10,000 basketball-starved fans wedged their way into Memorial Coliseum for the annual Midnight Madness festivities. The public address announcer served as timekeeper.

"Ladies and gentlemen, in just one minute the Rick Pitino era begins!"

The era would begin with eight scholarship players and little else. In the minutes leading up to the first official workout—televised locally—Pitino stood in a Coliseum tunnel and soaked in the energy and noise of those 10,000 fans. He was awed by their support but unsure what he could give them back. Pitino had a system, an innovative one, but he wasn't sure he had any players who could execute it.

Midnight Madness was exciting and a welcome relief (at last they were on an actual basketball court instead of that damn track, thought Pelphrey), but it wasn't a real Pitino-run practice. This was dunks and drills and a chance to play to the fans. In the privacy of a closed gym, the results were much less crowd-pleasing.

No matter where he coached, Pitino's first team practice always included time to install certain elements of his press. To run Pitino's press, you had to be able to deny the ball inbounds (in other words, guard your man so tight that he couldn't shake free to get an inbounds catch). If he did catch a pass, you had to contain him long enough for the defense to rotate and help. And if he broke containment, you had to be able to quickly run down the dribbler and tip the ball away.

The Wildcats couldn't do any of this. They couldn't deny the ball. They couldn't contain for more than one dribble. And they were too slow to catch the dribbler. When the staff convened in a meeting room after practice, Pitino asked his assistants, "Well, what'd you think?"

"Holy shit," said Willard, who, after seeing the Wildcats in action, thought they'd be lucky to win a single game.

"You're right," Pitino said. "And we've got to make them holy good. That's our job."

Willard argued that Pitino should consider running a different system with this team. These Wildcats, he said, weren't equipped to pressure and run. There weren't enough athletes.

Pitino knew the argument had merit. But what was the alternative?

"You know what?" Pitino told his assistants. "We're expected to win five games, so what's the difference? Let's get the style in, and at least it will be exciting to the fans, because the fans want to go back to a running style. Let's get our tails kicked, but let's incorporate our style."

Kentucky's new style required bodies. Pitino added five walk-ons to the roster so he'd have enough players for his grueling practices. Of course, the walk-ons were even less talented and less conditioned than the scholarship Wildcats. At times, those early UK practices were so horrifyingly comical that some of the assistant coaches wanted to burst out in laughter.

But Pitino was working on a secret weapon, which, if all went well, would be fully operational in 12 months. The weapon was from New York City—Harlem, to be exact—stood 6'8", and averaged 22.5 points a game for Cardinal Hayes High School. The weapon's name was Jamal Mashburn.

Forget the conditioning program. Forget the three elements of the press. Forget the philosophy behind shooting so many three-pointers. None of it mattered if you didn't have players who could make a difference. Mashburn, a top-70 talent who was being recruited by lots of major programs, could make a difference. Pitino had to have him.

At Cardinal Hayes, Mashburn was essentially a post-up forward. He dominated under the basket. But what made him so attractive to Pitino (other than the fact he was already better as a high school senior than anybody on the UK roster) were his shooting range, his ball-handling skills, and his athleticism. Mashburn, who liked to pretend he was Magic Johnson, was as comfortable from the three-point line as he was on the low post. He could drive to the hoop. He would be unstoppable in Pitino's up-tempo system. The only negatives: Mashburn was a little fleshy and a little immature, and word was that he didn't have much of a work ethic. The next weight he lifted would be his first.

Sendek, even before he joined Pitino at Kentucky, had been recruiting Mashburn for several years. Providence was a Big East program, and the Big East always worked the fertile basketball grounds of New York City. In an age before texts and tweets, Sendek would send Mashburn handwritten notes on Providence stationery with the Friar logo on top. *On a flight right now, but was thinking about you hitting a last-second shot for us*, wrote Sendek. That sort of thing. Mashburn read them and then tossed them. He thought Sendek was a nice, sincere guy, but corny. Which was true.

Mashburn had been born and raised in Harlem. He lived in Building 70, Apartment 80, of the Ralph J. Rangel housing project, about a block or so from the famed hoops oasis of Rucker Park and just across the Harlem River from Yankee Stadium. It wasn't the worst of the housing projects, but it wasn't a neighborhood for the weak. There were robberies, shootings, killings, drugs, and turf wars. There likely was more violent crime in the wee hours of a Harlem day than there was for a decade in Paintsville or Manchester. Put it this way: Helen Mashburn didn't make her son a bologna sandwich and then send him out to the backyard at the Rangel projects. There were no backyards.

Mashburn's father and mother had split up when he was 10. Robert Mashburn was a professional boxer who fought Ken Norton (Norton won by KO in the fourth round) and Larry Holmes (Holmes by TKO in the seventh), and who sparred with Muhammad Ali. He later became a special-service officer for the New York Police Department and stayed in contact with his son.

Mashburn kept to himself. He played ball, but he never bragged about his growing list of accomplishments and college suitors. Still, word spread in the neighborhood. Mashburn became a point of pride, and even the gang members looked out for him. If trouble was percolating around Rangel, it wasn't unusual for someone to tell Mashburn, "Jamal, it's time for you to leave." And Mashburn, knowing what it meant, would depart immediately, no questions asked.

Recruiters didn't come to Rangel. Mashburn wouldn't let them. He wasn't ashamed of where he lived, but he did fear for the safety of white (and black) college coaches in suits.

As a kid, he had rooted for Syracuse, a popular spot for New York City players (including Mashburn's favorite, Pearl Washington). But after a visit, Mashburn wasn't convinced the coaching staff could develop him into an NBA pro. Plus, they already had Billy Owens at his position.

His mom had only one recruiting rule: Mashburn couldn't go to nearby St. John's. It wasn't the program that bothered her but the program's location. A school away from New York meant less chance of her son having to deal with local hangers-on and "friends" more interested in Mashburn's future earnings than anything else. She wanted him to sign with Wake Forest and that nice man Dave Odom. Intrigued by the prospect of playing with Rodney Rogers and Randolph Childress, Mashburn seriously considered becoming a Demon Deacon. But he found the Winston-Salem, North Carolina, campus small and sedate. It was a lovely place, but it reminded him of his visits to his mother's hometown of rural Beckley, West Virginia, where the highlight of the night was catching fireflies and putting them into a jelly jar.

Kentucky? Mashburn had heard of the program, but he didn't know where the campus was located. He barely knew where the state was located. He didn't know Lexington from Louisville, bluegrass from Blue Cross and Blue Shield. Adolph Rupp? No clue who he was. Kyle Macy? Never heard of him.

Mashburn had read something about Chris Mills and the NCAA, but he hadn't paid much attention to the controversy. He was aware of the sanctions, but they weren't a deal-breaker. Mashburn was a pragmatist. He wanted to play for a coach and in a program that would prepare him for his chosen career, the NBA. He wanted to play in a system that would best develop and showcase his skills. And he wanted to play as a freshman.

That wouldn't be a problem at Kentucky. Mashburn had thumbed through the UK media guide and quickly realized the Wildcats' roster was sparse. He vaguely remembered Woods's name and saw that Farmer had put up some nice high school numbers. But Pelphrey? Feldhaus? The rest of them? No idea who they were. None of them were from NYC, he knew that. And in his mind, the best basketball was played in New York, not in the Maysvilles and Paintsvilles of Kentucky.

Sendek had switched schools and stationery, but Mashburn

remained his number-one priority. He arranged a meeting for Pitino, Mashburn, and Mashburn's mom at the Gauchos Gym in the Bronx, where Mashburn played his AAU ball. It was September in New York, and the thermometer was still stuck on hot and humid. You could have cooked a pot roast in the gym.

Mashburn, Helen Mashburn, Pitino, and Sendek found some space in the upper bleachers as a game began below. A public address announcer, his microphone volume at full capacity, decided to do play-by-play. Not a wisp of air blew through the gym.

Pitino began his presentation, practically having to yell over the noise in the gym. UK had a long tradition of basketball excellence . . . UK was a fine academic institution . . . UK could provide Jamal with the necessary tools for basketball and academic excellence. UK was a wonderful place to—

And then he stopped.

Uh oh, thought Sendek. *What's he doing?*

Pitino leaned toward Mashburn.

"Jamal, I'm going to be honest with you. You have a reputation of not always being the hardest worker. I have the opposite reputation. We have individual instruction. We work hard."

Sendek nearly fell off his bleacher seat. Was Pitino *trying* to blow it with Mashburn? Didn't Pitino know how badly UK needed Mashburn?

"Coach," said Mashburn, "I know if I'm going to make it I need someone like you."

It wasn't a commitment, but it also wasn't a refusal. Mashburn agreed to come to Lexington for an official visit.

In the meantime, Pitino called Mashburn's coach at Cardinal Hayes, Tom Murray. Pitino had coached one of his players, Darryl Wright, at Providence. Wright was a challenge; Pitino had almost redshirted him in 1987, and early in the season he kicked him off the team. But Wright regrouped, matured, and, along with Donovan, led the Friars to the Final Four.

Pitino wanted to know more about Mashburn. Murray told him.

"Rick, if you thought Darryl Wright was a pain in the ass, Mashburn will drive you crazy."

Murray's scathing evaluation caused Pitino to tell Sendek to pull the plug on Mashburn's recruitment.

"There's no way we can keep this guy," Pitino said.

"Coach," said Sendek, "Tom is an old-school high school coach. Mash will be fine."

Pitino calmed down. But when Mashburn arrived in Lexington for his official visit, he wore a Syracuse hat facing backward. It didn't go over well.

"Mash, it'd be a good idea here at Kentucky if you get rid of the Syracuse hat," said Pitino.

"Don't worry about it, Coach. I'm coming to Kentucky."

"What do you mean?"

"I'm coming to play for you."

Even Pitino was momentarily stunned. "Why would you want to do that?"

"Because everybody in New York tells me I should go play for the Knicks coach."

"But I'm not the Knicks coach anymore. I'm at Kentucky. Why would you want to play for the Knicks coach?"

"Because everybody says I'm lazy, and everybody says you won't allow me to be lazy."

"Are you lazy?"

"I don't think so."

"Well, are you willing to work hard, Mash?"

"I'm willing to do whatever it takes, Coach."

Mashburn asked Pitino if he'd start for the Wildcats. Pitino told him he'd be considered for a starting position if he earned it. It was a lie, of course.

"If he was just breathing, he was going to start," says Pitino. "I didn't tell him that. . . . But he looked at the team and he knew."

As it turned out, Mashburn led Cardinal Hayes to the Catholic High School Championship. Pitino called Murray, congratulated him, and said, "Not bad for a lazy kid, huh?"

Said Murray: "Ah, he's the best. He just needed to mature. He's the nicest kid in the world."

Mashburn was young—only 16 when he began his senior year of high school. He became the first player to commit to Pitino at Kentucky. The official announcement came 11 days after Midnight Madness.

In retrospect, it was an extraordinary decision by Mashburn. He could have gone almost anywhere, but instead signed with a school that he couldn't find on a map and a program that was under crippling NCAA sanctions. If it were similar circumstances today, says Pitino, "you couldn't get him. These kids today are so much into instant gratification. Their mind-set is one and done," referring to players who go into the NBA draft after their freshman year. "Mash was just a different breed of cat. Today, you don't get a Jamal Mashburn. The kids aren't like him."

But Mashburn wouldn't be in a UK uniform for another year. Pitino had to somehow put together a competitive team in time for the November 28 opener against Ohio University.

There were signs that the Wildcats were slowly adjusting to the Pitino way. As their conditioning became better, so did their practice sessions. Farmer scored 55 points in a scrimmage. Pelphrey was gaining confidence. Woods was beginning to assert himself. Feldhaus was as tough as Keightley had said. Miller could shoot. Hanson was the glue gun for the team. There was hope.

"I think the biggest mistake we made as a staff—those guys were better than we thought," says Oliver. "Those guys worked."

Those guys beat Ohio and then lost by only two points to powerful Indiana on the road. Those guys beat Mississippi State and Tennessee

Tech. Then those guys suffered the second-largest margin of defeat in Kentucky history—a 150–95 loss to No. 2–ranked Kansas at Allen Fieldhouse in early December.

"You'd think if you scored 95 points you're at least going to be in the game," says Farmer. "We lost by 55. I have never been beaten like that."

Three Wildcats fouled out. Pitino picked up two technicals. UK committed 27 turnovers. The Jayhawks broke Pitino's press at will. KU scored 80 in the first half and led by 19 at the break.

Pitino stormed into the visitors' locker room at halftime, picked up a Gatorade cooler, and slammed it to the ground. The top flew off, and Gatorade exploded out of the container and directly onto Donovan. Donovan didn't move an inch. No one dared to move during the tirade.

When the game resumed, Hanson quickly picked up his third foul.

"Rick, we need to get Reggie out," Willard told Pitino. "We need to slow it down."

Pitino looked at him as if Willard had just suggested that he eat spaghetti with motor oil, not red sauce.

"What? Slow it down? No."

The Kansas lead grew. UK was out of time-outs. Jayhawks coach Roy Williams yelled down to Pitino late in the game.

"Rick, what do you want me to do? We've got the third team in. . . . Do you want me to call a time-out for you?"

"Go fuck yourself," said Pitino, according to those on press row that day. "You know what you can do with your fucking time-out."

Pitino didn't like that Williams had kept several of his starters in the game when UK had been reduced to playing walk-ons. Williams didn't like Pitino's decision to keep pressing. The postgame handshake was icy.

Afterward, Pitino lit into his team. "You're soft!" he told his players.

Pitino's mood was no better on the flight home. He lashed out at Willard, telling him, "This was the worst scouting report I've ever had in the history of college basketball."

The Wildcats lost five of their next seven games, but UK fans didn't seem to mind so much. They were beginning to wrap their arms around this team—"Pitino's Bombinos," as *Herald-Leader* columnist John McGill called them—and its style of play. After the deliberate offense played by Sutton's teams, these Wildcats were a refreshing change. And they played with an enthusiasm that was understandably missing from the death march during Sutton's final year at UK.

"It's the most joy I can ever remember fans having in any season I've been around for," says Jerry Tipton, who has covered Kentucky basketball since 1981. "They were thrilled to, one, have a team and, two, have an entertaining team. It was one of the rare occasions when Kentucky was the little guy."

Pitino ran his players—and himself—into the ground. At times, the most fluid thing about them was their sweat. Pitino would return to the Kentucky locker room at halftime with his shirt and suit coat soaked in perspiration.

He was relentless. If his team made a costly error during a game, he would turn to Willard and hiss, "You're fired." And for that exact moment, Pitino meant it. He fired Willard at least 200 times during their time together.

A team trainer was instructed to have a fresh cup of root beer or cream soda on the sidelines for Pitino at all times. The soda kept Pitino's throat moist, allowing him to yell throughout the entire game. Once, he reached for the cup and it was empty.

"What do you think I am, a camel?" he screamed. "Get me a drink!"

No detail was too small. No dream was too audacious. Pitino would will the Blue Bloods to greatness. They had been beaten down by circumstances and chaos, but Pitino wasn't interested in pity parties. He was interested in only one thing: wins.

Bill Curry had been hired as Kentucky's new football coach in early January. When it came time to sign the contract, Curry noticed a mistake on the documents. They read: *Bill Curry, head basketball coach at the University of Kentucky.*

He called Newton. "C.M., I don't mind coaching both, but do you think we should let Rick know?"

Curry attended UK's basketball games and often had a seat near the Wildcat bench. He watched in amazement as Pitino yanked Pelphrey out of a game after the forward failed to take an open jumper. "Shoot the three or I'm going to take away your scholarship!" Pitino had yelled at Pelphrey.

Curry had played for Vince Lombardi, the great Green Bay Packers coach. He wasn't easily impressed. "But I could see halfway through the first season that Pitino was one of the best coaches I'd ever seen in any sport," says Curry. "A lot of the things I believed in, I learned from him."

Pitino's signature press didn't always work. The three-point shots didn't always fall. The thin rotation didn't always hold up. But when these elements were clicking, the results could be jaw-dropping, such as the signature victory of the 1989–90 season: a 100–95 win against Shaq, Jackson, Roberts, and the rest of the No. 12–ranked LSU Tigers.

The 6'7" Feldhaus, assigned to guard the massive O'Neal at times, outscored Shaq, 24–14. O'Neal had 21 rebounds, but Feldhaus had a creditable 10. Miller had 29 points, and Pelphrey, Woods, Farmer, and Hanson all scored in double figures.

"Those kids put on a clinic," says Pitino. "[LSU] couldn't guard the offense."

The Bombinos finished with a 14–14 record (13 wins at Rupp), exceeding Ledford's prediction by 9 wins and preseason expectations by infinity. By season's end, Rupp was again a madhouse. Pitino had been right: Those UK season tickets were precious things.

Eight scholarship players and a handful of walk-ons wound up fourth in the SEC standings. They had actually outscored their opposition for the season and done it with just one senior, Hanson. Most of all, they had survived.

Survived their schedule. Survived Oliver. Survived Pitino.

FIVE

October 15, 1989

Laettner was a happy man as he walked into the Duke locker room for the first day of practice. He had played in a Final Four as a freshman. He had seen his game improve exponentially. The way he looked at it, he was in the perfect program, with the perfect coach, under the perfect set of standards.

His freshman season had been a wonderful blur of wins, parties, coeds, classes, and intense, ballbuster practices—and Laettner had loved it all, even the humbling chores, such as carrying the dirty uniforms down to the laundry room or lugging Ferry's or Snyder's bags on road trips. That's what freshmen players did at Duke: They paid their dues and didn't say a peep.

Now that Laettner was a sophomore, it was time for someone else to be the grunt and replace him on the lowest rung of the Duke basketball food chain. He had served his sentence. That was the beauty of Krzyzewski's program: It didn't play favorites.

Until now.

Krzyzewski had spent nine grueling, work-intensive years turning Duke basketball into a self-sustaining program. Along with his family, his assistant coaches, and his players through those years, Krzyzewski had created a Duke basketball ethos. When talking about that ethos, Krzyzewski often asked his players to "jump all in." It was one of his favorite phrases. Of course, there was no mistaking his favorite analogy—that a team could be either like a hand or like a fist. A hand could create power, but a hand in the shape of a fist could do so much more. Krzyzewski wanted the Blue Devils to be an iron fist.

The former Army officer didn't believe in rules as much as he believed in self-empowerment. He had been ruled to death at West Point, and he despised that part of the Academy experience. What he had resented most about the seemingly endless list of regulations was that the rules were always written by somebody else.

Krzyzewski wanted his players to help determine their own guidelines. The more input they had, the more connected they would feel to the program. He liked to say that the growth of a plant placed in a container is confined by the size and shape of the container. Fewer rules meant a better chance his players could grow unencumbered by artificial boundaries.

It was New Agey, but it seemed to work. His players met as a team before the season began and came up with a short list of their own "standards," sort of a team constitution.

But the Duke coach also knew the fragile nature of major college basketball. His program was well established and highly successful. He was signing some of the best high school prospects in the country. His teams had reached three Final Fours in four years, but there were no guarantees it would continue. All it would take is a key injury, a series of recruiting miscalculations, or a missed NCAA Tournament or two, and Duke could fall from the elite. It had happened to other programs; it could happen to Duke.

That uncertainty is what helped drive Krzyzewski. He was allergic to complacency. Complacency was for losers.

Krzyzewski had also been profoundly affected by a comment in the

Blue Devils' locker room following their second-round loss to Boston College in the 1985 NCAAs. He had heard the pain in Dan Meagher's voice as the starting forward and senior captain told his teammates, "You guys don't understand. I don't get another chance."

Many of the same Duke players on that 1985 team—Jay Bilas, Mark Alarie, Johnny Dawkins, Tommy Amaker, and Billy King, among others—would reach the Final Four in 1986. But Krzyzewski remembered Meagher's words, and always would.

So Krzyzewski stood in front of his team on that October 1989 day fully aware he was about to break one of his most sacred pledges: that playing time was never given for free at Duke. But he was certain the step he was about to take would be in the best interest of his team.

No nimble-thinking CEO—and that's what major college coaches had become by then—could afford to let the ways of the past automatically determine his actions in the present. To succeed, you had to be willing to question everything, even your own methods, in search of a better path. Krzyzewski felt he possessed something—someone—for whom a break with tradition was the right way to go. So he did the previously unthinkable.

"This is your team," said Krzyzewski, handing a basketball to a 6-foot (maybe), 150-pound, handkerchief-white newcomer with sleepy eyes and a "Fuhgeddaboutit" Jersey accent.

Bobby Hurley took the ball and, without realizing it, instantly became the target of his teammates' cold stares. Krzyzewski had chosen him—a freshman!—over the three senior starters: Abdelnaby, Henderson, and Brickey. Brickey was the Duke captain (no small honor), while Henderson was the Blue Devils' leading returning scorer.

But by Krzyzewski's stunning decree, it was Hurley's team now. The announcement cut through the Blue Devils like a toothpick through a martini olive.

Laettner couldn't believe it. This was nothing less than an outright betrayal to him. He looked at Krzyzewski and then at the pasty-skinned freshman and thought, *You got to be frickin' kidding me. So that's how it is, huh?*

Hurley had been on the Duke campus for, what, two months? He had never played in a Duke game, had never felt the wrath of Krzyzewski during the heat of practice, had never earned the honor of wearing a Duke jersey. And now Krzyzewski was handing Hurley a basketball—and the Blue Devils with it—in some grand, symbolic bullshit gesture?

He had played in pickup games with and against Hurley for the last couple of months; everybody on the Duke team had. Hurley was good, but nobody had left the gym after those games raving about little Bobby Hurley of Jersey City, New Jersey.

How many times had Laettner and the rest of the Blue Devils heard Krzyzewski lecture them on the Duke basketball code? A hundred times? A thousand? Laettner knew the code by heart. He *loved* the equality of the code. Respected it. Believed in it.

Nothing is given to anybody . . . Every minute of playing time is earned . . . Doesn't matter if you're the number-one recruit in the country or the lowest man on the roster . . . You start each season as equals, and your performance determines if, when, and for how long you're on the court.

That's the way it had been for Laettner, Davis, and Palmer as freshmen. You worked your way into the lineup. You didn't show up the first day of practice and have the coach say, "This is your team."

Laettner wanted Hurley to be put through the Krzyzewski wringer, not just because he had been put through it himself a season earlier, but because *everybody* had. The wringer exposed your flaws, tested your resolve, brought you closer to your teammates. It was a shared suffering.

It was unfathomable to Laettner that Krzyzewski would make an exception. Not only was it unfair, thought Laettner, but it was borderline irresponsible for Krzyzewski to place those kinds of pressures on a freshman.

Laettner knew all about those pressures. He had played in all 36 games as a freshman and started 16 of them, including the Final Four semi against Seton Hall. He averaged 8.9 points and 4.7 rebounds but lost weight as the toll of the five-month season wore down his already slender frame. Krzyzewski was concerned about the weight loss, so he instructed Duke strength and conditioning coach Sonny Falcone to put 20 pounds of muscle on Laettner during the summer.

The 35-year-old Falcone, who had played defensive tackle for Duke in the mid-1970s, began working out with Laettner four times a week. Not supervising, but doing the same weight-lifting regimen as the sophomore center. It was Falcone's way of making sure Laettner didn't cut corners.

Fat chance. Laettner was a workout freak. When they were done with one weight-lifting circuit, Laettner would turn to Falcone and say, "What else we gonna do?"

Laettner arrived at that first official practice weighing 230 pounds. His body fat was down, his muscle mass up. He had done what was asked because, in his mind, that's how you earned your place in the program. Laettner had every intention of remaining a starter. Hurley? What had Hurley done other than sign his scholarship papers and play in some summer pickup games?

It was at the exact moment when Krzyzewski handed Hurley the ball—and handed over a roster of three seniors, three juniors, three sophomores, and three freshmen to the Jersey kid—that Laettner decided to make the basketball life of Duke's new point guard a daily hell. If Krzyzewski wouldn't do it, then Laettner would.

"From that day on," says Thomas Hill, one of those freshmen players that year, "Christian made him earn it every day."

Laettner wasn't the only player whose jaw dropped when Krzyzewski anointed Hurley. Brian Davis, who grinded his way through the 1988–89 season as the third or fourth man off the bench, fumed as the scene unfolded, muttering to himself, "This is *our* goddamn team. Isn't this some bullshit?"

Thomas Hill watched with envy and anger as Krzyzewski inserted Hurley directly into the lineup.

Man, this dude hasn't done anything, and it's his *team?* thought Hill.

But what was Hurley supposed to do, say no? Hurley too had been stunned by the announcement. After all, Krzyzewski told him what he tells everyone—that he didn't guarantee starting jobs—during the home visit in Jersey City.

The Duke coach knew he didn't have many options at point guard. He could move Henderson, who was a decent ball handler, from shooting guard to the point—but was that fair to Henderson in his senior season? He could go with Joe Cook, a junior who had zero career starts and who had played in only five games in 1989 because of academic reasons. Or he could start Hurley, giving the freshman valuable practice time with the first-teamers.

With the exception of Abdelnaby, who had known Hurley for more than 10 years and had played for his father in AAU summer ball, the Blue Devils looked at the newcomer and saw an undersized white point guard who admittedly had some talent. Krzyzewski looked at Hurley and saw a player who had more than talent: He had a gift. He realized Hurley needed freedom more than structure.

Hurley had starred at national power St. Anthony High School, played for his old man, the legendary Bob Hurley Sr., and had constantly distinguished himself among great players. So rather than have him worry about being a freshman and having to follow Duke protocol, Krzyzewski purposely removed the label and told him to be the same Hurley who had been so dominant at St. Anthony, the same Hurley who had planted himself in front of the oncoming Shaquille O'Neal during the McDonald's All-American game and coaxed a hard-earned charge call from the officials.

"He didn't earn that [starting job]," says Krzyzewski. "Yeah, I know that. . . . But he was coached in high school by a great coach who let him go. He also had really good players with him. In other words, if I'm a pitcher and I don't have a catcher who can catch a 95-mile-per-hour fastball, I can't throw it 95. I throw it 88, 85, so he can catch it. [Hurley] was always in a situation where he could throw his fastball. When he came here he had the same thing. He had a coach who understood that he needed to go—and he had good players around him."

Krzyzewski wanted Hurley to throw his heater. If Laettner, Davis, and the other Blue Devils wanted to pout about it, then they had better do it off the court. There would be no debate about the decision.

Hurley wasn't supposed to be a Blue Devil. He had made up his mind to stay close to home, which meant the Big East Conference and probably Seton Hall, where two of his St. Anthony teammates, Jerry Walker and Terry Dehere, had committed to play for P. J. Carlesimo. St. Anthony had finished the season 32–0, won the state championship, and earned *USA Today*'s No. 1 national ranking. There was pressure on Hurley to stay local and go to nearby Seton Hall, or at least to play in the Big East. Villanova was the other favorite, with Syracuse and St. John's as possibilities.

North Carolina was in the mix, too. Hurley grew up as a devout Tar Heels fan and attended Carolina's basketball camps when he was in elementary school. For decades there had been a New Jersey/New York basketball pipeline to Chapel Hill (Kenny Smith, Billy Cunningham, Sam Perkins, Mike O'Koren, Larry Brown, Mitch Kupchak, Jim Delany, among others), and Hurley envisioned himself joining the list. Carolina was his first choice, and everybody else was number two.

But Tar Heels coach Dean Smith's first choice was Kenny Anderson, the national sensation from Queens. Anderson, the consensus high school player of the year, was also a point guard, and he was being romanced by all the major programs, including Duke.

Bob Sr. encouraged Hurley to consider other options, including Duke and Krzyzewski, who had told him in the summer of 1988 that, yes, he was recruiting Anderson, "but I want your son." Bob Sr. knew his oldest son could play anywhere. After all, he had raised him on the game.

When Hurley was only a few years old, Bob Sr. brought him to a St. Anthony practice and set up his crib at courtside of the White Eagle Bingo Hall, where the playing floor stretched only 65 feet long, compared with the regulation 94. When Hurley was seven or eight, he and his younger brother Dan would steal the ball from the refs during time-outs at St. Anthony games and wow the crowd by shooting—and swishing—22-footers. When he was in junior high, Hurley would watch St. Anthony guards—small guards, such as David Rivers and Kenny Wilson—and imitate the way they handled the basketball. Hurley was small too, but he loved to figure out new ways to dribble the ball between his legs or behind his back. And when he was in high school, Hurley would go with Walker and Dehere and look for games in every part of the city: the Country Village Courts just blocks from their house . . . the YMCA in Jersey City . . . the CYO gym . . . Audubon Park . . . the rec-center gym and concrete courts near the projects.

Hurley would go from court to court, playground to playground, sometimes as many as three or four different places a day. Everybody would test him, especially the older guys. What they didn't know was that Hurley *wanted* to play against the bigger, older, stronger players. That's how you earned respect. Walker was there if things got out of hand, but Hurley didn't need a protector. When it came to basketball, he was scared of no one.

The great myth is that basketball is color-blind. It wasn't for Hurley. Even if the guys on the playground had heard of him—and he was a regular in all the local newspaper sports sections—they all wanted to see for themselves how good he really was. So they'd test him. Hard-foul him. Get in his face. And if they hadn't heard of him, they wanted to kick the little white kid's ass back to whatever Chrysler minivan suburb he'd come from.

But guess what? The fearless little white kid would kick *their* asses, and not with jumpers from the safety of the perimeter. Hurley would take it to the rim, cradle the ball like a running back carrying a football, absorb the fouls, and, more times than not, lay it in. And he could dunk, too. Jumpers were for suburban kids. Taking it hard to the basket was how you did it in Jersey City.

Hurley was anything but soft. He had grown up in the Greenville section of Jersey City. It was an ethnic, middle-class neighborhood dotted with redbrick row houses and their postage stamp–size backyards, like the one the Hurleys owned on 64 Ferncliff Road. The sound of sirens and church bells shared the same air space.

Everyone knew Bob Sr. He was a Hudson County probation officer, and the basketball coach of one of the best high school teams in the country. He'd pull up at a stoplight on Ocean Avenue, one of the grittier streets in one of the most unforgiving parts of Jersey City, and the corner hustlers would recognize him and yell, "Coach Hurley, how's the team doin'?" And the coach would roll down his window, stick his arm out, and wave.

Dan and Bobby shared a basement bedroom. Dan was a New York Knicks fan, so he had a poster of Bernard King on the wall. Bobby was a Boston Celtics fan, which meant Larry Bird posters. They would watch the great rivalries of college basketball—Indiana vs. Kentucky, UCLA vs. Notre Dame, Georgetown vs. Villanova—and wonder what it would be like to play in those games and on that national stage. As for the NBA, that was otherworldly, beyond their comprehension.

St. Anthony was their NBA and Bob Sr. was their Red Auerbach. Bobby took after his old man. Prideful. Competitive, almost obsessively so. Dan was a talented player in his own right, but he didn't live for the game. Bobby lived for it, needed it. He had to win or lose at something every day. Win a high school game. Win a pickup game. Win at his daily workout session. There had to be an outcome.

His old man got job feelers all the time. Would he be interested in the Rutgers coaching position? No, he wouldn't. Fordham? No. Fairleigh Dickinson? Hmmm. No. How about joining Pete Gillen's staff as an assistant at Xavier? That one Bob Sr. thought about. He and his wife, Chris, even flew to Cincinnati in 1985 and discussed the job with the Brooklyn-born-and-raised Gillen. Dan was all for the move (his favorite NFL team, oddly enough, was the Cincinnati Bengals), but his

brother actively rooted against it. Bobby was about to begin his freshman season at St. Anthony, and he wanted to play for his father. When
his parents returned from Cincinnati, Bobby tearfully asked his father,
"Who's going to be my coach? I wanted you to be my coach, and now
you'll never see me play."

In the end, blood was thicker than Xavier, and Bob Sr. stayed put—
and won the first of four consecutive Parochial B-class state championships with Bobby at point guard. Their record together: 115–5.

Had Bob Sr. taken any of those head coaching jobs after Bobby was
done at St. Anthony—Rutgers, Fordham, FDU—the two boys would
have followed him there as players. Duke or dad? Not even close. "If he
would have taken the job at Middlesex Community College, we would
have gone there," says Dan.

But he didn't. He stayed at St. Anthony, which was always on the
brink of financial insolvency, because he thought he made more of a difference there. In 2010 he became only the third boys' high school coach
to be inducted into the Naismith Memorial Basketball Hall of Fame. He
didn't believe he should tell his oldest son where to go to college. All he
asked is that he carefully consider his choices.

Bobby's first official recruiting trip was to Duke, though his heart
wasn't completely in it. He had talked to Krzyzewski several times in the
past and enjoyed the conversations, but Duke? He didn't know much
about the school. And while the Blue Devils had had success, there
wasn't anything particularly basketball-sexy about their style of play.
But his mom, who tutored students at St. Anthony, knew about Duke's
high academic standing and encouraged Hurley to take the visit.

He left on a Friday all but sure that he was Seton Hall–bound. He
returned on a Sunday as a Blue Devil.

It wasn't any one thing that convinced him; it was a hundred things.
The campus was unlike anything he had ever seen. The Duke players
were cool. The people were friendly, always asking him how he was
doing, if there was anything they could do for him. That didn't happen

in Jersey City. At Duke it was so quiet—no sirens, no honking of car horns, no traffic. And they had this strange delicacy called barbecue.

Hurley came from a tight-knit family, so he was quick to notice how comfortable it was during the visit to Krzyzewski's home that weekend for a team meal. He liked that it wasn't just players and coaches, that Mickie Krzyzewski and their daughters were involved. He knew Laettner a little bit from basketball camps, and Abdelnaby was a Jersey kid from Bloomfield.

Never a talker to begin with, Hurley didn't say much during the meal. If asked something, he'd duck his head and mumble an answer. He was polite, but he was also shy and not entirely comfortable in adult social settings.

"He's such a guy," says Debbie Krzyzewski, who entered Duke as a freshman that same fall. "Just a guy, not real sophisticated. . . . I just adore him. He was most comfortable on the basketball court or in the locker room. He just wasn't as comfortable sitting around a table of people where you had to have social etiquette and niceties."

This was in direct contrast to Laettner, says Mickie, who "was never uncomfortable in any setting, even though he made other people uncomfortable."

As the weekend continued, Hurley grew less attached to the original plan of playing in the Big East. And anyway, he thought, if he had been willing to play at North Carolina, then why not at Duke, which was only a few miles away from Chapel Hill?

Krzyzewski was the closer. He described exactly why and how Hurley and Hurley's game would fit at Duke. The more he talked, the more Hurley believed him. Hurley was careful by nature—not distrusting, but he was aware of the con job. It was the Jersey in him. Krzyzewski wasn't conning him. His basketball vision matched Hurley's. "I got a real strong feeling that he loved how I played, that he understood my game very well, that he was going to have a lot of confidence in me," says Hurley. "And there was something about his demeanor and his personality that I liked, that I thought would suit me when I played."

Krzyzewski considered himself a teacher, an educator. He taught basketball, but by doing so he also taught discipline, the importance of detail, and the intrinsic value of teamwork and family. He cared. But Krzyzewski knew all the four-letter words and could leave verbal scorch marks if necessary. It was the Army in him. Not once had he ever raised his voice in anger at his precious daughters. But to his "boys" (that's what the Krzyzewskis called the Blue Devil players) he could, when needed, unleash a mortar attack of expletives. Sometimes the boys understood that better than calm logic.

Hurley didn't want to play for a screamer. "I can't play under those circumstances," says Hurley. He wanted to play for someone like his dad. Bob Sr. could (and did) yell at his players, and his sarcasm was a form of weapon. But Bob Sr. was always about his players first, himself last. Krzyzewski reminded him of his old man.

No commitment was made, though. If Hurley was going to tell any-body of his college decision, it was first going to be his father, not Krzy-zewski. So he flew into Newark (Krzyzewski was right behind him for a home visit), and drove home to Jersey City. Later that Sunday morning, after Bob Sr. and Hurley had broken down the bingo tables at White Eagle Hall, they talked about Duke in the cramped basement weight room.

"I want to go there," said Hurley nervously. "I like everything about it."

Bob Sr. was shocked but also relieved. He liked his players to go on at least two recruiting visits so they had something to compare. But he also knew his son would never make an impulsive decision when it came to basketball. For him to feel this strongly about Duke meant something. Bob Sr. gave his blessings to the decision.

Hurley made it official and committed that day. He was exhausted, but also exhilarated. He called Seton Hall's Carlesimo and Villanova's Rollie Massimino with his decision later that night. Carlesimo wished him the best; Massimino was less pleased.

And Krzyzewski? "I felt damn good," he says.

Krzyzewski now had his point guard (Anderson eventually signed with Georgia Tech, not North Carolina, and stayed two seasons before leaving for the NBA). From Jersey City, Krzyzewski went directly to Allentown, Pennsylvania, to see a 6'3" shooting guard named Bill McCaffrey. Like Hurley, he was a McDonald's and *Parade* All-American. But unlike Hurley, who was a pass-first type of guard, McCaffrey had a refined jump shot and a 27.9 scoring average. Krzyzewski would sign him, too.

Thomas Hill was not a McDonald's or *Parade* All-American. He was from Lancaster, Texas, which, in the college basketball world, was a great place to play football. The 6'4" Hill played every position at Lancaster High School except point guard. Recruiters knew of him, but not all of them knew what to do with him.

Duke's Mike Brey was staying at Krzyzewski's beach house on the Carolina coast when he got a call from Bob Bender. It was August 1987.

"Hey, Thomas Hill's high school coach called," said Bender. "Should we have any interest in him?"

Brey had seen Hill play in Las Vegas during the summer. Hill was lean and fast and had a 40-inch vertical leap, but he had also spent too many minutes at Lancaster High as a center. The consensus among the Duke coaching staff was that Hill probably wouldn't compete for playing time as a freshman. But should they have any interest in him? *You're damn right we should*, thought Brey.

Roy Williams had an interest in Hill. The longtime North Carolina assistant coach had been recruiting him since Hill was a high school sophomore, a full year before Duke became involved. Hill was leaning heavily toward the Tar Heels, thanks primarily to the relationship he and his parents had built with Williams. "He was my guy," says Hill. "My parents loved him."

But shortly after Hill's junior season, Williams called to tell him he was taking the head coaching job at Kansas. If Hill wasn't 100 percent committed to Carolina, would it be okay to try to recruit him to

Kansas? Hill said yes. He would later verbally commit to Williams and the Jayhawks.

Still, he decided to go ahead and take a previously planned official visit to Duke. Of his three finalists, Kansas with Williams was his stone-cold lock, followed by Carolina and then Duke. Hill spent his first day in Durham with Buckley and junior forward Greg Koubek and the next day with Laettner and Davis. They spent hours talking about winning championships: not *a* championship, but multiple titles.

"You're just like me and Laett," Davis told him.

Hill told him he had committed to KU.

"Fuck Kansas," said Davis in his trademark indelicate way. "We're going to kick Kansas's ass."

When Hill returned to Texas, he called Davis.

"I'm coming," he said.

Williams was disappointed but wished Hill well. These things happened. (In fact, Williams still keeps in touch with Hill's parents.) But it was a double whammy of sorts: not only was Hill not going to Kansas, but he wasn't going to Williams's alma mater, North Carolina, either.

"To the nation I was probably ranked a second-tier player," says Hill. "That's the hype machine. I knew once I got on the court, I was going to be better than a lot of players. Wait until we get on the court."

In an early fall pickup game at Cameron, he earned the instant attention of Abdelnaby. The 6'10" center was about to retrieve a missed shot off the rim when Hill appeared out of nowhere. Hill, who as a kid used to practice hurdling over stacks of pillows in the family living room, leaped over Abdelnaby's shoulder, grabbed the rebound with one hand, and then moved down the court.

Abdelnaby traded looks with Brickey and said, "*This* is the guy we didn't even know about?"

Hill, Hurley, and McCaffrey weren't the only newcomers to the team. With Bender leaving to become the head coach at Illinois State, Krzyzewski had an opening on his staff. He had Brey, former Duke

All-American Tommy Amaker, and Pete Gaudet, who had been an assistant under Krzyzewski at Army and later succeeded him at West Point. So naturally Krzyzewski filled the assistant vacancy with a 26-year-old law student who had never coached but who had appeared on *Face the Nation* and in the forgettable sci-fi movie *I Come in Peace*, where he played Azeck, the Good Alien. (Sample dialogue: Evil Alien, snarling—"I come in peace." Detective Jack Caine [played by Dolph Lundgren], as he prepares to shoot Evil Alien—"And you go in pieces.")

The new Duke assistant coach's name was Jay Bilas. He had been part of Krzyzewski's job-saving 1983 recruiting class and later played in the 1986 Final Four. The Dallas Mavericks drafted him with the 15th pick in the fifth round of the '86 NBA draft, but Bilas took the guaranteed money and played professionally in Italy for two seasons instead before returning to the States and Duke's nationally acclaimed law school.

Bilas was essentially a glorified graduate assistant. He was there to learn, to do the coaching grunt work, and to spend the rest of his time at law school. He, too, had been surprised by Krzyzewski's decision to hand the ball to Hurley before the opening practice. And as the first week's worth of practices unfolded, Bilas was underwhelmed by Krzyzewski's handpicked freshman point guard.

"I didn't get it," says Bilas. "[Hurley] was throwing the ball all over the gym. And he was kind of whiny."

"In the beginning it was kind of shaky for me," says Hurley. "I was the kind of guy that until I feel comfortable in a situation, I'm more like, *I'm gonna take a backseat here and sort of feel this thing out.* I wasn't real assertive in the beginning. Maybe I was deferring more to the older guys on the team. . . . I was never a great player as a freshman. I was learning the whole year."

Duke won its first three games by an average of 46 points, but those blowout victories came against Harvard, Canisius, and Northwestern. Despite the easy wins, Laettner still tested Hurley whenever he got the chance. He chirped at him. Challenged him. He purposely tried to piss him off. He wanted to see how Hurley would react. He wanted—no, needed—Hurley to be able to handle anything.

Hurley's real introduction to big-time college basketball came in the Blue Devils' fourth game, a Big East/ACC Challenge matchup against top-ranked Syracuse.

The Orangemen were ridiculously talented. Forward Derrick Coleman would be the number-one overall pick in the 1990 NBA draft. Guard Billy Owens went number three in the 1991 draft, while center LeRon Ellis, who had escaped the meltdown at Kentucky and transferred to Syracuse, would be the 22nd pick the same year. They had the swagger and size of a pro team, and their athleticism stunned Hurley, who experienced his "I'm not at St. Anthony anymore" moment during the opening minutes of the game.

It happened during a Syracuse fast break so blindingly swift and well executed that Hurley could only think, *Oh, my god.* These weren't high school kids; these were pros killing time in college jerseys.

As for Hurley, he was an early mess. He nervously forced a long pass on a botched fast break that landed in the baseline seats of the Greensboro Coliseum.

"What the fuck are you doing?" said Abdelnaby.

Hurley stared back at him with eyes as wide as dinner plates.

Hurley scored 4 points and added 10 assists in 33 minutes. But he also had 6 turnovers in a game that had the feel of March Madness rather than early December. Syracuse won, 78–76, but Hurley's performance didn't go unnoticed. Watching the ESPN telecast from a seat in the Barbary Coast sports book in Las Vegas was UNLV coach Jerry Tarkanian, who took note of the freshman's play.

Duke dropped its next game, too, a 113–108 defeat at Michigan. But Hurley scored 19 points and had a half dozen assists. He was beginning to get it. The Blue Devils would win their next 9 games and 15 of their next 16.

With each victory, Krzyzewski's decision to place Hurley in the starting lineup was validated. Not even the upperclassmen could bitch about it anymore. "He was making our team so much better it was unbelievable," says Laettner.

Hurley was a pure point guard, which is exactly what the Blue Devils needed. He didn't have to score for Duke to win (but he could if necessary). He was creative, tireless, and, best of all, unselfish.

Laettner acknowledged Hurley's impact on the team, but he wasn't about to give him a break. Early in Hurley's freshman season, his brother Dan, only a junior in high school at the time, came to visit. Hurley invited him to the team training table. Standing near the doorway was Laettner, waiting, measuring the moment, deciding when he'd pounce on the already nervous Dan, who had been introduced to almost everyone on the team with the exception of the Blue Devils' sophomore center.

Bobby saw Laettner. Laettner saw Bobby. "And Bobby always had this look for me, like when he knew I was watching him too much, monitoring him too much, you know?" says Laettner. "The look on his face was, *Goddammit, just leave me alone. Can't you just leave me alone?* And I never left him alone. I never left any of them alone. If you can't tell, I loved that little bit of prickliness. It all has good intentions, to have fun. It's kind of my way of showing I love you. I'm not going to hug you all the time and say 'I love you' like a woman. I'm a man. I'm going to do it in my own way. It might be by slapping you on the back of your head, teasing you a little too sarcastically sometimes."

Or it might be what Laettner did that day at the training table, when Dan found himself standing in front of Laettner in the meal line.

"What the fuck are you doing here?" said Laettner icily. "This line is only for guys on the team."

Dan shrank in embarrassment. Hurley stepped in and told Laettner he was an asshole. Laettner, who had accomplished his goal of messing with not one but two Hurleys, loved the confrontation. To Laettner, it was good-natured fun, what an older brother would do to a younger brother. To Dan, who never forgot the incident, it was the act of a bully.

"I knew what Laett was doing," says Abdelnaby, who kept a watchful eye out for Hurley. "You should have seen them. It was like kindergarten, where there's only one juice box left. It was like that the whole year."

Hurley was sometimes easily provoked. He was a fearless player, but a sensitive one. Laettner fed on that sensitivity, reveled in Hurley's discomfort. On road trips, when the players were required to wear coats and ties, Laettner and Davis would tease Hurley about his selection of clothes. They'd ask him if he'd gotten a deal at the Chess King, a local discount department store. And it wasn't unusual for Laettner to jog past Hurley during a game and say, "You motherfucker, don't turn the ball over."

Hurley didn't always know how to handle Laettner's mind games. He thought Laettner didn't like him. At times he took the criticism personally. Hurley was developing a reputation as a whiner, a crybaby who would let the criticism or a mistake affect his next play.

"Bobby's not a real complicated guy," says Bob Sr. "He would just get pissed off."

Abdelnaby did what he could. If Laettner had been especially brutal to Hurley during a practice—and Duke practices were often more intense than the games themselves—Abdelnaby would stop by the freshman's room and try to talk him off the ledge. Sometimes it worked. Often it didn't, as the sensitive, edgy, and fiery Hurley tried to make sense of Laettner's relentless verbal barbs.

Of course, Abdelnaby had his own moments with Laettner. That fall in a pickup game, Abdelnaby popped Laettner twice with high elbows.

"Alaa, that's bullshit," Laettner told him. "You better keep your elbow down."

Abdelnaby wasn't going to let a cocky sophomore tell him what to do. So he hit Laettner again with an elbow. A series of wild punches followed, none of them landing. Ten minutes later they were in the locker room, exchanging bear hugs and blathering, "I'm sorry . . . I love you."

The battle for alpha-dog status was nothing new. The difference was that Laettner, in only his second season with the Blue Devils, was staking his claim. He stood up to the senior Abdelnaby. He challenged the freshman Hurley.

Krzyzewski saw what was happening and decided to let it play out. He knew Laettner could be an arrogant, demanding SOB, but for now that was okay. The more the coaches watched Hurley, the more they realized Hurley could take it and often needed it. Hurley played better when he was on edge.

Krzyzewski marveled at Hurley's intensity. During a practice session, he turned to his former point guard Amaker and said, "I can't believe how hard this kid works."

Hurley never tired. At the end of practices, when other players would head exhausted to the Duke locker room, Hurley made a beeline to one of the StairMaster machines and worked out for another 30 to 45 minutes.

"He was in marathon runner's shape," says Krzyzewski.

Adds Bilas: "He could run all day. *All* day."

Hurley was still a work in progress, but Krzyzewski quickly realized he had a player who felt the game, who approached it as an artist might approach a clean canvas. "Bobby is the player I would have wanted to be—and I coached him that way," says Krzyzewski. "Again, not to do him any favors, but to allow him to play uninhibited. I gave him as much freedom as I possibly could knowing that when I was a player—not that I should have been given all that—that's who I would have liked to have been. I would have liked to have been Bobby Hurley."

As usual, the final regular-season game was against archrival Carolina, this time at Cameron. The unranked Tar Heels had beaten 8th-ranked Duke by 19 points in the January meeting at Chapel Hill and, still unranked, were on their way to beating the now 5th-ranked Blue Devils by 12.

Hurley had played poorly in the first game, and Tar Heels guard King Rice had let him know about it. Now Rice was in Hurley's ear again, taunting and mocking him. But this time a Duke teammate stepped in and told Rice to shut up—or else.

That teammate was Laettner.

The Blue Devils entered the NCAA Tournament as the No. 3 seed in the East Regional. They had won 24 games, but lost 4 of their last 6 regular-season/ACC Tournament games. And like most teams, they had dealt with their share of inner strife.

Laettner had become a fan of his freshman point guard, but still resented the way Hurley had been given the starting position. Then, in January, Krzyzewski chewed out members of the Duke student newspaper, only to see his harsh comments printed in *The Chronicle*—one of the school's sportswriters had taped the exchange. In March, Henderson called his team out after the Blue Devils were upset in the ACC Tournament semis by Georgia Tech and their freshman star Anderson. "Too many quitters . . . a bunch of babies . . . cop-outs . . . with fake emotion, fake enthusiasm" is how he described some of his teammates to the media. And then there was Davis, who was angry that Krzyzewski hadn't given him more quality minutes.

"This is bullshit," he told Krzyzewski during a meeting in the coach's office. "Why is Koubek playing more than me? You told me you had to earn it, and he didn't earn it."

"This is *my* team," said Krzyzewski, whose patience had its limits.

"You said I could be honest with you," said Davis, "so I'm being honest with you."

Despite the late-season difficulties, the Blue Devils beat Richmond and St. John's in the first two rounds to advance to the Sweet 16 at the Meadowlands' Brendan Byrne Arena. It would be a homecoming for Hurley, whose Jersey City home was only about three miles away.

After defeating UCLA in the regional semifinal, Duke faced No. 1 seed Connecticut. Trailing by 1 point with 2.6 seconds remaining in overtime, Krzyzewski diagrammed a play, only to change it at the last moment when he and Laettner realized nobody was guarding the inbounds passer, who happened to be the Duke center.

"Special," said Krzyzewski to Laettner, who then yelled the audible to the rest of the Blue Devils. Laettner inbounded the pass to Davis, who immediately passed it back. Laettner dribbled once, created space between himself and UConn defender Lyman De Priest, faked, and then swished a 14-footer for the 79–78 victory.

"In terms of just utter, sheer burst of joy, there's nothing better than that feeling," says Laettner. "Hitting a shot for the school that you love, for the coach that you love, for all these guys on your team that you love . . . it's just the greatest feeling in the world."

Bonnie and George had made the drive from Angola to East Rutherford for the regional. Bonnie, a nervous wreck during games, never saw the shot because she was holding her daughter Katherine during the play. "I knew something great had happened," she says.

She worked her way down through the crowd and to the railing at court's edge. Her son had won the game, and she wanted to give him a hug. Instead, Laettner was swept away by teammates and then by CBS officials, who wanted him for a postgame interview. America needed to meet this kid.

"This is when I knew I'd lost him," says Bonnie, crying. "He didn't come to me. That's when I knew. He didn't come over. That's when I knew he was gone."

She watched a replay of the shot later that night.

Laettner was 7 of 8 from the field and finished with 23 points. Hurley had 8 assists and only 2 turnovers against UConn's press, but missed all 9 of his shot attempts. Krzyzewski didn't care—Duke was going to its third consecutive Final Four and its fourth in five seasons.

The Blue Devils beat Arkansas by 14 points in the national semis, which meant they would have to play tournament favorite UNLV, winners against Georgia Tech in the other semi. The Runnin' Rebels were stocked like a trout farm. The core of their 1989 West Regional final team had returned intact: David Butler, Anderson Hunt, Greg Anthony, and Stacey Augmon. And now they had bruiser Larry Johnson, the 1989 junior college player of the year.

They were coached by the ultimate rebel, Jerry Tarkanian, who had warred frequently with the NCAA and whose program was, at that very moment, the subject of a nearly yearlong investigation into alleged rules violations.

"We always felt like the N-C-two-A did not want us to win the tournament," says Tarkanian.

Because it was a convenient angle (and because it was partly true), the championship game was framed as Nice Guy Preppies (Duke) vs. Tire Iron–Wielding Hells Angels from Altamont (UNLV). But beyond the stereotypes, Vegas was a gifted, motivated team playing for its coach and for the right to tell the NCAA and its critics to stick it. Krzyzewski's daughter Debbie referred to the Rebels as "The Machine."

The main Duke traveling party—players, coaches, support staff, and immediate family—was housed on the same Denver hotel floor. And as usual, the players propped their room doors open with the security latch for easy in-and-out access. Thursday night, two days before the semifinal, Hurley began to feel sick with the intestinal flu. He still played 36 minutes in the win against Arkansas and, afterward, uncharacteristically popped off about the Razorbacks' lack of conditioning in the final five minutes of the game. ("Maybe they would have had some more breaths if they didn't do so much talking.")

But Hurley had to leave the game for some emergency bathroom breaks (each departure reported by CBS), and by Sunday his condition had worsened. "He had it coming out both ends," says Dan Hurley.

He received IV fluids, didn't practice Sunday, and wasn't any better on Monday. When Debbie Krzyzewski noticed his hotel door was open, she decided to check on the Duke guard. She almost recoiled at the sight of the bedridden Hurley, his eyes sunken and dark and his face as green as broccoli.

"And he has to play against The Machine," she says. "He looked like a little boy who needed his mom to take care of him. It was so sad to look at him."

The Machine annihilated Duke. Tarkanian, at the suggestion of long-time assistant Tim Grgurich, used a hybrid zone/man-to-man defense called "the amoeba" that confounded Duke. Hurley was virtually useless, pulled from the lineup with a little more than 12 minutes left in the first half. He would return—not that it mattered. UNLV won, 103–73, the biggest margin of victory in NCAA championship-game history.

"When they turned it up," says Davis, "guys just laid down."

Hurley finished with more personal fouls than points (3, 2) and was posterized on a dunk by Hunt, who scored 29 points and was named the Final Four Most Outstanding Player. The guy who could run forever suddenly couldn't run at all. He couldn't finish his cuts. He couldn't do anything.

Laettner, who verbally sparred with Hurley during the game (what else was new?), had 15 points. Henderson, in his final game as a Blue Devil, scored 21, but not before complaining to Krzyzewski that he couldn't get enough air in his lungs at Denver's altitude. Duke's coaches reminded him that UNLV's players didn't seem to have any lung issues.

Afterward, Tarkanian tried to ease the hurt by telling Krzyzewski that the score wasn't indicative of the difference between the two teams. He was right—Vegas might have been better than the 30-point margin.

Lost in the blowout was a telling personnel decision made by Krzyzewski in the final minutes of the game. Rather than replace Hurley with a backup, he kept the ill freshman in until the final horn.

"We were already embarrassed," says Krzyzewski. "We got beat by the most points of anybody ever to lose a national championship. I think Bobby had to feel things, so him feeling that meant he'd never forget it. . . . So I wanted him to experience the whole hurt, so to speak. His father would have wanted to do it, too."

Hurley wasn't the reason Duke lost the game. Vegas was relentless ("Like a tidal wave coming at us," says Hurley) and they were playing to prove a point to the NCAA. But it was the first time in Hurley's playing career that he had failed to respond in a big game. Yes, he was sick (he needed another IV after the game), but in that game, he says, "I didn't show up."

Says Davis: "He shit himself. Overwhelmed. Overwhelmed by Hunt and Anthony. Nerves. Altitude. Freshman. Sick. Pressure. I think he was nervous.

"But we also had a couple of guys saying, 'The ball is slippery.' Or, 'Is it cold in here?' No, motherfucker, it ain't cold in here. And the ball ain't slippery. So it wasn't just Bobby."

Laettner was more forgiving. "Look, man, he was young, they full-court pressed the whole time, they were the Runnin' Rebels and, Jesus Christ, they had Greg Anthony and Anderson Hunt, and they were just running circles around everybody," he says. "And they just kicked our butts."

Or, as Abdelnaby would tell reporters that day: "It was scary just watching them. They engulfed us."

Krzyzewski was publicly gracious in defeat. He was getting lots of practice at being gracious after losing Final Four games.

"I'm in awe of what they did tonight," said Krzyzewski to the media.

But in the privacy of the Duke locker room, Krzyzewski was livid. UNLV had dominated his team, demoralized it. It was as if the Blue Devils had merely hoped to win, nothing more. Hurley's illness had come at the worst possible time, but that was no excuse. He told his team that the loss—the way they lost—was unacceptable and it was not going to happen again.

After the game, Bob Hurley Sr. and his wife returned to the team hotel and stopped to say hello to some of the Iron Dukes boosters. Several of them were grousing about the loss, complaining that the Blue Devils had once again failed to win the championship.

Hurley Sr. was astonished. Didn't these people know anything about basketball? Duke's point guard was a true freshman. Their best inside player was a sophomore. The Blue Devils played hard and had talent, but Hurley Sr. wasn't sure they were a Final Four team. They had needed a last-minute comeback to beat St. John's and a last-second shot to beat UConn. How they beat Arkansas, he had no idea. And UNLV was in a class by itself.

It was time to educate the spoiled boosters. "This coach," said Hurley Sr. to the Iron Dukes, "just did a fantastic job getting this team here."

And then he walked out of the room.

A sellout crowd of 17,765 had squeezed into McNichols Arena for the game, including Krzyzewski's mother, Emily. Emily didn't like planes, which is why her older son, Bill, would always drive her in the family van from Chicago to Durham. But this time she made an exception, flew to Denver for the Final Four, and saw her younger son's team turned into mulch by the wood chipper that was UNLV.

Back at the hotel, she made her way to Krzyzewski's vast suite, where family and friends had gathered for food and postmortem talk. She walked up to the coach, patted him gently on the back, and said, "You'll do better next year, Mike."

Krzyzewski laughed, not unkindly. "Ma, we just played for the national championship. There's only two teams in the country that can do that. And it's going to be hard to do better next year."

There was more laughter. After all, UNLV was returning most of its lineup, including Johnson, Augmon, Hunt, and Anthony. The Rebels would be the prohibitive favorite to become the first repeat champions since UCLA won the last of its seven consecutive titles in 1973. Meanwhile, Duke was losing three senior starters: Brickey, Henderson, and Abdelnaby. It would be a rebuilding year of sorts for the Blue Devils; it had to be.

As people began to filter out of Krzyzewski's suite and back to their own rooms, no one was thinking that Duke, only hours removed from the worst championship beatdown in college hoops history, was heading toward a fourth consecutive trip to the Final Four.

No one except Emily Krzyzewski, who hadn't laughed when she told her son he'd do better in 1991. Perhaps she knew about Grant Hill.

SIX

August 1990

Kentucky's basketball Jesus arrived on campus three days before fall classes began. Less than a week later, Mashburn wanted out.

He had been told to report to Memorial Coliseum at 3 p.m. for his first conditioning session with his new team. Except that Mashburn didn't know that three o'clock really meant 2:45 in "Wildcat Time." In the world of Pitino, Wildcat Time was always 15 minutes before the scheduled event. Not only was Mashburn late for his first official team workout, he was nearly two miles away from where he was supposed to be.

"Where's everybody?" he asked a student manager.

"They ran to the track," he was told.

Ran? Holy shit, thought Mashburn. *Shouldn't that be the workout?*

Mashburn was issued a set of workout clothes that tellingly didn't include basketball sneakers. Instead, he was given a pair of running shoes. A student manager then drove him to the track, where he was introduced to Rock Oliver.

Oliver said the Wildcats were going to run a mile. Mashburn had played pickup ball all summer, so he figured he could do that. He was in decent shape. How bad it could it be, right?

He ran the mile. *That wasn't so bad*, thought Mashburn.

Then Oliver said they were going to sprint, not run, twelve 220s. Mashburn turned to one of the Wildcats.

"What's a 220?" he said.

"It's halfway around the track."

"And we're *sprinting* that?"

Nobody, certainly not Pitino, had mentioned anything about this during the recruiting process. Sendek had damn sure not written anything about running 220s on those corny postcards. Come to think of it, Mashburn had never met Oliver during his recruiting visit to UK.

Mashburn was able to complete two of the 220-yard sprints before his legs started to wobble. By the sixth or seventh sprint, his lungs felt like someone had pounded them like chicken fried steak. By the twelfth and final 220, Mashburn was useless. He was soaked in sweat and nauseated. Several times he had staggered to the side of the track and threw up.

"That was the first time I was ever drunk without alcohol," says Mashburn.

By the time the conditioning session finished, Mashburn was reduced to a puddle of agony. There was nothing left in his stomach to vomit. His legs were numb. He was still dizzy. Worse yet, he was supposed to return to Memorial to play in pickup games with the rest of the Wildcats. *Full-court* games. Mashburn couldn't run to the garbage cans to throw up, much less run the length of the gym. His body had shut down.

He wasn't alone. Fellow freshman Gimel Martinez, a center from Miami whose 6'8" frame was as thin as an eyebrow, couldn't move either. Even his sweat was sweating.

Only one UK teammate stayed behind to check on Mashburn and Martinez. That teammate was Farmer.

"They were in really bad shape, and everybody walked off, leaving 'em laying there," Farmer says. "And I turned around and I would go back. Every day that that happened, I would try to get them some water . . . or make sure they were okay, because I had been there and nobody stayed to help me. . . . I would talk to them and tell them, 'Guys, it will get better. You'll get stronger. You'll get through it—just hang in there.' Because I never had anybody to stay and tell me that, or just encourage me or whatever. . . . [I] would have loved to have had somebody help me when I was going through a difficult time, but there was nobody."

The two freshmen stayed sprawled on the infield grass for nearly an hour before trying to stand up. A UK maintenance man drove them back to Wildcat Lodge, where they collapsed in their dorm-room beds.

Mashburn had never lifted a weight in high school. He had never run 220s. On the AAU circuit, in high school, or at The Rucker, you were in basketball shape, not in win-an-Ironman-Triathlon shape. You were there to break ankles, take it hard to the hoop, keep the court. He had signed with Kentucky to play ball and prepare himself for the pros. He hadn't meant pro track.

"I didn't even know what conditioning meant," he says. "Conditioning? I thought that was some kind of hair product."

During those first few days on campus, when it hurt just to walk down a flight of stairs, Mashburn began to think he had made a huge mistake. Maybe some of his friends back in New York were right, that he belonged in the Big East, not the southeast. Everybody had told him that Pitino didn't churn out NBA types. And anyway, what kind of coach leaves the Knicks and the Garden for Lexington, Kentucky, and a program on life support?

One night during that first week at UK, Mashburn sat exhausted on his bed in his darkened dorm room. Martinez was on the other side of the room, in no better shape.

"What school are you transferring to?" Mashburn asked his roommate.

"University of Miami," said Martinez.

"You know what, screw what my mother said," Mashburn said. "I'm going to St. John's."

But they didn't leave. Mashburn, despite his brazen talk, couldn't defy his mother's wishes. He didn't want to let her down. And he didn't want to break a promise he had made to himself.

The projects were filled with could-have-beens and should-have-beens. Mashburn had seen them on the street corners and heard their sad stories and their tired excuses. He didn't want to become that person. In fact, he feared becoming that person, the guy about whom everybody in the neighborhood would say, "Yeah, he went to college, but he couldn't last and now he's back in the projects again."

But Farmer was right: It got a little easier each day. Very little.

"My first three weeks there, it was hell to pay," says Mashburn. "Most of those guys had been there the whole summer doing that stuff. I was the 'before' photo. Those guys had already had their 'before' and 'after' shots. Me and Gimel were the 'before' pictures."

Mashburn and Martinez weren't the only newcomers. Willard had left to become the head coach at Western Kentucky. It was assumed that Pitino would simply choose a new assistant from his and/or Newton's vast pool of candidates, but Pitino wanted to do something different. He wanted to hire a woman.

Pitino understood the value of keeping his program in the news. Hiring another male assistant would have made the Transactions agate of the newspaper sports pages. Hiring the first woman assistant coach in major Division I men's basketball would be a public relations bonanza, and UK could use the positive publicity.

The idea wasn't immediately embraced by the other Wildcat assistant coaches, who openly questioned the decision and argued that the program would be better served by hiring a male coach. But Pitino wasn't interested in their concerns. He instructed Tubby Smith to contact a University of Georgia Lady Bulldogs assistant named Bernadette Locke.

Locke, 30, had read a *USA Today* story several weeks earlier about Pitino's intentions to hire a female assistant coach. *Good for him*, she thought. And then she forgot about it.

When Smith's phone call came, her first reaction was that Smith had accidentally been given a message she had left recently for a member of the UK women's team staff. Smith assured her there had been no mistake; Pitino was interested in hiring her.

After a series of interviews with Smith and then Pitino, Locke was offered the job. She wouldn't be staff window dressing. Pitino expected her to coach (individual instruction, scouting, etc.), as well as oversee the players' academic progress, postgraduate job prospects, and on-campus recruiting.

If there was any question about her basketball bona fides, they were answered during her first appearance in Pitino's dawn-patrol pickup game. The former UGA All-American more than held her own. And in the ultimate sign of respect, Pitino cared enough to "fire" her on more than one occasion.

Kentucky remained ineligible for the SEC championship and postseason play, but its games could now be shown on live TV. The NCAA still allowed the Wildcats to play a series of intrasquad scrimmages in assorted towns around the state. After the first of those scrimmages, Pitino told Jerry Tipton and the other UK beat writers that Mashburn would become one of the greatest players, if not *the* greatest, to wear a Kentucky uniform.

It was a startling statement, even for the hyperbole-prone Pitino. But the quiet Mashburn—so quiet that UK coaches sometimes didn't realize he was in team meetings—instantly transformed the lineup and gave Pitino options he didn't have a season earlier. The more he watched Mashburn, the more Pitino was convinced that the UK rebuilding project might take only two years as opposed to his original four-year projection.

Oliver, too, was immediately aware of Mashburn's vast physical potential. "A genetic freak," says Oliver. "Finally, somebody I get to take a little weight off and there's muscle under there."

So vital was Mashburn to UK's success that Oliver made an unprecedented exception for the freshman. The Law of Rock dictated that all players had to run the mile in six minutes or less. Oliver arranged for Mashburn to run it in segments and then added the times together. He needed Mashburn to succeed, even if it meant bending the rules. A year earlier he likely wouldn't have made the same exception.

This didn't go over well with Pelphrey, who was sort of the mother hen of the team. Pelphrey always wanted the other Wildcats to follow his lead.

"What's up with this?" Pelphrey asked.

"Mind your own business," said Oliver.

The players recognized basketball greatness when they saw it. So did Kentucky's fans. When Martinez and Mashburn walked into Commonwealth Stadium that fall to watch a UK football game, the entire student section stood up and applauded. Martinez knew they weren't clapping for him.

Mashburn could score so effortlessly. He did things on the court that they couldn't do—and never would be able to do. Hanson, who battled Mashburn every single day in practice, could only shake his head at some of the freshman's moves.

"We would have never been able to do the things we did without [Mashburn]," says Pelphrey. "Before him, we were just a bunch of white guys with bad haircuts. He changed our program. We had a few good players and then we had Jamal. If you took away Jamal from us, we were Vandy. . . . He was a guard who played at the center spot, and nobody could guard him."

Kentucky won its first three games of the season and entered its fourth game against Kansas intent on exacting revenge. They met on December 8, one day short of the anniversary of UK's 55-point humiliation at Allen Fieldhouse.

"That was bloodlust," says Pat Forde, who had just begun his first season as the UK beat reporter for the Louisville *Courier-Journal*. "Pitino wanted that badly. So did the fans. . . . With Pitino it's always about payback."

Pitino has a long memory. He is a master at creating an enemy that doesn't necessarily exist. But the grudge against KU and Williams was no invention. It was real, and a Rupp Arena crowd of 24,175 made sure to remind the Jayhawks that they weren't in Kansas anymore.

Moments before tip-off, Pitino huddled his team at courtside. Locke leaned in, but it was no use. The UK fans had become human Harley-Davidsons, gunning their voices into one overpowering roar. Locke could see Pitino talk, but she couldn't hear a word. "And I was standing right there," she says. "I don't know how the guys heard him."

Kentucky forced 20 Kansas turnovers, had five players score in double figures (Woods had a career-high 25; Mashburn had 15) and won 88–71. "I would have liked to have been able to beat them by 55," says Farmer.

Next, Pitino turned his attention to Dean Smith and North Carolina, who had beaten the Wildcats last December by 11. This time they would play at Chapel Hill. And once again Carolina would win, the result of UK foul trouble and the Wildcats' inability to hold a late lead.

Lazy fouls and blown leads were the symptoms of a tired team. Afterward, Pitino snapped at Oliver. "This is the worst-conditioned team I've ever seen," he said.

Later, Oliver made his way to the team bus for the ride to the local airport. As he began to board the vehicle, Pitino said, "What are you doing on the bus?"

Oliver had to catch a ride back to Lexington with a UK booster. He didn't get home until 4:30 the next morning. As he walked into his house, Oliver nervously rehearsed the speech he was going to give his wife when she woke up. He had been fired, he would tell her. But he'd get another job somewhere and they'd be fine.

Then the phone rang. It was Sendek.

"Where are you?" said Sendek, who was in the UK basketball office.

"Herb, I got fired," said Oliver.

"You'll get fired every day. Now get back in here."

Pitino fired someone almost daily, sometimes hourly. He could be caring, dictatorial, and impossible in the same five minutes.

That Christmas he invited Mashburn and Martinez to dine with his family, since the two players couldn't afford to fly home for the holidays. As Mashburn sat at the dining-room table, he remembered there was a practice scheduled for the next day.

"Uh, Coach, what kind of practice are we going to have tomorrow?" said Mashburn. The harder the practice, the less Christmas dinner Mashburn was going to eat.

"Jamal, it's going to be light," said Pitino. "So just eat up."

Mashburn dug into the massive food spread. He even went back for seconds.

The next day, he walked onto the court and saw that team managers had set up garbage cans near each basket.

Holy shit, thought Mashburn.

"We start practicing and he's running the shit out of us," says Mashburn. "The only thing I can feel is my stomach cramping. You saw people throwing up [including Mashburn]. Obviously they ate a lot during Christmas break, too."

UK beat Louisville in late December at Freedom Hall. It opened its SEC schedule in early January by beating defending conference champion Georgia, 81–80, in Athens. Mashburn had 17 points and 15 rebounds, and he hit two free throws in the final 5 seconds to help seal the win.

In its next game, UK defeated O'Neal and LSU at Rupp. Shaq had 28 points and 17 rebounds against his undersized defender, Feldhaus. But Feldhaus confounded O'Neal by stepping out to the three-point line and hitting six treys. He finished with 27 points.

Something weird and unexpected was going on. Kentucky, the program everybody assumed would be roadkill for at least three years, was on its way to winning the SEC regular-season title.

"They were the best team in the league," says Forde. "Their style of play drove everyone crazy. Pitino was way ahead of everyone with the three-point shot, the tempo, the everything."

The SEC office wasn't exactly embracing the surprise resurgence. Despite the Wildcats' move toward the top of the standings, the weekly release from the conference listed UK in last place with a notation explaining their ineligibility. An SEC assistant commissioner would later remind reporters that the Wildcats could win the conference only "in their minds." An infuriated and insulted Pitino called the remarks foolish.

Pitino didn't pick his fights; he took on all comers. He was a 24/7 coach who subsisted on little sleep, who craved exercise (he had a treadmill at his home), and who considered no detail too small. He pushed himself, his staff, and his players to and past their limits. He was impulsive. He was emotional. There was no such thing as a comfort level.

You never told Pitino something wasn't possible. You never said, "Well, that's the way it's always been done here." If you did, Hurricane Pitino would quickly gather strength and reach landfall, and all hell would break loose.

Pitino wanted the annual UK basketball awards banquet, previously a private affair, to be held in Rupp Arena and open to the public. It happened. He wanted a louder, more NBA-style music selection piped over the arena speaker system during pregame, halftime, and time-outs. It happened. He wanted his postgame radio show to be done at courtside, to make the show and the Wildcats coach more accessible to UK fans. It happened. He wanted Newton to purchase 15 very expensive, state-of-the-art stationary bikes for team conditioning purposes. It happened.

His preparation for a game was meticulous, if not obsessive. His assistants knew better than to submit a scouting report that didn't address every nuance of the opposing team. By the time his Wildcats were done with a Pitino-approved scouting report, he wanted them to be able to run the other team's offense better than the opponent could.

The UK players who had been there since the beginning of his reign could now predict his volcanic eruptions. Repeated mistakes would often result in banishment from a team huddle. He wore a thick, heavy ring on his right hand, and when he wanted to make a point, he would rap it against a player's kneecap as he sat on the bench. The Pitino Pinch was another of his favorite tactics, undetectable to fans and TV viewers. Pitino would put his arm around a player's waist during a time-out or a quick sideline exchange and pinch his skin at the hips as he talked—just to make sure he had the player's full attention. Players compared their Pitino Pinch bruise marks in the locker room.

One player—Woods—almost had the distinction of receiving a Pitino Shoe mark.

With only seconds remaining in a February 9 game at Mississippi State, Woods easily weaved his way through the Bulldog defenders, converted a layup, and then raised his arms in triumph. Kentucky had overcome a 12-point deficit in the final 10 minutes to tie the game and send it into overtime.

Or so Woods thought. In one of the great UK brain cramps, Woods hadn't realized the Wildcats needed a three-pointer, not a two, to tie the Bulldogs. Pitino had painstakingly diagrammed the play in the huddle—Woods would drive to the basket, then dish the ball to one of the Wildcats fanned out at the three-point line—but then watched in horror as his point guard forgot how to count.

Mississippi State 83, Kentucky 82.

A livid Pitino made his way to the tiny visitors' locker room at Humphrey Coliseum, but not before stepping on a piece of gum. Once inside the locker room, he angrily handed his gummed-up loafer to Keightley and then began yelling at an embarrassed Woods.

Keightley pulled out a pocketknife and began digging deep into the heel of the expensive shoe. He handed the loafer back to Pitino, who looked at it disgustedly and then fired it toward Woods. The shoe whizzed past the point guard's head.

"It was one of those times you want to laugh so bad, but you can't," says Martinez.

Pitino composed himself, put on his carved-up shoe, and met with the media. There was no mention of the flying loafer.

Three weeks later, a record crowd of 24,310 fans crammed themselves into Rupp for Senior Day and the Wildcats' final game of the season. Everybody but Ledford scored for UK as the Wildcats beat Auburn, 114–93, and unofficially clinched the league title with a 14–4 record (22–6 overall). Because of the sanctions, 13–5 Mississippi State and LSU were officially recognized as co-conference champions.

Nobody in Big Blue Nation was buying it. After the blowout victory, the Wildcats gave Pitino a shoulder ride to the basket, where he snipped away at the nets. Cheerleaders unfurled a banner that read "SEC No. 1—1991." Rings for the players were already in the works.

Afterward, Pitino reminded everyone that "championships are won or lost on the court, and no matter what anyone thinks or what anyone says, we won the championship." Newton announced that there would be a parade through downtown Lexington and "the dad-gummest pep rally ever held at the University of Kentucky. We want these guys to know what they have done. They've got Kentucky back on top."

A team that wasn't going to the SEC Tournament, wasn't going to the NCAA Tournament, and wasn't officially found on top of the league standings got a parade, complete with fire trucks and fan-lined streets. UK followers wore "Kiss Our Asterisk" T-shirts. "It was like we had won the national championship," says Woods.

They had finished 10th in the final regular-season AP poll. It was the first time in three years that the Wildcats had ended their regular schedule in the top 10. Maybe Kentucky wasn't "back on top," as Newton had proclaimed, but they were trending that way.

Pitino had achieved hero status in Lexington. His new restaurant, Bravo Pitino, was doing brisk business. UK hoops tickets were scarcer than royal flushes. A waiting list of 6,000 people vied for 10 season-ticket openings.

"That was a great time," says Oliver. "It was like Camelot then. When we got good, it was awesome. It was like we had a military presence."

Pitino's preseason wish list had included a 16-win season (check), a top-4 finish in the SEC (check), and a 95-point scoring average (whoops—UK missed by 9.1 points). Kentucky had survived the two-year postseason ban better than anyone had expected, Pitino included.

But he wasn't satisfied. Nor were his players. Late that March, Pelphrey decided to take his spring-break trip not to the warm and sun-drenched beaches of Florida or Mexico, but to . . . Indianapolis? He and his brother drove to Indy, bargained their way to a couple of tickets, and watched Duke, UNLV, Kansas, and North Carolina vie for a national championship.

Pelphrey wanted to know what it looked like in person. He wanted to know because he had every intention of playing in the Final Four next year.

SEVEN

April 1990

Hurley returned to New Jersey after the Final Four debacle against UNLV and tried briefly to go into hiding. Good luck. Everyone in Jersey City knew Hurley, and worse yet, everyone had seen him bomb on national television. They knew about his in-game sprints to the bathroom in the semi and his virtual no-show in the championship game.

No, Hurley wasn't going to receive any sympathy or tender, understanding hugs. After all, this was Jersey City, home of the unfiltered thought. Instead, he was peppered with "What were you *doin'* out there?" Or "What *happened*, man?" It was as if they couldn't believe Hurley—their Hurley—had stunk it up so bad.

For weeks, even months, Hurley was haunted by his performance against Vegas. It didn't matter that he had been ill or that Duke would have been lucky to beat Tarkanian's team once out of 10 times. It was the *way* he had played that bothered him. There were no guarantees he'd ever get another opportunity like that, and he had blown it. He had never felt that kind of failure before—which is exactly why Krzyzewski had kept him in the game and forced him to endure the carnage.

Dan Hurley had attended the Vegas beatdown. He saw how the stomach virus reduced his brother's effectiveness by, what, 25 percent? 50 percent? The Runnin' Rebels had taken care of the rest.

"They were monsters," says Dan. "Me, if I played in that UNLV game and we lost like that, I don't know if I would have come out of my room for months. I might have gone into a death spiral through the clouds, through the ocean. But not him. He's not wired that way. . . . He's like The Terminator. Bobby was a driven guy, a Schwarzenegger type."

But The Terminator who came home to Jersey City was physically worn down and mentally exhausted from a stressful freshman season. Slowly—and it took time—Hurley began to recover from the Vegas hangover. And not surprisingly, he used the UNLV loss as motivation for the upcoming 1991 season; all the Blue Devils did.

It was the third consecutive year Duke had lost in the Final Four. The program was making progress—at least it had reached the championship game in 1990—but the 30-point loss negated that accomplishment. All anyone remembered was the Vegas rout, not the 29 wins it had taken to get there.

At school year's end, Thomas Hill returned home to Dallas. When he walked into his local gym to play in the daily pickup games, he—and Duke—were the punch line of every joke. Vegas's Johnson, who also was from Dallas, played in the same pickup games, as did UNLV's Augmon.

The verbal abuse was relentless. It wasn't so much Johnson and Augmon who did the talking, but everyone else who was in the gym. Hill had no choice but to take the insults. But inside he was reaching 212 degrees—boiling point.

If we ever get a chance to see these guys again, he said to himself, *it's going to be a different story.*

For the most part, the Duke players actually liked the UNLV players. They admired the team's work ethic, intensity, and killer instinct.

The Rebels had a coaching staff willing to trust them, just as Krzyzewski trusted the Blue Devils. And sure, UNLV's players had that swagger, but they'd earned it. All in all, the Rebels were good guys.

Of course, the NCAA was less enamored of Tarkanian's program. It had investigated it for years and eventually found it guilty of an array of rules violations. A deal was struck: the NCAA would allow UNLV to defend its title in 1991, but the Runnin' Rebels would be ineligible for the 1992 postseason and prohibited from appearing on television. Tarkanian forever refers to it as "that horseshit ruling."

At least UNLV would have a chance to repeat. And given its returning lineup, it was a virtual certainty that the Rebels would be back in the Final Four.

But without knowing it, Tarkanian's team had done Duke a favor. The blowout gave the Blue Devils a cause that would sustain them through the entire off-season and into the 1991 schedule. It also gave Krzyzewski a button to push whenever necessary.

"Worst sports experience in my life," says Davis. "If we didn't get back [to the 1991 Final Four], we'd be viewed as the biggest suckers. After we lost to UNLV, we all turned it up. We trained and prepared that summer like we were going to be playing them again."

As the Blue Devils trained, Krzyzewski, 43, faced a pivotal career decision. He had been approached and pursued by other college and NBA teams in the past, but always politely dismissed the advances. This time, however, it was the Boston Celtics, led by new team president (and Krzyzewski friend) Dave Gavitt, who wanted to talk to him about their coaching opening.

It was an intriguing opportunity and gave Krzyzewski and Mickie pause. A storied franchise. A man they trusted in Gavitt. Lots of money.

Krzyzewski met with Gavitt to discuss the job, but eventually withdrew his name from consideration. He had unfinished business at Duke and the timing didn't feel right, so he stayed put.

During that off-season, Krzyzewski coached the USA National

Team, which included Laettner (a bronze medal at the FIBA World Championships) and Hurley (a silver medal at the Goodwill Games). McCaffrey played for the ACC All-Stars in a tour of then West Germany. Thomas Hill played in the U.S. Olympic Festival.

Davis played for nobody. He spent the early part of his summer recuperating from a hernia operation that required 91 stitches and two weeks in a hospital bed. He wasn't even allowed to laugh, in fear that the sutures would tear.

It was during those two bedridden weeks that the always intense Davis had an epiphany. As if the UNLV experience wasn't enough of a motivating factor, Davis decided he would measure his value to the Duke program by the number of players, coaches, and staff members who came to visit him. Only four did so: Krzyzewski, Mickie Krzyzewski, trainer Dave Engelhardt, and Laettner.

The small turnout wounded Davis. After all the support and encouragement he had given his teammates, he expected more than just one teammate to stop by and see him. In his mind, he had become an afterthought—again.

This was the final insult. For two years he had been the good Duke soldier. He was the one who had had to recruit Krzyzewski, not the other way around. He was the one who had played in 66 games for the Blue Devils, but never as a starter. And he was the one who had apparently been forgotten by almost all of his teammates as he recovered from surgery. Had it been one of his teammates in the hospital—from the lowliest walk-on to the biggest star—Davis would have been the first one at his bedside.

By the time he was released from the hospital, Davis had vowed his days as a supporting cast member were done. Somehow, some way, Davis was going to become more, much more, than another name on the roster.

"That's when I became a complete monster," says Davis.

The transformation wasn't limited to Davis. The Duke roster was undergoing seismic change. Abdelnaby, Henderson, Brickey, and even Cook were gone. The two remaining seniors, captains Koubek and Clay Buckley, were featured on the cover of the 1991 media guide, but they weren't expected to be starters.

Hurley, McCaffrey, and Hill had survived their freshman seasons (Hurley was named to the freshman All-America team), and Laettner had blossomed into a bona fide star. In addition, five new recruits had joined the program: guards Marty Clark and Kenny Blakeney, forwards Antonio Lang and Christian Ast, and an elegant, unassuming, and deceivingly lethal swingman whose arrival would tip the balance of college basketball power toward Durham and Duke for the next several years.

His name: Grant Hill.

"Christian is the best player," says Davis. "Grant is the best talent Duke ever had."

Krzyzewski first saw Grant Hill at Garfinkel's Five-Star camp. A handful of campers were rated higher by the scouting services, but none of that mattered to the Duke coach. He walked away thinking, *This kid could be one of the best players to ever play the game.*

Grant Hill was 6'8", strong, and intuitive, and he had the ballhandling skills of a point guard. Most of all, he was ungodly athletic, in a way that had rarely if ever been seen in a Duke uniform. Best of all, his ego could be detected only with the aid of a microscope.

His parents, Janet and Calvin Hill, had raised him to embrace diversity, challenges, and success—because that's the way they had been raised. Janet, who had attended predominantly white Wellesley College in the 1960s (she was a dormitory suitemate of Hillary Clinton), would often tell her son, "The pursuit of excellence differentiates you."

Excellence ran in the family. Calvin had earned a history degree at Yale, where George W. Bush was a Delta Kappa Epsilon fraternity brother. He spent 12 years as a running back in the NFL, where he was a four-time Pro Bowl selection and a member of the 1971 Super Bowl champion Dallas Cowboys.

Grant grew up in Reston, Virginia, near Washington, D.C., the only child of only children. When he was six, he traveled to Europe and was bored to tears as his mother and grandmother drank afternoon tea in London. Nor was he impressed with a visit to the office of Kingman Brewster, the former president of Yale who was serving as U.S. ambassador to the Court of St. James's. Little Grant did headstands there.

By the time their son was 13, the Hills knew he was an athlete of extraordinary potential. Not ones to brag, they were careful about their comments to others about Grant. But when Janet saw Verne Lundquist that fall—the CBS sports broadcaster knew the Hills from their days together in Dallas—she confided in her longtime friend.

"Our son's going to be pretty good—and it's not going to be in football," she told him.

She was right. The 13-year-old Grant was part of an AAU national championship basketball team and named to the all-tournament team. He later played AAU ball with Davis and Blakeney (also from the D.C./Maryland area) and became friends with Chris Webber and Jalen Rose. (Webber was recruited hard by Duke, but like Rose signed with Michigan.)

A McDonald's All-American, Grant was recruited by 85 schools, whittled his list to 10, and settled on 5 finalists: Georgetown, Michigan, Virginia, North Carolina, and Duke.

Janet, a longtime Georgetown season-ticket holder (second-row seats), was hoping her son would sign with the Hoyas. But Grant, who had attended dozens of Georgetown games, ruled them out: He loved John Thompson's program, but the campus was too close to home. He didn't want helicopter parents hovering over him.

He eliminated Michigan partly because of the frigid weather and partly because he preferred the ACC.

Virginia was crossed off the list because coach Terry Holland was departing and a replacement hadn't been named yet. That left North Carolina and Duke.

Grant had always followed Carolina basketball. His father bought a big-screen TV and one of those huge Betamax video recorders in 1982, just in time for the classic UNC–Georgetown NCAA championship game. It was the first program the family ever taped on the machine, and Grant watched the game over and over again.

Calvin was a Yalie, but when it came to basketball he bled Carolina blue. Had it been up to Calvin, there wouldn't have been a list of five finalists; Grant would have signed with Carolina, sight unseen.

He and Grant went to Chapel Hill for an unofficial visit and spent part of the day with Tar Heels coach Dean Smith. The next morning, Calvin told Grant, "Look, we've been to the Promised Land. Let's get on a plane and go home."

But Grant had promised the Duke coaches he'd give equal time to the Blue Devils. So they drove to nearby Durham, where they met with Krzyzewski. Later, Billy King and assistant coach Amaker walked the campus with Calvin. They discussed basketball, of course, but also politics and world issues. Calvin came away intrigued. If Duke could produce the likes of Amaker and King, what might it do for his son?

Still, Calvin remained committed to North Carolina and Smith. His son wasn't so certain.

"We are confused," Calvin said when he talked to his wife that night about Grant's recruiting mind-set.

"*We* are not going to college," said Janet sternly.

Later, during his official visit to Duke, Grant called a friend in Virginia he had known since high school. She asked him if he was going to sign with the Blue Devils. "Nah, I'm just making a visit," he told her. "Don't worry, I'll be a Tar Heel."

Forty-eight hours later, he had fallen in love with Duke.

Laettner and Davis hosted Grant during the visit, and as usual, Davis sold him hard that weekend (and in earlier phone calls) on creating a basketball dynasty, just as he had done with Thomas Hill. Davis had that knack. He could sell a fur coat to an animal-rights activist.

The pitch worked. Everything worked—the campus, Krzyzewski, the assistants, the camaraderie, the location, the weather, the conference.

Grant returned from the trip on Sunday ready to commit to Duke. He canceled a planned visit to Michigan, but his father insisted he at least keep an appointment for a Tuesday home visit by Dean Smith. Two hours into the visit, Grant politely excused himself from the meeting to go upstairs and do his homework. Smith left the house knowing he had lost Hill to Duke. So did a heartbroken Calvin.

However, when it came time to drive to Duke late in the summer of 1990 for freshman orientation, Grant had a panic attack. He called Amaker shortly before the orientation session began and asked to be released from his scholarship.

"I don't think I'm ready to go to Duke," he told the Blue Devils assistant coach, whose uncle owned the barbershop where Grant got his hair cut. "I don't know if I can compete on and off the court at Duke. I want to go to George Mason."

Amaker nearly fainted. Grant was one of the most coveted recruits Duke had ever signed. When Krzyzewski promoted Amaker from graduate assistant to full-time assistant in 1989, the former Duke star tried to thank his boss for the opportunity. Krzyzewski cut him off.

"That's fine," said Krzyzewski. "Now get your butt back home. We've got to get Grant Hill."

Amaker earned his entire 1990 salary by convincing Grant that he was suffering from a simple case of freshman nerves, that everything would be fine. But it wasn't until Grant actually arrived on campus that Amaker could finally breathe a sigh of relief. Kids.

It wasn't the first time Grant had wrestled with his place in the world. He was bright, talented, unfailingly nice and grounded, but at times also conflicted and confused.

His father had been a star NFL running back and moved on to the front office of the Baltimore Orioles. His mother had her own consulting firm on Capitol Hill. But Grant didn't always feel as if he fit in with white kids, because of his African-American heritage. Nor did he always feel he fit in with other black kids, because of his parents' social and economic standing. He sensed he was being judged, that he wasn't considered "black" enough, because his life hadn't been undercut by tragedy. "The more you've gone without and had to struggle, then that's almost like a badge of honor," says Grant.

When Grant was 12 or 13, his father was asked to address the student body of his middle school. Grant pretended to be sick and spent the entire speech in the school infirmary. He was embarrassed and uncomfortable with his dad's success—or more accurately, how that success would reflect on Grant. And it was Grant who asked his father to take him to basketball practice in the older, more worn family Volkswagen instead of Calvin's Porsche.

Grant wanted to fit in. But he would eventually realize there was a difference between fitting in and disavowing the accomplishments of his family. A breakthrough came one summer when Grant was at the Five-Star camp. An African-American player from inner city New York couldn't understand why Grant was subjecting himself to the grind of basketball.

"Why are you even playing?" said the camper. "You live in a mansion."

Grant was insulted by the question. First, he didn't live in a mansion—he wasn't Will Smith in *Fresh Prince*. Second, even if he did, why would it matter? To Grant it was reverse stereotyping. Because his parents were prominent, well-educated, and well-compensated, some African-Americans looked at him as less black. So Grant resolved to use his basketball game as a way to prove otherwise.

"I don't know if it was insecurity or just the struggle to fit in," he says. "But I said, 'Okay, I may not fit in when you guys tell stories about this and that and the other, but I'm damn sure going to fit in on the basketball court. I'm going to have a street game. I'm going to cross over. I'm going to get to the hole. I'm going to dunk on you.'"

By the time he reported for his first practice at Duke, Grant had become a devastating slasher and finisher—something the Blue Devils lacked in their lineup. And at 6'8", Grant was a matchup nightmare, both on offense and defense.

Grant had watched the UNLV–Duke game at a high school teammate's house. His first reaction: Vegas could have beaten an NBA team that night. His second reaction: Vegas broke Duke's spirit.

Marty Clark had had the same thoughts, that the Runnin' Rebels looked like they belonged in the NBA's Western Conference. Immediately after the loss, Clark's friends mocked him about his college destination.

"Nice choice," said one buddy.

"Way to go," said another. "Your guys look really good."

Clark didn't care. A year earlier no major basketball program east of his Denver home was recruiting him. Then he attended the July 1989 session of Five-Star, played well, and suddenly was on the recruiting short lists of Krzyzewski, Knight, Fisher, and Illinois's Lou Henson.

A nine-year-old boy approached Clark at the camp and said, "See that guy over there in the yellow shirt?"

Clark glanced up and saw a man waving to him. "Yeah."

"He said you've got a scholarship to Vanderbilt University."

The man in the yellow shirt was Commodores coach Eddie Fogler. Under NCAA rules, coaches weren't allowed to talk to players, so Fogler had recruited a nine-year-old to make the scholarship offer.

But Clark liked Duke's motion offense, the school's academic reputation, and that Johnny Dawkins had played there. Even better, he liked that Grant Hill, now a Five-Star legend, was on his way to play at Duke.

"It didn't take too much to convince me," says Clark.

Kenny Blakeney, from inner city D.C., was another Dawkins and Duke fan. As early as fourth grade he had decided he would one day play for the Blue Devils. He wore Duke T-shirts as a kid and later attended DeMatha, the same school that had produced Danny Ferry and lots of championships.

There was no recruiting war with Blakeney, because there was no doubt where he would sign. Maryland, Georgetown, and Georgia Tech wanted him, but the feeling wasn't mutual. Oklahoma was recruiting him and his cousin, but Blakeney wasn't interested.

"Man, I want to win championships," Blakeney told his cousin.

But UNLV, not Duke, had won the 1990 title. And Blakeney's friends weren't about to let him forget it. For months they reminded him of the final score and ragged on the Blue Devils.

Despite the loss of three senior starters, there was no confusion about Duke's goal. Krzyzewski and the Blue Devils were tired of being Final Four floor mats. There was a time when they were thrilled just to reach the Final Four, but that time was done. The 30-point loss to Vegas changed everything.

Krzyzewski kept telling his team, "We want more. Don't you guys want more?"

Laettner wanted more. He would listen to Krzyzewski and get so amped up that he'd want to run through a locker-room wall for the Duke coach. Laettner judged almost everything by wins and losses. Otherwise, what was the point? Life was a zero-sum game for him. Finishing second was no better than finishing 122nd.

Hurley wanted more. He was consumed by competition and now by the memory of the UNLV defeat. But first he had to fix a gaping hole in his game.

Hurley was a whiner. He didn't do it intentionally, but his freshman season had been full of pained looks, crybaby faces, and negative body language. ESPN's Vitale had roasted him during broadcasts. Krzyzewski and his assistants talked about it in staff meetings—what to do about Bobby? Opposing fans were calling him "Bart Simpson." He was projecting a bad attitude on the court, and it had to stop. Krzyzewski believed a team's success was dependent more on trust and relationships than X's and O's. So the Duke staff assembled a videotape of Hurley's worst on-court reactions and showed it to him.

Your teammates take their lead from you, the coaches told him. If their point guard whines, you make it easier for them to do the same. And if you show weakness, you give our opponents hope.

Hurley got the message.

Nothing less than a national title would do. There were those who considered Krzyzewski the college basketball equivalent of Marv Levy or Bud Grant—two very good NFL coaches who reached Super Bowls but could never win one. Koubek and Buckley were 0–3 in Final Fours. Laettner, Davis, and Palmer were 0–2. Hurley, Thomas Hill, and McCaffrey were 0–1. They all had been on the wrong end of a national humiliation and had had enough.

Koubek and Buckley were the seniors, but Laettner considered himself the de facto leader of the team. He was Duke's best player, and he was also Duke's best conduit to Krzyzewski. And nobody could annoy, provoke, and antagonize better than Laettner.

Laettner was charismatic, but not in a traditional sense. Quin Snyder—now there was a natural leader. Everyone wanted to be around Snyder. He was exceptionally smart (an academic All-American as a senior), famously cool, and universally liked. Laettner wasn't universally liked. He lacked the easygoing charm of Snyder, but there was something about him that kept your attention.

Krzyzewski recognized Laettner's particular brand of charisma early on. It was raw and different, but it was there. He also recognized Laettner's toughness. You could yell at him and yell at him hard, but Laettner wouldn't flinch, just as Krzyzewski hadn't flinched when Knight had ripped into the Army cadet. So Krzyzewski would sometimes use Laettner or Davis as sacrificial lambs, picking apart their play in front of the entire team as a way to send a message to the other, perhaps more sensitive Duke players.

Laettner didn't mind. He treated Krzyzewski's words as basketball gospel. Despite his irritation with how the Duke coach handed the ball to Hurley as a freshman, Laettner never said a peep to Krzyzewski. He questioned the decision, but he didn't question Krzyzewski's right to make it. He simply couldn't see what Krzyzewski saw in Hurley—at least, not at first. But he trusted Krzyzewski implicitly. And Krzyzewski trusted him back, giving Laettner the latitude to impose his considerable will on his teammates. Krzyzewski monitored Laettner's methods, but rarely interfered.

"I understood that they were beautiful to coach together," says Krzyzewski. "I loved every day coaching them. You have to allow them to be themselves. I allowed Christian to say things whenever he wanted."

The truth was that Krzyzewski liked and encouraged Laettner's arrogance and ego. Used properly, it was a powerful weapon. He wanted his team to exude an aura of confidence and intimidation. Laettner had that in spades and wasn't afraid to show it.

"The first year and a half, I thought he was the biggest prick I'd ever met," says Clark. "I think a lot of people thought the same way."

Laettner could be as oppressive as a Third World dictator. A year earlier, Hurley's instant ascension into the starting lineup had angered Laettner and his teammates. It took time for Hurley's value to emerge, which didn't help matters.

But Laettner was becoming a pragmatist. In Grant Hill he saw a player whose impact could be immediate and profound. Hurley had arrived at Duke barely as tall as the student managers; Grant arrived a grown man. Hurley struggled during the first week of practices; Grant quickly established himself as a game-changer, impressing even Laettner in pickup games and practices with his stunning playmaking skills.

It was obvious to Laettner and everyone in the program that Grant was going to play lots of quality minutes as a freshman. But this time Laettner didn't hold a grudge against the newcomer. He had pushed Hurley hard, often too hard, but he learned that he couldn't push Grant's buttons as easily. The freshman wasn't as tightly wound or as emotional as Hurley, and he often seemed more amused by Laettner's antics than annoyed. Laettner could zing Hurley and usually get an instant reaction. Not so with Grant. Grant would process Laettner's insults or challenges and then decide if or how to react.

Grant had never met anyone as complex as Laettner. He assumed that since Laettner had attended a well-to-do private high school, he had come from money. If so, Grant had never met a rich white kid with such a hard edge. Actually, he had never met *anybody* with that kind of edge.

Laettner decided that Grant needed to be toughened up. So he played older brother to Grant—*his* older brother. He would beat him in Ping-Pong and crow about it. He would slap box with him. He would walk into the locker room, pick up a shoe, and throw it hard at Grant (or other players) as a test. Would the freshman stand up to him or skulk away? Grant never skulked away.

There were epic one-on-one games between Laettner and Grant. After each victory, Laettner would brag about his domination, that the great and heralded blue-chip recruit Grant Hill could beat everyone else on the team but not him. And Laettner loved challenging the freshman to dunk contests, but with a twist: Laettner would stand under the basket, toss Grant the ball, and say, "Come dunk on me." And then as the phenom soared high toward the rim, Laettner would hard-foul him, or block his shot and then talk trash after the rejection. But sometimes Grant would lay down a thunder dunk, and the other Blue Devils would howl and chirp at Laettner. And Laettner, who despised losing, would walk away satisfied.

Hurley had dreaded the confrontations with Laettner—and still did. But Grant, the human shrug, played along. He knew his place on the team: He was the freshman; Laettner was the junior. He thought Laettner had some odd qualities to him, but more than anything he thought the Duke star was ultracompetitive and ultraconfident. Could he be a jerk? Sort of, but Grant didn't think about Laettner in those terms. He actually thought Laettner was funny, even silly. The freshman had a good feel for people, and his instincts told him that Laettner, at his core, cared about his teammates, that he was a better guy than he let on.

But also, just below the surface, Grant wanted Laettner to like him. He wanted everyone to like him. He didn't want to seem selfish, overbearing, or privileged, so his default position was to cede to others, in this case to Laettner and Davis.

Not all the freshmen were transitioning as well to the college game as Grant. Then again, none of them had his kind of talent. Ast, a 6'8" German whose father had been a mathematics professor at the University of Heidelberg, came to the States in 1988 and played two years of high school ball. He was fluent in four languages, though several of the Duke players quickly questioned if basketball was one of them. They liked him, but he had end-of-the-bench status written all over him. Ast had skills, but he was having trouble adjusting to the ultracompetitive basketball environment of Duke. He was in way over his comfort level.

Meanwhile, Lang was simply trying to survive. He had come to Duke from Mobile, Alabama, the first player Krzyzewski had ever signed from the state, after declining an offer to join O'Neal, Roberts, and Jackson at LSU. Kentucky's Pitino had also made a home visit, but Lang wanted no part of a program on NCAA probation. He was still uncommitted when Krzyzewski phoned him from a team dinner at the Final Four in Denver (a savvy recruiting touch) and reiterated the program's interest in Lang.

"Coach, I got one question," said Lang.

"What's that?" said Krzyzewski.

"You never allow any of your players to wear undershirts under their jerseys."

"You're right. I haven't allowed that yet."

"Well, if I came to Duke, could I wear an undershirt?"

"Let me put it this way: Your first game is the Blue–White scrimmage. If your teammates say it's okay for you to wear a T-shirt, I'm okay with you wearing a T-shirt."

"Is that true?"

"Yeah, it's true."

The 6'8" Lang, with a 165-pound body as thin as a half-court line, committed a week later. He chose Duke because of its rising basketball status and its family atmosphere, and because his parents, who were high school teachers, were impressed with the school's academic rankings. But the possibility of wearing a T-shirt over his concave chest helped.

Of course, none of that mattered during Lang's first practice. By session's end, Lang looked like his hero Muhammad Ali did during the latter rounds of the Thrilla in Manila, staggering and stumbling about, his body exhausted. Duke's coaches wondered if Lang would be able to finish.

The competition for playing time was fierce, even cutthroat. Laettner, Hurley, and Grant Hill were the only ones guaranteed starting spots. Davis, Thomas Hill, McCaffrey, Koubek, Palmer, and Lang would fight for the other minutes. The scraps would go to Clark, Buckley, and Ast.

"It's probably the least mature team age-wise that I've had since 1983," Krzyzewski told reporters. "We have kids who all can play. It's just a matter of, How old are they? We actually start out with a younger team, but have more anchors than a year ago."

Despite the young roster, Krzyzewski didn't consider it a rebuilding year. "For our program," he said before Duke's first practice, "to use that word is a cop-out. Will we get back to the Final Four? I don't know about that. I think we'll be good. I hope we'll be."

Vitale liked the Blue Devils' potential and said so. But he also said he had concerns about their size and depth. Not surprisingly, North Carolina was the preseason favorite to win the ACC. Krzyzewski, at least publicly, agreed with the predictions.

Grant Hill's considerable skills were unveiled in the Blue–White scrimmage about a week after practices began. He led all scorers with 14 points in the 20-minute game. (Lang, 15 pounds heavier from a weight-lifting program, didn't wear a T-shirt during the scrimmage. Afterward, Krzyzewski grabbed him by the upper arm and said, "It

would have been an injustice not to show the world these biceps.")
During the closed practices, Grant and the rest of the second-teamers
on the Blue squad would often beat the starters. It wasn't an exaggera-
tion to say he could be Jordanesque at times. And team managers, who
charted a Duke-invented stat called "efficiency points" (e.g., offensive
rebounds that led to assists, deflections, steals, etc.), soon discovered
that one player kept dominating the competition. "It wasn't close at the
end of practice," says former Duke manager Ashok Varadhan. "It was
always Grant."

Grant Hill and Lang were roommates, and despite competing for
the same position, the two freshmen became instant friends. Grant
called him "Cotton" or "The Great T-Lang." Lang's Alabama accent
confounded Grant at first. He would spend those early conversations
asking, "What'd you say? Huh?" But they were Velcro'd at the hip. If
you saw Grant at a party, Lang would be there, too. If you saw Grant
hanging out between classes, Lang would be in the vicinity.

"Grant's as nice a person as I've ever met," says Bilas. "But Grant's
not nicer than Tony. They had empathy for other people."

Still, Grant was starting and playing considerable minutes and Lang
wasn't. Lang had the most contagious smile and the gentlest soul on
the team, but he began to wonder if he'd made a mistake in coming to
Duke. The campus was in the South, but it wasn't *the* South. The student body had a decided New York/New Jersey influence to it and was
predominantly white. There was nothing about Durham or the campus
itself that reminded him of Mobile. He was used to Southern accents as
thick as the mustard you slopped on the hot dogs at Mobile's famous
Dew Drop Inn. Duke seemed so foreign. And it didn't help that playing
minutes were hard to come by.

Krzyzewski was busy mixing and matching lineups. Laettner, Hurley, and Grant were the constants, but the other two starting spots were
always in play. Davis started the opener against Marquette, shot 1 for 7,
grabbed just 1 rebound, and was back on the bench for the second

game against East Carolina. McCaffrey worked his way into the starting lineup and then out of it. Palmer was a starter in December and a reserve by early January.

The Blue Devils were winning games (10–2 as ACC play began, their only losses coming to second-ranked Arkansas and sixth-ranked Georgetown), but the rotation remained in flux. Practices were daily wars. Clark lost several teeth when Davis elbowed him in the mouth, but he didn't dare miss any time: Krzyzewski rarely used more than an eight-player rotation once the conference season began. "The number nine and ten players were going to be pissed," says Clark. He didn't want to be one of them.

Duke was three days removed from a 54-point win against Boston University when it opened its league schedule at Virginia. So, of course, UVA crushed Krzyzewski's team. The Blue Devils committed 24 turnovers, were burned by Stith's 20 points, and lost, 81–64.

When the team returned to Cameron after the three-hour bus ride from Charlottesville, Krzyzewski ordered a late-night practice. Krzyzewski wanted to make a point, but it came with a price. Grant broke his nose during the physical practice and would miss all but two minutes of the next three games. The irony? Lang took his place in the lineup and stayed there through the next eight games—seven of them wins.

An identity was slowly beginning to emerge. Grant (and to a lesser extent Thomas Hill and Lang) had upgraded the Blue Devils' versatility and athleticism, but perhaps equally important was Duke's on-court disposition. They were becoming—and this was a good thing—sons of bitches.

Thomas Hill, who had forced his way into the starting lineup on a semi-regular basis, was motivated by a dozen different demons. He never forgot that the Duke student newspaper had once referred to him as "a project." Or that Krzyzewski and his staff hadn't considered him an elite recruit. Or that they never ran any plays for him. He spoke when spoken to, but it was sometimes difficult to get him to smile or to joke that season. It was as if he didn't have time to do anything else but prove people wrong.

"He would rip the skin off your teeth in order to stop you defensively," says Laettner. "And I loved that about him."

Thomas Hill was afraid of no one. He was quiet, but he played with such ferocity that Duke coaches sometimes worried that he was *too* competitive during practices. He would fight anybody on the team, including Laettner. McCaffrey was his main competition for playing time, so if they faced each other during practice, Thomas was almost manic in his effort to shut down the sweet-shooting sophomore.

Davis, too, was beginning to make good on his promise to become a factor. He was getting more minutes and a few starts here and there. But unlike Thomas, Davis wasn't afraid to speak his mind. He saw that the Duke coaches had recruited over him—that is, brought in new players at his position—and added it to his laundry list of motivators.

"They used to tell guys, 'You'll play ahead of Brian Davis and Thomas Hill,'" says Davis.

Maybe they did, maybe they didn't, but Davis used the slights, true or not, to his advantage.

Hurley also wasn't the same player from a season earlier. He wasn't even the same player from pickup games earlier in the fall. He was more assertive, more confident. Laettner had seen to that.

Months earlier, during unsupervised and unrefereed pickup games, Laettner's team kept beating Hurley's team. And after every win, Laettner taunted Hurley, reminding him that it was he, Laettner, who was the biggest, baddest, and best player on the court.

"Bobby, you'll never beat me," announced Laettner.

Hurley said little, but Laettner could tell he was upset. During the next game, the point guard dipped his shoulder, dribbled past his defender, drove down the middle of the lane, and found himself confronted by Laettner, who had left his man to help stop Hurley's clear path to the basket. Hurley had two options: attempt a floater/

Mike Krzyzewski *(kneeling)* and his staff of *(from left)* Chuck Swenson, Tom Rogers, Pete Gaudet, and Bob Bender in the mid-1980s. If some powerful Duke boosters had had their way, Krzyzewski would have been fired in 1983.

Courtesy Duke University Athletic Association

Tom Butters: the man who hired the little-known Krzyzewski—and stuck by him.

Courtesy Duke University Athletic Association

Jay Bilas was part of the 1982 Duke recruiting class that transformed Krzyzewski's program from ACC afterthought to national powerhouse.

Courtesy Duke University Athletic Association

The most humbling and humiliating experience of Bobby Hurley's Duke career: UNLV 103, Duke 73, in the 1990 NCAA Final Four championship.

Courtesy Duke University Athletic Association

After stunning unbeaten UNLV in the 1991 NCAA Final Four semis, the Blue Devils give Duke and Krzyzewski their first-ever basketball national championship.

Courtesy Duke University Athletic Association

His own Duke teammates nicknamed him "Asshole," but Christian Laettner never apologized for his methods or his results: four consecutive Final Fours and two consecutive national titles.

Courtesy Duke University Athletic Association

Brian Davis had to beg Duke to sign him out of high school. He used the slight as constant motivation. And no one understood Laettner better than The Mayor.

Courtesy Duke University Athletic Association

If Krzyzewski could have come back in another life as a point guard, it would have been as Bobby Hurley. He marveled at the way Hurley played the game.

Courtesy Duke University Athletic Association

Thomas Hill *(left)* quickly earned the admiration of the hard-to-please Laettner. Said Laettner: "He'd rip the skin off your teeth."

Courtesy Duke University Athletic Association

Grant Hill and the rest of the Duke players underestimated just how good John Pelphrey and the other Wildcats were.

*Damian Strohmeyer/*Sports Illustrated/*Getty Images*

Pound for pound, Deron Feldhaus might have been the toughest Wildcat. Here he battles Grant Hill.

*John Biever/*Sports Illustrated/*Getty Images*

As Kentucky made its second-half comeback against Laettner and Duke, the Wildcats bench erupted in emotion.

*John Biever/*Sports Illustrated/*Getty Images*

The shot that everyone, including the Duke players, thought had ended the game and their quest for back-to-back national titles: Woods's bank-shot floater over Laettner with 2.1 seconds left in OT.

John Biever/Sports Illustrated/*Getty Images*

Even the president of the United States was talking about The Shot the next morning. A Kentucky thoroughbred owner was so upset that he named a horse LaettnerBeGone.

©*Chuck Liddy*/The Herald-Sun 1992

Grant Hill made The Pass. Laettner made The Shot. College basketball had its greatest game.

Courtesy Duke University Athletic Association

Kentucky athletic director C. M. Newton: the reluctant hero who guided UK basketball through the dark days of NCAA sanctions.

John Biever/Sports Illustrated/*Getty Images*

Newton actually tried to tell Rick Pitino *not* to take the Kentucky job. In the end, Pitino couldn't turn down "the Roman Empire of college hoops."

David E. Klutho/Sports Illustrated/*Getty Images*

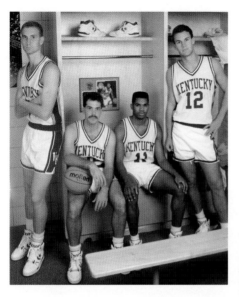

The Ones Who Stayed: John Pelphrey, Richie Farmer, Sean Woods, and Deron Feldhaus.

Courtesy The Cats' Pause

The two most gifted players on the floor that night at the Spectrum: Duke sophomore Grant Hill and Kentucky sophomore Jamal Mashburn.

Damian Strohmeyer/Sports Illustrated/
Getty Images

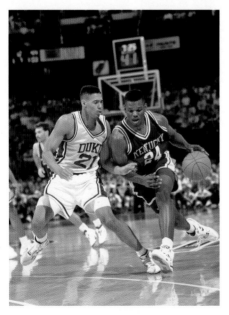

Antonio Lang tried, but nobody could stop Mashburn. He finished with 28 points and 10 rebounds before fouling out.

Damian Strohmeyer/Sports Illustrated/*Getty Images*

Kentucky's players didn't know it as they stood on the floor of Rupp Arena,
but The Unforgettables were about to get their jerseys retired. It was Newton's version
of a lifetime thank-you note.

Courtesy The Cats' Pause

pull-up jumper over Laettner, or complete a wraparound pass to the guy Laettner left unguarded for an easy dunk or layup.

Hurley chose an unusual third option: He threw the ball flush into Laettner's face from three feet away. And then he sprinted out of the gym.

Laettner's eyes watered up, and you could see the red mark on his face from where the ball had struck him. But even through the pain, Laettner had to give Hurley credit: The little guy had stood up to him. It was a big brother–little brother moment.

Laettner didn't chase after Hurley; the point guard was long gone. Even if he had caught him, the punishment would have been light: Put Hurley in a headlock, sit on top of him, and make him promise he'd never do it again. "But I wouldn't hit him," says Laettner.

Flash forward to the January 19, 1991, game against the Tar Heels at Cameron. This time when Carolina's Rice woofed at Hurley, Hurley woofed back. Rice scored just 2 points and Duke won by 14. Laettner beamed with pride.

"If those guys could handle me, the overbearing, anal-retentive, obsessive-compulsive me . . . they could handle everything," says Laettner. "If they could handle me and my chip on my shoulder, they could have a little chip on their shoulder when they went into Carolina, where they all want you to die and want to beat you by 40 points."

Krzyzewski wasn't above pressing a few buttons, too. Two days before the Carolina game he had watched with disgust as one of his players nonchalantly went after a loose ball. Krzyzewski stopped practice and ripped into the Blue Devils. As an exclamation point, Krzyzewski then dove at a ball on the court, his body slamming against the wooden floor, his bare knees screeching across the surface. He got up clutching the ball. His wide-eyed players couldn't help noticing the fresh floor burns on his bloodied knees.

By Laettner's doing, by Krzyzewski's coaching, or by the natural progression of things, the Blue Devils were developing into a very tough out. They had been hardened by the Vegas experience and energized by Grant's arrival. In fact, when Krzyzewski asked Hurley and Laettner to name the best player on the team, the two had the same answer.

"Grant," said Hurley.

"Grant," said Laettner.

Krzyzewski agreed. It didn't matter who the Blue Devils played, Krzyzewski was convinced there was no opposing player any more talented than the only child of Calvin and Janet Hill. His preseason hopes for excellence were coming true, mostly because he now had a core group of three emerging stars: Grant, Hurley, and Laettner.

"We have the most intense competitor," says Krzyzewski of Laettner. "We have Bobby. We have Thomas Hill, who's this fighter. Brian Davis—who thinks that he's Marvin Gaye, but he's really a background singer. He's got the biggest ego on the team. And everyone on our team recognized how exquisite Grant was as a person and as a player."

But the best player on the team was, as Amaker put it, "unselfish to the point of being selfish." Grant had been taught—actually, self-taught—to defer to others. He had programmed himself to wait his turn, but Krzyzewski wanted him to push to the front of the line. He constantly reminded Grant that it was okay to be better than everyone else. And he asked Laettner, Hurley, Davis, and Thomas Hill to remind Grant of it, too. "Otherwise, he'll let you guys do things a little bit more because he doesn't want to steal the show from you."

Lang was assigned to room with Laettner on the road. "And the bags would drop—ding, ding—and we'd start wrestling," says Laettner. "Not fighting, but I'd just grab him to see how tough he was, see if he could get me off of him, the same things my brother did to me when I was young. He knew it was coming. . . . Some of the guys would put their bags down and hear us wrestle and come down and watch. And sometimes I would end up between the wall and the bed, or he'd end up between the wall and the bed. And everyone would laugh, then we'd hug each other, slap each other on the back of the head a little bit, and then we'd go to practice. All that is still some of the greatest times of my life."

The wins and the team-building continued. A 29-point road blowout against Clemson. A 2-point road squeaker against Georgia Tech (thank you, Thomas Hill, who came off the bench to score 20 points, including the game-winner with one second on the clock). A 13-point road win against Notre Dame. A revenge victory against Virginia. A 20-point blowout against Maryland. An 18-point win over Shaq and LSU (Laettner outscored O'Neal, 24–15, and outrebounded him, 11–10).

Victories were one thing. But there was another storyline emerging in the Blue Devils' season: the beginnings of celebrity status.

The now annual Final Four appearances by Duke had given the program a national presence and, as was becoming clearer each week, a national following. It didn't hurt that Laettner looked like he belonged in an Armani ad campaign, or that Grant Hill was the son of a famous Dallas Cowboy, or that Krzyzewski's relationship with the sports media was charmingly disarming. And there wasn't a mom in the country who hadn't wanted to give Hurley a hug and fix him a glass of hot chocolate after the disaster against UNLV.

The Blue Devils were becoming cool—no small accomplishment in the fickle world of sports. From the outside looking in, Duke was a program worth rooting for. The coach seemed like a nice, self-deprecating guy. Their star center was easy on the eyes. Academics mattered. And despite all those wins, they always seemed to be the underdogs come tournament time. America loved underdogs.

After the early February win at South Bend, dozens of people, mostly girls, crowded the exit area outside the Duke locker room. They were there for autographs and to catch glimpses of the Blue Devils players. It was semi-bedlam.

Hurley wanted no part of it. Shy by nature, he had a low tolerance for crowds, strangers, and postgame attention. He simply didn't think he was worth the fuss.

One by one, the Duke players and coaches emerged from the visitors' locker room. Each passed through the gauntlet of autograph seekers. But still no Hurley.

Even as the charter bus pulled away from the Joyce Center, there was no sign of the Duke point guard. That's because the Duke student managers, at Hurley's request, had stuffed him into an equipment bag, zippered it shut, and then carried him onto the bus.

There were hiccups later that month (losses at Wake Forest and Arizona in an eight-day span), but those were forgotten when Duke beat Carolina on the Tar Heels' Senior Day in the regular-season finale at Chapel Hill. This time Hurley let his box score do the talking. He had a career-high 18 points, made 4 of 6 three-pointers, and added 6 assists as Duke clinched the conference title. Rice scored 7 points. "I like the toughness of my team," said Krzyzewski.

He liked it for seven days. Then North Carolina crushed the Blue Devils, 96–74, in the ACC Tournament. Hurley finished with no field goals and 5 turnovers, while Rice scored 12 points with 7 assists and no turnovers. Laettner received a technical foul for chirping at an official and afterward said the Blue Devils had too many "whiny faces out there today."

The Blue Devils held a team meeting and vowed to each other that there would be no more letdowns. Their season, they decided, officially began March 14—opening day of the NCAA Tournament.

After the loss to Carolina, Bonnie and George Laettner, who had driven to Charlotte for the ACC Tournament, found themselves in the same elevator as Krzyzewski. Almost matter-of-factly, as if he were telling them what floor the hotel restaurant was on, Krzyzewski said, "We're going to win the national championship."

After the Duke coach left the elevator, George turned to Bonnie and said, "What's he smoking?"

When Duke, a 2-seed in the Midwest Region, took the court for its first-round game against Northeast Louisiana, its lineup included

Koubek, the once forgotten senior. He had nearly quit the team during Christmas break because of lack of playing time. Against the Indians, he grabbed exactly one rebound and took the scoring collar in the victory.

But he wasn't the only one who struggled. Duke led by just 6 points at halftime, prompting an angry Krzyzewski to beat up an innocent chalkboard. Final score: 102–73.

Meanwhile, Thomas Hill, who had replaced McCaffrey in the starting lineup three weeks earlier, scored 18 points against NE Louisiana and 17 in the second-round win against Iowa. On defense, he was ripping skin off teeth.

Next up was a rematch against Connecticut, the team Laettner had denied a Final Four spot a year earlier. And just to make sure that the Blue Devils didn't suffer from any overconfidence, Krzyzewski volunteered during a news conference earlier in the week that the 1986 Duke team, his first to reach a Final Four, "would kick our ass. This year's team has a ways to go."

If there was one thing that drove the Blue Devils nuts (other than Laettner sometimes), it was Krzyzewski's constant references to his No. 1–ranked 1986 team. To hear Krzyzewski tell it, the '86 team could walk on water and do it while playing man-to-man defense on Jesus. Everyone understood why Krzyzewski adored that team so much, but if it was so good, wondered some of the current Blue Devils, then how'd it lose to Louisville in the championship game?

In a chippy Sweet 16 win against UConn, Koubek, still starting, scored 18 points in the 81–67 victory. But the story would eventually settle around a series of skirmishes involving Laettner and UConn forward Rod Sellers. CBS replays showed Sellers slamming Laettner's head against the court several times, but no fouls were called by officials.

In retaliation, Laettner elbowed Sellers as they ran down the court. Sellers responded with shoves, received a technical foul, and then fouled out. Two months later, the NCAA ruled Sellers ineligible for UConn's opening game of the 1992 tournament.

With Duke and UNLV on the same side of the tournament draw, the two teams would meet in the semifinals if they both reached the Final Four. Some experts considered the Runnin' Rebels to be the best team of all time. Vegas routed Montana in the first round, but looked surprisingly mortal in its 8-point win against Mourning's Georgetown team in the second round. The Hoyas trailed by as few as 4 points in the final minutes and became only the second team that season to lose to UNLV by single digits.

"From reading the papers, you'd think they were Superman and Batman," said Mourning. "They're not invincible."

This was news to UNLV's Hunt. "He can say what he wants. But we're advancing and they're going home."

Hurley watched the Vegas–Georgetown game with considerable interest. "And to be honest, I wouldn't have minded if they lost; I wasn't going to be crushed," he says. "But I knew deep down that they were going to be there at the end. They were that good."

UNLV wore down Utah in its Sweet 16 game and then secured its place in the Final Four with a 77–65 victory against Seton Hall. That same day, Kansas beat Arkansas to advance.

But Utah's Rick Majerus, whose scouting and preparation were second to none in the business, was convinced even after his team's 17-point loss to Vegas that the Runnin' Rebels were capable of beating themselves. He had spent nearly four days watching game film of UNLV and was the first to admit that the Rebels and Tarkanian were a basketball tornado. But for all of their talent, Majerus thought UNLV had too many players who needed the ball to be effective. Unlike previous Tarkanian teams, they didn't seem to have a "blender" type of player, a non-star who could do lots of little things. He also wondered if the weight of a national championship in 1990 and the expectations in 1991 were beginning to take their toll on UNLV.

The next day, North Carolina beat Temple to return to the Final Four for the first time since they won the championship in 1982. And with its 17-point win against St. John's, Duke became the first program since the John Wooden dynasty to reach four consecutive Final Fours.

Not that it mattered. Few gave the Blue Devils much of a chance against mighty UNLV. The smart guys in Vegas made the Runnin' Rebels 7½-point favorites—a huge spread for a national semifinal game. But it made sense: UNLV was The Machine, and after all, there was the 30-point win against Duke a season earlier. Even the U.S. Postal Service thought Tark's team was a lock. A postmark—*UNLV National Champions, Las Vegas, NV*—had already been stamped on about 400,000 pieces of mail.

Krzyzewski gathered his team together and laid out his Final Four plan. He told his players to ignore whatever he said to the media during the week. He intended to smother UNLV with basketball love and downplay his own team's chances. For good measure, he would also talk up Smith's Tar Heels and Roy Williams's Jayhawks.

True to his word, Krzyzewski laid it on thick.

"The last time we played Vegas, they beat us by 30," Krzyzewski told reporters. "The last time we played North Carolina, they beat us by 22. And I just found out that Roy runs the same system as Dean. So what the hell are we doing here?"

A year earlier, Krzyzewski and his staff had had about 36 hours to prepare for their game against UNLV. This time they had nearly six days to dissect the Runnin' Rebels like they were frogs in a high school biology lab. Krzyzewski hunkered down in his Indianapolis airport hotel suite, curtains tightly drawn, notepad on his lap, and watched tape after tape of UNLV.

The more Krzyzewski studied film of the 1990 nightmare loss to Vegas, the more he realized it wasn't as awful as the final score indicated. Yes, UNLV's effort and emotion had overwhelmed Duke, but Krzyzewski could correct that. Yes, UNLV had routed the Blue Devils, but it had done so against a sick freshman point guard and a team that had overachieved. And yes, the 1991 version of UNLV was undefeated, but it was also untested. Its strength—its ability to bury teams early—could become its weakness if only Duke could force the Runnin' Rebels into the unfamiliar territory of late-game pressure.

UNLV was an extraordinary team, but those six days allowed Krzyzewski and his assistants to find its weaknesses and determine ways to exploit each of them. A game plan emerged: Koubek would front Johnson, with Laettner available to sag off UNLV center George Ackles when needed. (The assignment was so stunning that student manager Ashok Varadhan, sipping on a Gatorade near the back of the meeting room, passed the drink through his nose when Krzyzewski announced the Koubek–Johnson matchup.) Grant would be assigned to Augmon, who was nicknamed "Plastic Man" because of his wingspan and ability to defend. Grant would also help handle the ball, to take some of the pressure off Hurley and perhaps create some offensive mismatches. Thomas Hill and Hurley would match up against Vegas's guards, Anthony and Hunt.

To prepare for UNLV's full-court pressure, which had helped force 23 costly Blue Devil turnovers in the 1990 game, Krzyzewski had his starters practice against six and sometimes seven Duke defenders. And each day he kneaded into his players' minds that UNLV was not only vulnerable but beatable.

The night before Duke played UNLV, Lang and Grant decided to get haircuts. Lang got his first, followed by Grant. As the barber trimmed away, Lang kept saying, "He's messing your head up."

Grant laughed it off until he looked in the mirror and saw the damage. His high-top fade looked like a mini-version of Christopher Reid from *House Party*. Grant's ears stuck out like a pair of monarch butterflies.

"Just cut it all off," said Lang.

But the Blue Devils had a team rule: no drastic haircuts going into a tournament game. This was a butcher job, but a bald-headed Grant would have violated the rule. He was stuck with it.

Calvin and Janet Hill hated their son's new haircut. But Calvin was really worried that Grant and the other players were too relaxed. In less than 24 hours they were going to face The Machine.

"You ready?" said Calvin.

"Dad, we're gonna win."

And then he explained Krzyzewski's strategy.

Janet listened to her son as he confidently explained all the reasons why Duke would upset UNLV. Janet nodded her head, all the time thinking, *These guys are dreaming.*

Carolina played Kansas in the first semifinal game. The storyline was obvious: Williams vs. his longtime mentor Smith. Debbie Krzyzewski sat in her Hoosier Dome seat quietly saying to herself, "Please, God, don't make us play Carolina for the national championship." Three games against the Tar Heels had been stressful enough; a fourth meeting would be too much. So Debbie rooted for Rock Chalk.

A nervous Emily Krzyzewski sat next to a nervous Debbie as the Jayhawks defeated Carolina, 79–73. A few minutes later, the Blue Devils and Runnin' Rebels emerged from the tunnels for pregame warm-ups.

"I think this is a day of miracles," said Emily.

"Grandma, with Carolina losing, maybe you're right."

Debbie saw the faces of Duke's players and instantly saw a difference from 1990. *They're not afraid.*

Afraid? They were almost cocky. Davis glanced at the Runnin' Rebels during warm-ups and almost felt pity. *You are all about to lose,* thought Davis, *and y'all don't even know it.*

Duke took a 15–6 lead in the opening minutes, forcing Tarkanian to hurriedly alter his defensive assignments. Johnson, the consensus player of the year, couldn't handle the quicker, more athletic Grant. Augmon was switched to the Duke freshman. The change didn't go unnoticed by Krzyzewski and the Blue Devils assistants; unlike a year earlier, UNLV had to react to what Duke was doing.

UNLV slowly steadied itself, went on a run of its own, and led,

43–41, at halftime. But the aura of Vegas invincibility had been burned away. Krzyzewski's decision to double Johnson and dare Ackles to shoot 12- to 15-foot jumpers was working perfectly. Ackles didn't know what to do. Even worse, he struggled to contain Laettner, who scored 20 first-half points.

Johnson was becoming frustrated. Augmon had his hands full with Grant. Anthony began collecting fouls.

Meanwhile, if there was any doubt about Hurley's resolve, it was answered early in the second half when Hunt broke free on the wing during a Vegas fast break. For 12 long months Hurley had replayed those same UNLV layups and dunks in his mind. This time Hurley sprinted toward Hunt and hard-fouled the Vegas guard as he went up for the shot. The Rebels' bench screamed for an intentional foul, but the officials took a pass.

A message had been sent not just to UNLV but to Hurley's own teammates: This wasn't 1990, wasn't the same Duke team, and it sure as hell wasn't the same Hurley. There would be no freebie dunks this time.

"Bobby wasn't no punk," says Davis. "He's from Jersey City. . . . That was his moment: 'I'm Bobby Hurley and I'm for real.'"

During a UNLV possession in the same half, Hurley, crouched low and hard as he played defense, thought he had forced a 5-second call. When he heard no whistle, Hurley, still in his stance, growled at a nearby official, "I'm working my *ass* off here."

But the Runnin' Rebels hadn't won 45 straight games by accident. They were in trouble, but thanks to superior rebounding and Hunt's shooting they still held a 74–71 lead entering the final four minutes. Nine seconds later Anthony was called for a charge—his fifth foul—while driving in for a layup. UNLV was without its point guard.

Still, Vegas held a 76–71 lead with 2:32 left to play as Hurley dribbled the ball downcourt. At the last moment, Tarkanian switched his defense from man-to-man to its famed amoeba, prompting Krzyzewski to stand up so he could call a new play to Hurley.

But before Krzyzewski could make the call—and before Hunt could rotate over in coverage—Hurley sank a three-pointer with 2:14 remaining, a three-pointer that to this day Krzyzewski calls one of the most important shots in Duke basketball history. "Bobby just said 'Screw you' [to Vegas]," says Krzyzewski.

On their next possession, the Rebels committed their first 45-second shot-clock violation of the season (late-game pressure?) and then fouled Davis as he converted a baseline drive. A free throw later, Duke had a 77–76 lead with 62 seconds to play.

With 49 seconds remaining, Johnson tied the game with a free throw. Laettner sank two free throws with 12 seconds left to put Duke ahead. And then, in the final seconds, Johnson passed up an open three-pointer and swung it to Hunt, who, with Laettner and Hurley closing fast, chucked a desperation shot at the buzzer that eventually landed in Hurley's hands.

Hurley, like a fighter who doesn't hear the final bell, began to make a move downcourt, unaware the game had ended. Grant grabbed him.

"It can't be over, right?" said Hurley, in a daze. "We just did this?"

"It's over," said Grant. "We got it."

Hurley, who played all 40 minutes of the game, nearly floated back to the Duke locker room. Laettner, the only other Blue Devil to play 40 minutes, and Krzyzewski reported to a postgame CBS interview, but not before the Duke coach grabbed his star center and said, "We've got one more game; don't forget that."

In the 1990 game, Johnson and Augmon had combined for 14 of 19 field goals for 34 points against Duke. In 1991, they were a combined 8 of 20 for 19 points. Hurley and Laettner in 1990: 5 of 15 for 17 points (15 by Laettner). In 1991: 13 of 21 for 40 points.

Grant shut down Augmon. Davis came off the bench and scored 15 points. The Las Vegas post offices had to cancel those 400,000 pieces of specially marked mail.

Tarkanian calls his 1991 UNLV squad "the best team I'd ever been around." But he had feared a rematch.

"I didn't want to play Duke again," he says. "I was pulling like hell for [St. John's]. I knew our kids would think it would be easy."

The charging foul on Anthony? "Such a horseshit call," he says. "We probably would have won the game."

The difference maker? "Grant Hill. He could create his own shot. To me that's the most important thing in college basketball."

The bottom line? "We didn't play very well. Duke played great."

The Blue Devils returned to their hotel near the Indianapolis airport. Joyous Duke fans had overrun the lobby and atrium area, giving it the feel of the French Quarter during Mardi Gras. Hurley squeezed his way through the madness and celebrated one of college basketball's great upsets by playing cards with his parents in his room. But the talk never wandered far from that 79–77 final score. Hurley kept saying, "I can't believe we've done this."

To watch the sea of Duke humanity celebrating in the lobby, you would have thought the Blue Devils had won the national championship. All they had really done was put themselves in a position to win their first title or to suffer a colossal post-Vegas letdown. That's why Krzyzewski had spent part of his postgame speech telling "the boys" there was still one more game to be played. And the next day, during a Sunday afternoon practice, Krzyzewski was still on full UNLV hangover alert. "I don't like the way you guys are walking," he said. "I don't like the way you guys are talking. I don't like the way you guys are dressing. You think you're too big right now."

Tarkanian knew better. After watching the Blue Devils in person, he knew Kansas didn't have enough to beat Krzyzewski's team. KU didn't have what Duke had: a Laettner, a Hurley, and a Grant Hill. Most of all, it didn't have the same motivation. Duke . . . Krzyzewski . . . Hurley . . . Laettner . . . Davis . . . they *had* to win. Tark had seen the same body language from his own team in 1990.

It wasn't much of a game, more a procession and coronation than anything else. Two minutes into it, Hurley and Grant Hill broke free on a fast break, with the point guard dribbling once past the half-court line and then lofting an alley-oop pass that sailed just a little too high and a little too far right. It was clearly uncatchable.

Except that Hill, who had already sprinted past three KU defenders and then another two as he neared the basket, gathered himself, and then defied the laws of physics as he sailed higher and higher toward the rim. He cupped the ball with his right hand, and in one thunderous motion jammed the ball through the hoop to extend Duke's lead to 6. CBS's Billy Packer nearly fell out of his courtside seat, telling play-by-play man Jim Nantz, "That ball was thrown to the point that it was going out of bounds. I don't know how he got up there to get it!"

As Grant Hill pointed to Hurley and acknowledged the pass, you could almost see the KU players' shoulders sag. They had no defense for that kind of greatness.

Duke won, 72–65, and afterward Davis rushed up to Krzyzewski, pressed his sweat-soaked uniform into the coach's expensive suit, and yelled into his ear, "We finally got it for you, baby!"

It was a night of hugs. Hurley and his frequent tormentor Laettner embraced in an emotional bear hug on the court. Hurley had gone from televised bathroom breaks to raising a national championship trophy over his head in almost exactly a year. He had gotten a rare second chance at a national title and delivered (43 assists, just 10 turnovers, in 219 minutes of playing time during the tournament). Laettner, voted the Final Four Most Outstanding Player, had fulfilled the goal he set when he signed with Duke: be part of the program's first title team.

Thomas Hill, who nearly signed with Williams and the Jayhawks, had proven everybody wrong, perhaps even Krzyzewski. But not Davis, who had foreseen this two years earlier. He told Thomas after the game, "Call your dad. Tell him we beat Kansas."

Koubek, who had come this close to quitting during the holidays, got a championship in his final game as a Blue Devil. So did Buckley.

Grant, bad haircut and all, had gone from a panicked incoming freshman to the player whose amazing talents filled the one remaining hole in the Duke lineup. Without him, who knows if Krzyzewski and the Blue Devils would have gotten their one shining moment.

An hour or so after Krzyzewski took his turn climbing up a ladder and snipping a piece of precious net from the rim, he and his family finally made their way out of the Hoosier Dome. They left with their shoulders lighter, their smiles wider. At last, there would be no more "Can Krzyzewski Win the Big Game?" stories.

Sports Illustrated writer Alex Wolff walked with Krzyzewski as he left the building.

"Did you see their faces?" said Krzyzewski, referring to his players. "They were so happy. Gee, I'd like to do this again. When will we do it again?"

A year earlier in a Denver hotel suite, Emily Krzyzewski had told him the 1991 season would have a happier ending. Now, as everyone gathered in the coach's Indianapolis hotel suite to celebrate, Emily was there to remind him that mother knows best.

"See," she said, "I told you you'd do better next year, Mike."

EIGHT

October 15, 1991

itino was now on the coaching clock, which is how he preferred it. His program wasn't completely out of NCAA prison (UK had one more year of probation to serve), but it no longer had to walk around wearing an orange road-gang jumpsuit.

The scholarship restrictions were gone. The asterisks were history. The Wildcats were now March Madness approved. For the first time since his arrival, Pitino could look at his roster and see more than slivers of hope. At last he saw expectations.

Every ingredient for success was in place. Kentucky had the makings of a college superstar in Mashburn. It had four seniors—Pelphrey, Farmer, Feldhaus, and Woods—who would start or get massive minutes. It had experience (a total of seven juniors and seniors and ten lettermen). It had motivation. And it had Pitino and his driven staff.

The program had some scores to settle. Even its preseason media guide had a certain "F— you" editorial quality to it. On page 15 of the guide was a UK team photo accompanied by a copy block with a message as subtle as Bruce Willis in *Die Hard*:

Wait just a minute here. Did you say Kentucky would be ranked SECOND in your preseason basketball poll?

SECOND, as in one place lower than first?

Kentucky? A sleeper for the Final Four? A team of destiny?

How could this have happened so soon? Okay, okay, so last year was great fun. But only yesterday you said it would take YEARS to rebuild this program.

YEARS, as in more than one. Only yesterday, your friends from Sports Illustrated *used the word "shame" in reference to Kentucky. But this . . . SECOND?*

What will people think? What will they say?

Take that. Kentucky was suddenly Officer John McClane and *SI* was terrorist Hans Gruber. "Yippee-ki-yay" and all that.

Pitino's original three-year rebuilding plan called for the Wildcats to challenge for the SEC championship and to play in the NCAA Tournament. But the plan was outdated. UK had already won its version of an SEC title, and it was good enough to do more than just play in the NCAA Tournament. Pitino knew it and so did Kentucky followers.

The UK roster that Pitino had carefully reshaped and assembled was an eclectic mix of personalities, accents, and playing styles. There were five Kentuckians, two players from New York, two from Mississippi, two from Florida, and one apiece from Indiana, Texas, Illinois, and Tennessee.

Martinez and Mashburn were inseparable. They had come to Kentucky together, roomed together, configured their class schedules together. Worked out together. Barfed together.

Mashburn was the Grant Hill of the Wildcats, a player whose refined skills, size, and physical abilities simply made him better than anyone else. And like Hill, Mashburn deferred to the upperclassmen and considered himself an overachiever. "I always had that mental concept in my head that I had never arrived," Mashburn says.

At Kentucky, the talent difference between Mashburn and the rest of the UK roster was much more pronounced than between Grant Hill and the Duke lineup. Because of that, Mashburn wasn't hesitant to try to take over games. Nor was he afraid to respectfully challenge Pitino on coaching matters. He showed up at Pitino's office one day to argue that the UK press was configured wrong, that he should be at the back end of the press, conserving his energy and acting as a defensive safety net. Pitino had him scrambling the entire length of the floor.

"Coach, you know and I know that I need to score about 20 points a game this year," said Mashburn. "But you've got to take me off the front of the press. It doesn't make sense."

Pitino changed the press. Mashburn's scoring average went from 12.9 to 21.3.

Martinez was the first of his family to be born in the United States. His mother had come from Cuba when she was nine, his father at age ten. His grandmother, who also had fled the Communist-ruled island, was a sweet woman, unless you mentioned Fidel Castro.

His father had wanted him to sign early with Massimino and that nice Catholic school, Villanova, but Martinez decided to wait. Villanova moved on. Sendek invited him to UK for a visit, and by the time Martinez returned home he was hooked.

He knew almost nothing about the state except that it had the Kentucky Derby. He could barely understand a word of Farmer's Kentucky accent, and Kentucky didn't have any Cuban restaurants. On the flip side, Kentuckians didn't know much about Martinez. One well-meaning caller to the weekly *Big Blue Line* radio show said he and his friends had given nicknames to each Wildcat player. "We call him 'Pierre,'" the caller said of Martinez. "You know, since he's Spanish."

Martinez came to UK as thin as coaxial cable. He was placed on a 5,800-calories-a-day diet and ordered to chug down protein drinks that tasted like crushed chalk. With the staff's blessings, he was a regular at the nearby McDonald's.

On the court he was a grinder who was prone to fouls and a nasty temper. His teammates loved pressing his anger button.

Feldhaus wasn't skinny. Pound for pound, Feldhaus was the Wildcats' toughest and strongest player. The UK sorority girls loved him for his looks, but Pitino loved him for his fearlessness. Only 6'7" and 210 pounds, Feldhaus didn't blink when assigned to LSU's massive O'Neal. He backed down from nobody. If there was a wall to run through, the usually reserved Feldhaus would be the first to slam his shoulder into the plaster.

"If there ever was a Kentucky ballplayer who you could build out of clay, it was Deron Feldhaus," says Pitino.

Woods was his roommate as a senior. It was an odd pairing. Feldhaus chose his words carefully. Woods chirped like there was an expiration date on his voice. He was brash, noisy, and friendly, but it drove him nuts that the Wildcats were perceived as a soft, gimmicky team, all three-pointers and mad sprints up and down the court. Soft? Gimmicky? Try saying that after watching one of their brutal practices, after an Oliver-led workout, or after a session with Coach Buddy.

Woods's jump shot was a constant work in progress, and Pitino would sarcastically ask him, "Why do you shoot from the outside?" But Woods had no conscience. His theory: You can't score if you don't shoot.

Woods might have been the most talkative of the Wildcats, but Pelphrey had developed into the team lawyer of sorts, the brains of the roster. All of the regulars had become adept at memorizing Pitino's scouting reports and game plans, but Pelphrey was a film-room junkie.

"If you put him in a suit," says Mashburn, "he looked like he was part of the coaching staff. He didn't look like a basketball player. If you looked at him, got up close to him, you're like, 'Nahh . . . he's not a basketball player. Is he an assistant coach?'"

He was part player, part on-court coach. Pelphrey was image-oriented, but he wasn't above a little trash-talking. More than a few opponents (and UK staff members) had underestimated him and had paid for it.

"When I first saw him I thought he was Ichabod Crane," says Oliver.

"He was tall, lanky, skinny, and slow. What I found out was that he was tough, gritty, smart, a great leader, and a great teammate. The best captain I've ever seen."

Farmer, at last in Pitino-type shape, had long ago earned the respect of his teammates. They had watched him put on otherworldly shooting displays in practices, scrimmages, and games. They had seen him endure as Oliver and Pitino tested his will daily. "They did everything they could to make him quit," says Tubby Smith. And with the game on the line, Farmer was the team's best free throw shooter.

But Richie could still be Richie. He was, says Feldhaus, "the god of high school basketball in the state of Kentucky," and he liked the attention that came with it. He was the favorite son of eastern Kentucky, and the sports talk radio shows were often flooded with calls from those mountain towns, asking, "How much is Richie gonna play tonight?"

Farmer thought he had been singled out by Oliver and Pitino—and he was right. He was more than willing to do the work. All he wanted was some recognition for the effort. But Pitino wasn't the warm and fuzzy type.

Some players thought his parents were around the Wildcat Lodge just a little too much—doing his laundry, doting on him. But his teammates loved his goofy vocabulary, his tobacco-dip-scented, cement-thick twang (even Pelphrey had trouble understanding him sometimes), and his loyalty. Farmer lived for UK and for his teammates.

Jeff Brassow had freakish physical skills that seemed to translate better in practice than in games. He wasn't much of a ball handler, but he could shoot threes and jump out of Rupp. And nobody out-hustled him (he was voted the team's Mr. Hustle in 1990). Oliver called him "Cyborg."

"He'd do whatever I'd tell him," says Oliver. "'Brassow! I want you to go to Iraq, rescue those prisoners, and bring them back home.' He'd do it. 'Brassow! I want you to swim the English Channel.' He'd do it. He was the one guy, I couldn't get to him. It was like he had two sets of lungs."

His teammates adored him, but he played out of control at times and he was a bit of a lovable space cadet. At least once a practice, Pitino would say, "Earth to Brassow."

In Dale Brown's brief bio in the 1991–92 UK basketball media guide, one sentence read, "Coach Rick Pitino was impressed by his three-point shooting touch." Funny, since Pitino never saw Brown play in person.

Brown, an all-state selection at Pascagoula (Mississippi) High School, had originally signed with Mississippi Valley State, but was forced to sit out his freshman year for Prop 48 reasons. He transferred to Gulf Coast Junior College and became a juco All-American. One day he walked into the basketball office at Gulf Coast and his coach said, "Guess what? Rick Pitino called about you."

"Get out of here," said Brown.

"No, he said he's going to send some people to watch you."

Tubby Smith saw him play and returned to Lexington with glowing reports of Brown's jumper and one-on-one defensive skills. Pitino then sent Sendek and Donovan to Perkinston, Mississippi, for confirmation. At the time, UK also was recruiting blue-chip guards Jimmy King, Eric Brunson, and Donald Williams. King signed with Michigan, Brunson with Temple, and Williams with North Carolina. And Brown signed with Kentucky.

"I came from a family, man, that was poor," he says. "My mom had seven kids. I was the baby of the family. I was looking for an opportunity to get an education. I was mainly there to go to Kentucky, play for a coach like Pitino, try to get to the NBA, and take care of my mom. We didn't have a lot of things. Nobody else in my family had a college degree. Sisters had kids early. Half of them were lazy—I can't lie."

But Brown, like Farmer, actually quit the team briefly because it was simply too hard. He couldn't handle the conditioning, the practices, and the pressure Pitino applied daily. He cracked, but just for a moment. And then he was back.

As usual, it was Pelphrey who had helped ease the transition. He came to Brown's dorm room and told the nervous juco transfer, "Dale Brown, you've got to settle down. You've got a lot of talent. But you've got to listen to Coach."

Says Brown: "He was like a big brother to me, man."

Brown settled down. "And once he got it, he was a confident guy," says Woods.

Travis Ford had transferred from Missouri a year earlier (and paid his own way that first year) but now was eligible to play for UK. He had grown up in Madisonville, Kentucky, and averaged 31.7 points as a senior at North Hopkins High School. The 5'9" Ford was never seriously recruited by Sutton's UK staff. It wasn't personal; the Wildcats simply had too many point guards on their roster.

Duke was interested, but only if Hurley didn't sign with the Blue Devils. So Ford went to Mizzou and started at times for the No. 1 team in the country, but he began looking for an exit strategy when the program became the target of an NCAA investigation. He had played for LSU coach Dale Brown in the Olympic Festival, and LSU and Carolina made runs at him, but Ford was intrigued by Pitino's system at Kentucky. When they met, Pitino half-kiddingly said that Ford wouldn't have time to visit Chapel Hill and Baton Rouge.

Ford rubbed some of his teammates the wrong way when he first arrived in Lexington as a transfer. He had a personalized license plate (FORD5) on his late-model car and wasn't in a hurry to lend out his ride to the other Wildcats. Early on, he ripped teammates in practice. Some of the UK players thought he was a spoiled brat, that he acted as if he had done them a favor by transferring to Kentucky.

But he could shoot and he had a Mensa-level basketball IQ. Once he bought into the Pitino way of doing things, he became invaluable. The Wildcats nicknamed him "Doogie Howser" because of his baby face, but few players were tougher than Ford. He cracked his kneecap in half during the Blue–White Game; it was so severe that the team physician blurted out "Wow" when first examining it.

Rather than undergo surgery, Ford played the entire season with the injury. He wore an elastic sleeve over the knee, never took painkilling shots, and gutted it out, even though "it felt like 100 knives were shooting into it." His effort didn't go unnoticed by his teammates.

Andre Riddick, a 6'9" freshman center from New York, was a top-50 recruit who had played AAU ball with Mashburn. Riddick was a shot blocker and capable rebounder, but he wasn't a versatile offensive player. Like Brown, he didn't automatically trust people. He had had a sometimes trying childhood, and he took his time before confiding in outsiders. He often wore headphones on campus, as if he were still in a New York City subway station.

Freshman guard Chris Harrison, from Tollesboro, Kentucky, surprised his teammates with his play in practice, but he wasn't expected to contribute much. The same went for hard-luck redshirt sophomore guard Henry Thomas, who had been plagued by knee injuries. Carlos Toomer, a hyperactive sophomore better suited for football, was destined for third-team point-guard duties.

Freshman forward Aminu Timberlake came to UK from Chicago. Mashburn immediately recognized Timberlake's basketball potential, but the freshman wasn't prepared for Pitino's in-your-face methods. Pitino was a yeller, a verbal blowtorch. Timberlake had trouble adjusting to Pitino's volume level.

Junior guard Junior Braddy had joined the team as a walk-on in 1989 and earned a one-year scholarship in 1990. He might still own the record for Shortest Time as a Pitino-coached Wildcat. Braddy overslept on the first day of practice in '89 and Pitino immediately dismissed him from the team. He begged Pitino to reinstate him, and the coach did allow him to return, but not before telling him to buy two backup alarm clocks.

"Those guys, they would have died for Kentucky," says Oliver. "Never seen anything like it."

The Wildcats bought into the preseason hype. At Midnight Madness they carried themselves like a confident, accomplished team, a far cry from the nervous, unsure group of 1989. "We'd been through every war you could think of," says Woods. "Our whole goal was to get to the Final Four. We were ranked in the top five, and everybody was telling us how good we were. We went from blue collar to white collar. We thought we had it made."

And then UK, ranked fourth in the AP poll, played unranked Pittsburgh at Rupp in the second game of the Dodge Preseason NIT.

If a season is a series of defining moments, then the 85–67 loss to Pitt was on the short list. You could have measured Pitino's anger level with a Richter scale.

It wasn't just that Kentucky had lost at home, ending a 22-game win streak at Rupp. Or that the Wildcats couldn't hit the side of the arena (21 of 77 from the field). Or that UK had been blitzkrieged by a more physical and determined Pitt team.

It was all those things and then this: New York.

With the victory over UK, Pitt was bound for Madison Square Garden and the semifinals of the NIT, where it would play Eddie Sutton's Oklahoma State team.

The Wildcats were bound for Pitino hell.

"Do you know my life would have been better if I had died then?" says Oliver.

Pitino's dream of a triumphant New York homecoming vanished on that November 22 evening at Rupp. He had planned to see old friends and family in Manhattan. Maybe he and Joanne would sneak in a dinner or two at their favorite restaurants. Maybe see a Broadway show. And nothing beat playing a game in the Garden, especially against the coach he had replaced at Kentucky.

That's all Pitino had talked about during the summer—taking the Wildcats to the NIT in New York. Feldhaus's mom and aunt had already purchased plane tickets to attend the game.

Instead, Pitino and the Wildcats stayed home, and Feldhaus's mom and aunt, stuck with nonrefundable tickets, flew to New York, went shopping, and saw a couple of plays. Sutton's Cowboys went on to win the preseason tournament.

"We can stop talking about going to the Final Four and we can stop all the talk about being a top-five team," Pitino said in his postgame news conference. "We are not."

There was no 20-hour-a-week practice limit during the Thanksgiving break. Pitino ordered three-a-day practices for nine consecutive days. (Once the limits kicked back in after the holiday, he scaled back the workout time.)

"That was a week or so that I think everybody who was there will remember as long as they live," says Farmer. "It was kind of a lesson for all of us. I think even Coach had probably overlooked [Pitt] a little bit."

The practices were brutal. Brown suffered full body cramps. Garbage cans were hosed out every day. And yet, says Feldhaus, "it was probably the best thing that ever happened to us that year." Adds Farmer: "It kind of refocused us, that's for sure."

The Wildcats grew closer through the shared hell. They also began tightening up the loose lug nuts in their offense and their press. They were getting good.

Pitino was a man possessed, but he found time to support UK football coach Bill Curry, who was struggling through his second season, going 3–8 (0–7 in the SEC). "[Pitino] would come to the football games, and there were times when we were blown out," says Curry. "That was a very difficult time for me. But not only would he not say anything negative, he would never leave the games early. I never forgot that."

Kentucky's next hoops game wasn't until December 4, when it faced Pitino's alma mater, Massachusetts—and the man he had recommended for the coaching job, John Calipari. But the day before the game, Brassow, who had started the first two games and scored 23 points against

West Virginia, tore the ACL in his right knee during practice. He needed surgery and was lost for the season.

Brown took Brassow's place in the lineup, and the Wildcats beat UMass by 21. Then, in one of Pitino's signature UK wins, the 14th-ranked Wildcats upset Knight's 9th-ranked Indiana team, 76–74, at the Hoosier Dome in Indianapolis.

UK lost just once in December (to No. 13 Georgia Tech), twice in January (to unranked Tennessee and No. 9 Arkansas), once in February (to unranked LSU), and once in March (to unranked Florida) to finish the regular season atop the SEC's Eastern Division. Pitino never took losses well, but the 21-point defeat in Baton Rouge resulted in a nearly four-hour film session when the Wildcats returned home at about 1 a.m. By the time the UK players plopped exhausted in their beds, the sun was on its way up.

There would be no corners cut, no letdown. Pitino wouldn't allow it. He knew his team was top 10–worthy, but only if all the parts worked. Even with Mashburn, the Wildcats didn't have much margin for error.

But Pitino had his soft side. Before the regular-season finale against Tennessee, he had fought a losing battle against tears during the Senior Day ceremony at Rupp Arena. Under normal circumstances, UK's Senior Day celebration is like no other. But this farewell was especially emotional. These were the boys who'd been there for the worst of times and stayed to help bring the Wildcats from shame back to pride again. So many people cried during the singing of "My Old Kentucky Home" that vendors could have sold boxes of Kleenex.

In their first postseason game since Sutton's final year in Lexington, the Wildcats beat Vandy in the SEC Tournament opener and then got a Shaq-sized break when LSU's O'Neal was ejected in the Tigers' quarterfinal victory for fighting and was automatically suspended for the semifinal game against UK (Kentucky won, 80–74).

In the locker room before the start of the league championship game, Pitino asked if anybody wanted to say anything. The quiet Mash-burn cleared his throat and told his teammates, "You know, I don't have a lot of money. I can't give you anything like that, but what I can give you is an SEC championship against Alabama."

Mashburn made 12 of 14 shots from the field, scored 28 points, and grabbed 13 rebounds as UK routed Alabama, 80–54. The Wild-cats scaled a wooden ladder and snipped away the nets. They posed for photo op after photo op with the SEC Tournament trophy.

Pitino's team hadn't just challenged for an SEC title, it had won it—and even the SEC said so this time. With a 26–6 record and a con-ference tournament championship, it was only a question of how high the Wildcats would be seeded and in what NCAA Tournament region they'd be placed.

On the day the SEC Tournament started in Birmingham, the nine members of the all-powerful NCAA Men's Basketball Selection Com-mittee began to arrive in Kansas City. They were sequestered in the downtown Hyatt Hotel, where the entire 40th floor, complete with security personnel, was reserved for their exclusive use.

Chaired by SEC commissioner Roy Kramer, easily the biggest mover and shaker in college sports, the committee's proceedings were as trans-parent as mud. Kramer was occasionally made available to the media in the weeks leading up to Selection Sunday, but his comments were predictably and purposely bland.

Critics of the process wonder if it is a coincidence that the commit-tee has the exact same number of members as the U.S. Supreme Court. They consider the committee too secretive, the equivalent of a college basketball star chamber. So far-reaching was the secrecy that former committee member and chairman Dave Gavitt declined to discuss the inner workings of The Nine with reporters that March—even though Gavitt had left college athletics to become vice president of the Celtics.

The committee included Kramer, Mid-Eastern Athletic Conference commissioner Ken Free, Syracuse athletic director Jake Crouthamel,

Fresno State AD Gary Cunningham, Kansas AD Bob Frederick, Houston AD Rudy Davalos, Arizona State AD Charles Harris, and two others—Duke AD Tom Butters and Kentucky's Newton. If the merits of a committee member's own basketball program came up, the member was required to leave the room.

Duke, ranked No. 1 in the AP poll the entire season, wouldn't have to sweat out a bid. Barring a colossal collapse in the ACC Tournament, the Blue Devils were all but guaranteed a No. 1 seed. Shortly before 6:30 p.m. Sunday, when the committee's selections would be announced, the NCAA provided its broadcast partner, CBS, with the tournament bracket. Sure enough, Duke was the No. 1 overall seed and assigned to the East Regional, while UCLA (West), Ohio State (Southeast), and Kansas (Midwest) were the other number ones.

Pitino's Kentucky team was given a No. 2 seed. That was the good news. The bad news: UK had been placed in the same region as Duke. The Blue Devils would begin their tournament against 16th-seeded Campbell in Greensboro, North Carolina, only 55 miles from the Duke campus in Durham. Kentucky would have to travel 731 miles to Worcester, Massachusetts, for its opening-round game against No. 15 seed Old Dominion. Didn't matter. The Wildcats were so confident after winning the SEC Tournament and so happy to finally be in the NCAAs, they would have pushed Coach Buddy there.

Kentucky had little trouble with ODU, winning 88–69, and then wore down Iowa State, 106–98, to reach the Sweet 16. (Pitino had convinced the Wildcats that Old Dominion was the equal of the Celtics and that Iowa State was capable of beating the Los Angeles Lakers.) A rematch against UMass was next.

The Wildcats had crushed Calipari's team, 90–69, nearly five months earlier in Lexington. But this wasn't the same UMass team. Back in December, the Minutemen were running on fumes. They had come directly from the Great Alaska Shootout tournament, first spending two hours on the tarmac at the Anchorage airport, then flying to Seattle, connecting to Cincinnati, and taking a budget-rate school bus from Cincinnati to Lexington. (Rather than hire a driver, a UMass assistant coach had driven the bus.) They never had a chance against Pitino's team, which hadn't played in 12 days.

This time the 3rd-seeded and well-rested UMass team had only 261 miles to travel and was in familiar surroundings—its conference tournament was also played in Philadelphia. Calipari had kept his March practices short (usually no longer than 45 minutes) and the mood light. While answering questions at the off-day news conference, Calipari held a cutout face of Pitino in front of him. He wanted to project a sense of relaxed calm to his players. But deep down?

"For me, we were taking on Goliath," he says.

When the 6'3" Will Herndon outjumped the 6'9" Martinez for the opening tap, UMass fans thought it was a sign that their undersized but ultra-athletic team could pull off the upset. Instead, Kentucky needed just 12½ minutes to build a 21-point lead.

But UMass fought back, and when Jim McCoy, who had never made a three-pointer in his college career, heaved in a 62-foot shot at the first-half buzzer, the Minutemen trailed by only 8. "And we raced off the court like we were going to win," says Calipari. "We raced off the court like, 'It's on now.'"

And it was. Anton Brown's three-pointer with 6:18 remaining in the game cut Kentucky's lead to 70–68. Thirty-one seconds later, the Wildcats received a gift from the basketball gods.

The gift's name: referee Lenny Wirtz.

With 5:47 left to play, Calipari gestured that Woods had come over the top of a UMass player for a rebound. Wirtz instantly wheeled around from almost the opposite diagonal end of the court and whistled the Minuteman coach for a technical foul. According to Wirtz, Calipari had left the confines of the coaching box.

"What did you just do?!" said Calipari, looking down at his feet, which were within the coaching boundary.

It was a bizarre, game-changing call made by a ref with a reputation for attention-grabbing decisions. How Wirtz, from his distant position on the court (and with the Spectrum's confusing array of on-court decorative lines), could have detected the infraction remains difficult to understand. And from that distance, he couldn't have heard what Calipari was saying.

"I had said some things that probably deserved a technical," says Calipari, who became Kentucky's coach in 2009. But, he adds, "I knew I didn't step out [of the box]."

The technical gave the Wildcats some elbow room. Farmer (who else?) sank the two free throws, UK got the ball back, and Feldhaus scored to turn a 2-point game into a 6-point Kentucky lead.

"I can't tell you the feeling when the technical was called," says Calipari. "It took the air out of me. Because I knew that was it."

Kentucky won, 87–77. Mashburn, the player UMass had no answer for, scored 30 points.

And Wirtz? That summer, Wirtz would be asked to referee games for an American all-star team playing in Europe. The coach of the team? Calipari. "One time he was late for a bus and I did leave him on purpose," says Calipari. "Other than that, I was good to him."

The Wildcats had reached the Elite Eight. They were a win away from a Final Four.

Pitino and Calipari shook hands at game's end. Calipari leaned in and said what would have been unthinkable at UK three seasons earlier: "Go win this whole thing."

Julius Erving, a UMass alum and former teammate of Pitino's, came into the Kentucky locker room after the game. A beaming Pitino told his team that UMass had been the tournament matchup that concerned him most. They had survived (with the help of Wirtz) a furious Minuteman comeback. This had been their test. They'd be fine now.

"Coach Pitino was so happy," says Pelphrey. "He was so certain we were going to the Final Four."

Pitino and his staff stayed at the Spectrum and watched Duke beat Seton Hall, 81–69. On the bus back to the UK hotel, the mood was joyous and upbeat. Even Pitino, the ultimate worrier, couldn't contain himself.

Pitino noticed that Sendek, who was in charge of putting together the Duke scouting report, wasn't celebrating. Instead, he was sitting quietly by himself, seemingly lost in thought.

"Herb?" said Pitino.

Sendek looked up.

"Coach," said Sendek. "Duke is *really* good."

NINE

April 1991

Several weeks after winning the national championship, Duke's players were asked to autograph a stack of commemorative team posters. When Hurley arrived at the signing session, he noticed someone had already scribbled a signature over the point guard in the photo. So Hurley found another spot and signed his name.

When Hurley went to sign the next poster, the same signature appeared over his face. It was that way on every poster.

Hurley examined the autograph.

Laettner.

Hurley couldn't take it anymore. He called Krzyzewski to complain about his teammate/tormentor.

"Coach, can you believe he did this?"

Krzyzewski sighed. Big brother and little brother were at it again.

"Why do you think he did that, Bobby?"

"I don't know. I don't know what's going on with him."

"Well, he always does something like this if he doesn't feel you're at his intensity level."

"I don't care. I've had enough of him."

"Well, tomorrow when you're in the gym, you go tell him in your own words that if he ever does that again, you're going to punch him in the mouth. You understand?"

"Huh?"

"Do exactly that: Tell him you're going to punch him right in the mouth."

The next day, Hurley confronted Laettner. He told him to expect a fist in the jaw if he ever pulled another stunt like that. Laettner nodded and walked away.

Later, Krzyzewski asked Hurley about Laettner's response.

"He didn't do anything," said Hurley. "He just said okay."

Krzyzewski smiled. Hurley still didn't get it.

"Of course that's what he said," Krzyzewski said. "All he wanted to know is that you would punch him in the mouth. He wanted to see that."

"Oh," said Hurley, who didn't have the patience to translate the motivational language of Laettner.

But Krzyzewski understood it. Laettner and Hurley were the Lennon and McCartney of the Blue Devils. Their personalities were so different and their relationship so complex, but they shared a common love for the game. And they were obsessed with winning.

"There were some people Christian got on and would never let off, like Bobby," says Mark Williams, the Duke team manager. "He'd do it to get them to perform. . . . I think he was in complete control in that relationship."

"I always felt like Bobby was looking for Laett's approval and Bobby was looking to be accepted by Christian, and Christian kind of kept him on edge and never really let Bobby in," says Grant Hill. "I don't know if it was that he didn't like him or he just felt, 'If we're going to win, I need Bobby to be tough and I'm making him tough.'"

Hurley would roll his eyes at Laettner's remarks. Laettner would pick on Hurley. Team meetings would be called; Laettner would sometimes use them as another opportunity to criticize Hurley.

"He'd pick on guys and use the excuse, 'I'm just trying to get you ready,'" says Varadhan. "Only with Grant was it genuine. At the end of the day, even Christian, he would look at some of the things that he would do—holy shit. You'd see him do things that were almost inhuman."

There was a love and respect, however hidden, between Laettner and Hurley, but Laettner didn't always know how to articulate his side of it. He wouldn't come right out and say it—at least, not to Hurley—but he had realized long ago that Duke couldn't win and Laettner couldn't realize his full potential without the Jersey kid. Hurley was the perfect player for Krzyzewski and the perfect point guard for Laettner: a fearless, pass-first, shoot-second star.

Still, Laettner wouldn't release his grip on Hurley. He wanted to calibrate him just so. And there was still the lingering resentment from when Krzyzewski had deeded the team to Hurley at the first 1989 practice. Some of the Blue Devils called him "Coach's son." They would tell him, "You've got two fathers."

Part of it was jealousy. Part of it was good-natured kidding. But there was no denying that Krzyzewski had a different kind of relationship with his point guards, especially Hurley. At Army, he had played the same position as Hurley, but he hadn't played it the same way, or been allowed to try. So he let Hurley drive the team without wearing a seat belt.

Krzyzewski saw what Laettner was doing: finding the fine line between what made Hurley very good and what made him great. When Hurley played with just the right amount of anger, he was an extraordinary point guard. And nobody could make Hurley angrier than Laettner.

Instead of tossing the ball downcourt to Hurley on an inbounds pass, Laettner would wave for him to come back and get it. Or he'd roll the ball to him. It drove Hurley nuts.

It wasn't an accident that Laettner's teammates nicknamed him "Asshole." He could be engaging, charming, and even sweet at times. Or he could be distant, cold, abrasive, and borderline cruel. You never knew which version of Laettner you'd get in a given day. He might be your best friend in the morning and not acknowledge your existence in the afternoon.

"He was sort of the dad," says Clark. "He took on sort of the parental role, whether we wanted him to or not. . . . I ignored him, and that was the thing that he hated most. I wouldn't give him the time of day. He'd say, 'Hey, so-and-so, you going to let him shoot over you like that?' He was the first to get on you, but the first in line to cheer for you, too."

"Christian is one of the nicest guys you'll know," says Williams, "but you'll only know if he lets you in."

Laettner was choosy about whom he let in. He had been carefree and gregarious as a child, but much less so at Duke. His own mother had seen the transformation.

"I don't know what changed him," Bonnie Laettner says. "I think he did not really like all the attention he got in college."

The paradox is that Laettner loved Duke, loved playing for Krzyzewski, loved basketball, loved winning, and, believe it or not, loved his teammates. He just didn't know how to show it.

"He was like the popular girl in the sorority," says Varadhan. "He could be demeaning, a little bit arrogant. People didn't necessarily like him but everybody wanted to be loved by him. Everybody wanted Christian's approval. He was despised and at the same time revered."

Says Bilas: "He was the leader, without question. He had some reluctant followers. They followed him on the floor."

Laettner had returned to the gym and to his workouts almost immediately after Duke won the national championship. He expected Hurley to be there, too, and wasn't pleased by the point guard's absence.

Of course, Hurley wasn't the only Duke player to take some post–Final Four R&R—not that that mattered to Laettner. The way Laettner looked at it, if the Blue Devils were going to pull off the rare championship repeat, then they couldn't afford any downtime, especially by Hurley.

There was a certain truth to Laettner's concerns. To win consecutive championships, Duke would have to have overcome two enemies: history and complacency. Not since UCLA's 1972 and 1973 teams had a program won back-to-back titles. In fact, not since the 1984–85 Georgetown teams had anybody won a championship and reached the title game the following year. For the Blue Devils to repeat, they'd have to pretend they hadn't won the 1991 title. They'd have to work harder, be mentally tougher, and absorb the best shots from everyone on their schedule. After all, a magnificent UNLV team had tried and failed to do the same thing.

Laettner couldn't stand the idea of not winning what he believed belonged to him and Duke. Nor could he stand that Hurley wasn't putting in the same gym time he was.

So he wrote his name over Hurley's face on the posters. That would get his attention, Laettner figured. And he was right. Hurley reacted exactly as Laettner had hoped. The "I'm going to punch you in the mouth" threat was comical, but Laettner admired Hurley's nerve. Best of all, Hurley was back in the gym—which was the whole point.

But not everyone was like Laettner. Actually, *nobody* was like Laettner. Hurley wanted to win. But he also wanted some Me Time. After a long and ultimately redemptive championship season, Hurley needed to decompress. For the better part of six months he had spent the majority of his days connected to his teammates and to the Duke program. He had loved it, but now he wanted to give his body and his mind a brief break from the grind.

Laettner didn't believe in breaks. Me Time? What was that? The Blue Devils had won, partied, been feted at Cameron, and even been greeted by President George Bush at the White House. Now it was time to work again.

Not everyone was interested in winning a second championship ring. McCaffrey, Duke's second-leading scorer during the 1991 season and an All-NCAA Final Four selection, informed Krzyzewski that he was transferring to Vanderbilt. The decision caught everyone by surprise. Blakeney had been with McCaffrey the day before the announcement, and McCaffrey had said nothing about leaving the program.

The official reason for his departure: McCaffrey wanted to play point guard on the college and NBA level. With Hurley a fixture at the position, McCaffrey had to go elsewhere.

The unofficial reason: Thomas Hill. Not only was McCaffrey never going to unseat Hurley at point guard, but Thomas Hill had all but locked down the off-guard starting spot. McCaffrey had a better shooting stroke, but Hill was better at everything else. So the 21-game starter transferred to Vandy.

Palmer also left the program, transferring to Dartmouth, where his older brother Walter had played. As an incoming freshman, Palmer had been considered by some Duke coaches to be more game-ready than Laettner—but that was then. Only three players on the 12-man roster played fewer minutes than Palmer in 1991. With big-man recruits Cherokee Parks and Erik Meek joining the team later in the summer, Palmer's playing time was in serious jeopardy.

"[The transfers] do not change the team at all," Laettner told reporters. "We have an incredibly large amount of basketball talent on our team."

Davis looked at the Duke schedule and didn't see a game the Blue Devils shouldn't win. "We never thought we were going to lose again," he says.

Krzyzewski didn't disagree. He knew the Blue Devils were good enough to win a second consecutive national title. And while he would never say so publicly, he also knew they were good enough to win every game—and win each one big.

A season earlier, he had used the embarrassment of UNLV's 30-point victory as a major motivator. He had kept that memory in his pocket like a wallet photo, pulling it out whenever necessary to remind his team of that defeat and that feeling.

But the dynamic had changed. Krzyzewski could no longer use failure to push his team. Now he had to use the idea of success, but in an unconventional way. So he compartmentalized the 1991 title. He told his team and the media that the Blue Devils weren't defending the 1991 championship. After all, it had been bought and paid for with victories, and nobody could take it away. Duke's name would be on the trophy forever.

Instead, he said Duke would try to *win* another NCAA championship. Not defend, but *pursue* and *add*. Big difference.

By separating 1991 from 1992, Krzyzewski was trying to reduce the pressure on his team. In addition, he dialed down the Blue Devils' off-season conditioning program. Krzyzewski wanted his players to report to the October 15 opening practice in shape, of course, but he didn't want them overtrained and overtired before they even started.

Duke's schedule was adjusted for another championship run. A season earlier, the Blue Devils had played 10 games before Christmas. This time they would play half that many. Krzyzewski didn't want his team to burn out, increase the chances of injuries, or develop bad habits before the ACC schedule arrived in January.

Laettner and Krzyzewski weren't the only ones who thought Duke was the best team in the country. The preseason Associated Press poll had the Blue Devils ranked No. 1, followed by Knight's Indiana team. Kentucky was ranked No. 4.

It was difficult to dispute the voting. Duke returned four starters from the 1991 championship game (Laettner, the Hills, and Hurley) as well as Davis, who would join the starting lineup. They had one of the best coaching staffs in the business, one of the best home-court advantages, and one of the best centers, point guards, and swingmen in Division I. They had Final Four and championship experience. They had attitude. And they had the 6'11" Parks, considered one of the best freshmen prospects in the country.

Both Parks and fellow freshman Meek were from southern

California—Parks from Huntington Beach in Orange County, the 6'10" Meek from Escondido, near San Diego. Parks was a consensus high school All-American who had visited Kentucky and was expected to sign with nearby UCLA, but instead he committed to Duke in October 1990. "Offensively he is the best big man produced on the West Coast since Bill Walton," said recruiting guru Bob Gibbons.

Meanwhile, the 1991–92 Duke basketball media guide also invoked the big redhead's name when describing Meek as the "most recruited basketball player from San Diego since Bill Walton."

But Meek arrived at Duke still dealing with the aftereffects of injuries suffered when a drunk driver hit him from behind as he jogged home late in his senior year of high school. His left hamstring had been punctured, and he had cracked his left shoulder blade after bouncing off the car windshield. Meek attended his June graduation in a wheelchair and was on so many painkillers that he could barely recall the ceremony.

That left Parks to receive the full brunt of the Laettner Mentoring Program. Or as the Duke media guide gingerly put it, "Top level impact player that should develop well in first year under tutelage of Christian Laettner."

Parks was part surfer dude, part free spirit, part basketball star. His mother had a sweet, flower-child, peace-and-love way about her. Parks inherited his parents' laid-back style. He had All-American hoops skills, but his intensity level paled in comparison to that of Laettner, Davis, Thomas Hill, and Hurley.

His nickname was "The Chief." He liked basketball, but it didn't define him. His favorite gesture was a shrug. Parks cared about his new teammates and about winning, but he wasn't consumed by it. You could find him volunteering at the Safe Sex information booth near the Duke student center just as easily as you could find him in a gym.

It was hard not to like Parks. He was West Coast smart, cool, and hippie-ish—the exact opposite of many of the type-A personalities who attended Duke. But he had chosen both the exact right and the exact wrong time to become a Blue Devil. Right, because Duke was poised for another title run. Wrong, because his first season would be played under Laettner the Merciless.

They were born three years, 2,600 miles, and two worlds apart. Parks wanted to play well and often did play well. Laettner wanted to dominate you, win the game, tear your still-beating heart out of your chest and then toss it into the garbage disposal. He was a basketball perfectionist.

Pity the student manager or teammate who threw Laettner a lazy chest pass during a practice drill. He'd fire the ball back so hard that the logo would leave an imprint on your skin. If there was a big-man drill and he had his guy pinned on his right hip, Laettner wanted the entry pass firmly on his left side so he could catch and dunk. God help you if the pass wasn't just so.

There was no ambiguity with Laettner. He wanted to beat the shit out of you in every drill, every scrimmage, every pickup game, every real game, every slap fight, every egg fight, every wrestling match, every tennis match, every Ping-Pong game, every air-hockey game, every team bowling outing, every everything. He didn't have Shaq's size and power or Mourning's strength. He survived and excelled because he never took a nanosecond off. He squeezed everything he could out of a 90-minute Duke practice and then stayed afterward to work some more. He might have been an asshole, but he was a relentless asshole devoted to making himself and his teammates unbeatable.

Parks didn't have that basketball gene. He worked, but he couldn't match Laettner's intensity. Nor did he try. Meek did, but he didn't possess Parks's skills. Parks was extremely coordinated for a big man, almost fluid for someone his size. Meek was a worker bee destined to be a backup's backup that season.

Pete Gaudet coached the Duke bigs. Laettner would ask Gaudet, "Why don't you work with Cherokee like you work with me?" And Gaudet would tell him, "Because he's got to get the work ethic."

Parks was often one of the first players off the court after practice. The quick exits astounded Laettner.

"Where the fuck is Chief?" he'd say. "Why isn't he out here?"

And then he'd go into the Duke locker room and drag the freshman back onto the court for more drills. That was the thing with Parks—he needed someone to tell him where to be and when to be there. For two weeks straight, Laettner practiced a turnaround jumper after every workout. And for two weeks straight, Parks had to make sure he got a hand in Laettner's face when he shot it—or else.

During the November 2 Blue–White Game, Laettner bodied Parks to the ground. The Cameron crowd booed its disapproval. After the game, several fans asked the freshman, "Do you and Laettner hate each other?"

"That's just him," said Parks.

Added Meek, who didn't play because of a knee injury: "Basically that's the way it is every day in practice."

Laettner took it to Parks and Meek on a daily basis. For the most part, Parks wasn't bothered by Laettner's intensity, his elbows, his comments, and his criticisms. (A Laettner favorite: "Chief, you're playing like a girl.") It was the California in him. *Whatever, dude.*

But there were times when even the carefree Parks was pushed to the limit and Duke coaches had to step in.

"I think Christian felt it was his mission that, 'I'll make [Hurley] tougher, more ready; I'll make him more like me,'" says Brey. "And he did that with Cherokee Parks as a senior, where the kid was in tears. I had to tell [Laettner], 'Back off. We're going to have to flush him. We're not going to get anything out of him.'"

So Laettner backed off, but only by inches, not feet. He had to make sure Parks was ready. And anyway, he hadn't stiffed the NBA and its millions so he could *maybe* win another NCAA championship during his senior season. He wanted the repeat. (As a precaution, Laettner's parents took out a Lloyd's of London insurance policy for him.)

"When I went out of the game, I didn't want us to go down 10 points every time," says Laettner. "And when I went out, he's the person that came in there, so he had to hold the fort down a little bit. And as a freshman to be able to hold down the fort in the ACC, you had to be tough. . . . We were like, 'Cherokee, when you frickin' step between the lines with us, you better bring it and you better bring it hard and tough and intense, because that's what we do here at Duke.'"

Bilas had a soft spot for Parks. Maybe it was the California connection (Bilas had attended Rolling Hills High School in the Rancho Palos Verdes area), the big-man connection, or the empathy he had for anyone who had to endure Laettner's toughening-up process. Parks, says Bilas, "had the body of a 40-year-old when he was 18." He also had a tattoo on his lower back, possibly the first tramp stamp in Duke basketball history. It was an Aztec face. When Bilas asked him about it, Parks said, "It's the face of pain."

The other Duke newcomer had been recruited by exactly nobody out of high school. His name was Ron Burt, a 6-foot senior engineering student who had answered a cattle call for Duke walk-on candidates the night of October 15. Krzyzewski was down to 11 scholarship players, and he needed another body on the practice floor, preferably a guard.

Thirty-eight players had shown up for the tryout, including a future *Sports Illustrated* writer named Seth Davis, who had been cut from his high school team as a senior. A series of scrimmages reduced the number of candidates to 12 and then to 1—Burt, who got a call from Amaker several hours after the tryout. He was the first Blue Devils walk-on since 1987.

As the season approached, Krzyzewski began to reach into his motivational toolbox. During a late October practice attended by sportswriter (and Duke alum) John Feinstein, Krzyzewski halted practice after an hour and called the team together.

"You know, I've been reading and listening to interviews you guys have been giving this fall, and I keep hearing over and over again that this could be the best team defensively that Duke has ever had," said Krzyzewski in a calm, even voice. "So far, of what I've seen, that's just lip service."

Practice reconvened a few minutes later. For the next half hour, reported Feinstein, every pass and dribble was frantically challenged by a Duke defender.

If Krzyzewski had any doubts about his team's commitment to back-to-back championships, they didn't last long. No. 1 Duke began the season by beating East Carolina by 28 points without Laettner, who missed the opener because of a foot injury (Parks started for him). Five days later against Harvard, this time with Laettner in the lineup, the Blue Devils won by 53. So meticulously played was Duke's first half against the visiting Ivy Leaguers (Duke led, 59–28) that Krzyzewski walked into the locker room at halftime and told his team, "I have nothing to say."

It was as if Duke was playing not against Harvard but against its own standards. The sellout crowd of 9,314 at Cameron thought it was watching a mere blowout, but the Duke staff knew better: It was witnessing the closest thing to basketball perfection. It was an esoteric experience, a rare time when the opponent didn't matter. Harvard or Carolina, it would have made no difference that night. The Blue Devils were nearly flawless.

Parks had now played in two games and hadn't missed a field goal. He was 5 for 5 against ECU and 6 for 6 against Harvard. Maybe tough love worked.

Something was working. When Duke improved to 3–0 with a win against St. John's, SJU coach Lou Carnesecca said, "The only part I'm proud of is that we didn't die."

Whenever possible, Krzyzewski liked to schedule a nonconference road game in or near a player's hometown. This time it was Laettner's turn. The Blue Devils were going to play Canisius at the Buffalo Memorial Auditorium, better known to the locals as The Aud.

George Laettner was a local. When he was a kid, he would sneak into The Aud to watch games. Years later he would bring his own children to the old arena and buy $4 tickets to see the NBA's Buffalo Braves.

There was snow on the ground when the Blue Devils arrived in town the day before the December 7 game. The mayor presented Laettner with a key to the city.

Laettner took the team to his uncle's modest house in the First Ward neighborhood of south Buffalo. There was a snowball fight. Pizzas from Bocce's were ordered and devoured. So were buffalo wings. Teammates and student managers marveled at how nice, even relaxed, Laettner was during the visit.

The game was a big deal not only to Laettner and his family but to Buffalo. Duke hadn't been to the city since 1951. Now the Blue Devils were ranked No. 1 and their star center was one of Buffalo's own.

Canisius, a small Jesuit college with an enrollment of 4,700, hadn't reached the NCAA Tournament since 1957. There was a definite sense of civic pride on Laettner's part when the game sold out, making it the largest crowd (16,279) to see a college hoops game in western New York history.

Two years earlier, Duke had beaten the Golden Griffins by 36 points at Cameron. The margin of victory would be no different in 1991 as the Blue Devils won, 96–60. But Laettner was different. He didn't attempt a shot in the first half as Duke built a 47–25 lead. Krzyzewski grabbed him as they walked into the visitors' locker room.

"What's wrong?" said a perplexed Krzyzewski. "Why aren't you scoring? It's the one time in your whole career at Duke you get to play in front of your home crowd."

"Coach, I get so much attention and so much credit," said Laettner. "I want my hometown to see how good my teammates are."

Krzyzewski was amazed. The same Laettner who demanded so much of his teammates had subjugated his own game so they could shine in his hometown. In most cases, it would have been the other way around.

"Well," said Krzyzewski, "next half *you* show off. You show off to me."

Laettner finished with 19 second-half points and the grudging admiration of his teammates, who had rarely seen this side of their senior center.

"He was sort of showing us off, like, 'Look how lucky I am that I get to play with these guys,'" says Grant Hill. "And the mystery surrounding Christian, that was kind of who he was. He kind of had a firm exterior—he came across as cocky, like, 'I'll be the guy; I'll be the one who takes the hit; I'll be the one that puts myself out there.' But he was a great leader and he was a great teammate."

Says Krzyzewski: "I'm telling you, there's nobody who loved his teammates more than Christian."

And yet, at one time or another, every one of those teammates wanted to smack him.

"He was unusually brilliant, with quotation marks around *unusual*," says Krzyzewski.

Krzyzewski controlled the minutes, dictated the basketball strategy and tactics, and cultivated relationships between teammates, but the Blue Devils' personality wasn't a reflection of him. That's one of the great myths in the game, that a team takes on the personality of its coach. Krzyzewski knew better. Great teams take on the personality of their best players and of their best traits. In Duke's case, it took on the combined personalities of Laettner, Davis, and Hurley. Krzyzewski simply put their arrogance, toughness, and fearlessness into a martini mixer, shook it, and poured out a team intimidated by no one. Laettner and Davis ruled by the power of those personalities and now their senior standing. Hurley ruled by the artfulness and spontaneity of his play.

"Bobby didn't need to play off sheet music," says Krzyzewski. "He just played. Christian could play, too, but he needed sheet music."

The Blue Devils were a functionally dysfunctional team, often succeeding in spite of themselves. They loved one another but didn't necessarily always like one another. There was another incident of Hurley throwing a ball in Laettner's face and then running out of the gym. Parks was occasionally a mental mess. Grant was uncomfortable taking over games. (Laettner: "You're the best player on the team and you don't even realize it." Grant: "Am I really that good?") Krzyzewski sometimes had to toss the team out of Cameron for not practicing hard enough.

Laettner thrived on the conflict. But his personality and his quest for perfection could overwhelm his teammates and confound the coaching staff. On occasion Davis, Laettner's roommate and best friend, would tell the Duke assistants, "I know you guys are frustrated with the big guy. What do you need me to do to get through to the big fella?"

Other times the Blue Devils would take matters into their own hands. Once, Laettner looked up and found eight of his teammates standing in front of him. Davis and Hurley were the mutiny leaders.

"Let's get him now," said Davis. "He can't stop all of us."

And the Blue Devils piled on top of Laettner, wrestled him to the ground, and took turns giving him noogies. They laughed as they did it, but there was a message conveyed.

"The point they wanted to get across was, 'Stop fucking with us so much,'" says Laettner. "I loved that they did that. It meant a lot. It still means a lot."

They were college basketball celebrities, winners of a national title, the No. 1–ranked team in the country. But they were also kids, capable of doing kid things. Sometimes a couple of the Blue Devils would carry a cooler filled with ice and water and throw it on, say, Hurley as he took a shower after a game. And then there was the night Laettner drove to Lang and Grant's apartment with some exciting news.

"Guys, I found this great new parking lot," Laettner said. "The pavement is so slick. C'mon."

So Lang and Grant squeezed into Laettner's Honda Accord, drove to a nearby rain-slickened parking lot, and sat wide-eyed in the car as the likely player of the year gunned the engine and did doughnuts. As they spun around, Grant thought, *This dude is crazy.*

Despite the personality conflicts, the kid factor, the expectations, the pressure, the lingering resentment over who had earned their starting positions and who hadn't, the publicity, the demands of school, the travel, and the tribulations, the Blue Devils were scarily resilient. "There were days when I marveled at how good they were," says Bilas.

Meanwhile, 700 miles away in Ann Arbor, Michigan, a team like no other ever assembled counted the days until it faced the Blue Devils in a mid-December game at Crisler Arena. The Fab Five and its University of Michigan teammates didn't marvel at Duke. Instead, the five heralded freshmen—Chris Webber, Jalen Rose, Juwan Howard, Jimmy King, and Ray Jackson—all but sneered at the Duke hype.

"They won a national championship," says Jimmy King. "They hadn't seen us yet. It's a new time. It's our time."

It wasn't that the Fab Five hated Duke. On the contrary, Webber had seriously considered signing with the Blue Devils before committing to the Wolverines. (He apparently wasn't impressed with cozy Cameron during his recruiting visit. As they toured the famous old arena, Webber had asked Blakeney, "Where do you play?")

Duke recruited Webber hard, and with good reason. He was phenomenally gifted, a 6'9" forward who immediately made his way into the Wolverine starting lineup. In Michigan's first three games, Webber averaged 18 points and 11.7 rebounds. He was a game- and program-changer.

Many of the Blue Devils players had met Webber during his recruiting visit to Duke and liked him. At his parents' insistence, Webber attended Detroit Country Day, a private, predominantly white school whose parking lot featured its share of Mercedes-Benzes, according to Rose. Even the mailing address for the private high school was ritzy: Beverly Hills, MI.

Webber and Grant Hill were friends from the AAU basketball

circuit. Their families were friends with each other. Webber had even spent a weekend at Grant's house in Virginia when they were in high school. During that trip, Webber and Grant attended a party; as Grant's midnight curfew approached, he told Webber they had to leave. Webber said he was staying. So Grant drove home, only to be ordered by his mother to return immediately to the party, retrieve Webber, and do it all before the midnight curfew.

Webber fit in at Duke, not just because of his immense basketball IQ but also because of his personality. He could have been a Dookie with ease. Instead, he signed with Michigan and helped create an instant basketball phenomenon.

Rose, who was never on Duke's recruiting list, also played AAU ball with Grant and was friends with Hill and his family. "To be honest, I wanted a lot of the things that he had," says Rose.

Rose's estranged father was, like Grant's dad, a pro athlete, the former NBA star Jimmy Walker. Rose had a mother he adored, who worked as a key puncher tracking auto parts at a Chrysler plant. Grant had a comfortable, well-to-do life. Rose, well, didn't.

"I wasn't envious at all, because I actually liked [Grant]," says Rose. Rose had considered going to UNLV, but the chance to play at Michigan and in front of his family was too much to ignore. He wore No. 42 in high school to spite Walker, whom he had never met (Walker wore No. 24 in the pros), but switched to No. 5 at Michigan because he was the last of the Fab Five to sign his letter of intent. Now he would face the same Duke program that UNLV humbled in 1990 and lost to in 1991.

Rose was impressed with Laettner's overall game, as well as his attitude. Laettner didn't take shit from anybody; Rose liked and respected that. Hurley and Laettner were two white players who, in Rose's mind, played "black." Of course, Rose also thought Laettner was probably the kind of guy who would spend too much time fixing his hair after a game.

The Michigan freshmen actually preferred the nickname "Five

Times" rather than the Fab Five name they made famous. Whatever they were called, they had definitely caught the attention of the Blue Devils. The Duke players were aware of the hype, of their longer, baggier game shorts (the black socks would come later in the regular season), of their growing popularity, and their swagger, which some of the Blue Devils thought was undeserved. After all, they had played only a few regular-season games against mediocre opposition.

"It was like the anti-culture from what our culture was," says Krzyzewski. "We looked at it as two different worlds . . . and I think the public looked at it that way, too. Whether they liked them or liked us, it was a huge game."

Krzyzewski never shied away from scheduling difficult nonconference games. The Michigan game meant a national television audience, more exposure for his program, and a chance for potential Midwest recruits (especially in talent-rich Detroit) to see the Blue Devils program. Plus, it was the kind of game that could help Duke months later during the NCAA Tournament.

Laettner and Davis almost didn't make it to the game in one piece. The night before, they were at a party near the Michigan campus when several Wolverines football players decided it was time to teach the two stars a lesson. Says Davis: "They were out front trying to kick our ass." Laettner and Davis escaped, but only after crawling through a backyard, sneaking into a car, and lying on the car floor until the football players abandoned the chase.

Michigan students began lining up outside Crisler in the cold and sleet as early as 5 a.m. on game day. It was only December 14, but there was almost a postseason feel to the matchup. The subplots (the Webber factor, Duke No. 1, the Fab Five hype, the cockiness of both teams, the preppy image of the Blue Devils, national television) all contributed to the intensity.

"I think Duke got a lot of credit of being so straightlaced and All-American," says King, who was recruited briefly by Duke. "We stepped on the scene, and we felt like we could play with those guys, that we were just as good."

It was a sometimes chippy, verbal game. After a Webber jam, the freshman glared at Laettner and said, "You just got dunked on, on national TV!" And, according to Webber, when Laettner dunked on him, the Duke star said, "That's how you do it, little kid." (Laettner later disputed the quote, saying he asked Webber where the U of M defensive rotation had been on the play.)

Duke led by 10 at halftime, 43–33. But Michigan reversed the numbers in the second half and forced the game into overtime, before the Blue Devils prevailed, 88–85.

Webber fouled out, but not before scoring 27 points and grabbing 12 rebounds. Laettner also fouled out, with 24 points and 8 rebounds. Michigan blocked 8 shots. Rose, Webber, and King accounted for 60 of the Wolverines' 85 points.

Says King: "It's early in the season and nobody really knew us. Then you've got the superpower coming in, and we're just going to bow down and show respect? Nuh, uh. That wasn't our mind-set."

"We should have beaten them by 20," says Davis.

Duke won its two November games, its four December games, and its ten January games, including a victory at Florida State, the newest member of the ACC, where Laettner both complimented and half-mocked the Seminoles fans' tomahawk gestures. "When they do that little chant thing, that was excellent," he said.

After crushing Notre Dame by 29 points on February 1, the Blue Devils were 17–0, ranked No. 1 in the country, and had won over even the most casual college basketball fan. They were mainstream America's team.

On road trips, coeds and even older women would leave notes and phone numbers for the players under the windshield wipers of the team bus. Some women sent roses. Or panties. Or love letters—from as far away as Hawaii. Sorority girls would bake them cookies or even serenade the Blue Devils at their off-campus houses and apartments. Hurley had boxes of fan mail waiting for him at the Duke basketball office. Fans from Japan wrote him.

"If there was a Fab Five," says Davis, "it was us. We had the biggest following in college basketball history."

It was a simpler time. ESPN had just begun to truly flex its college basketball biceps. Most Duke students couldn't get cable in their campus dorms. The Internet was in its infancy. Relatively speaking, cell phones were cinder-block huge. Nobody texted, tweeted, or Facebooked. People still read newspaper box scores.

And on February 5, 1992—the date of the season's first Duke– North Carolina game—Duke students definitely read the Wednesday edition of their campus paper, *The Chronicle*, or, as its editors renamed it that day, *The Daily Tar Hole*—mailing address: Chapel *Hell*, North Carolina.

The Duke student newspaper poked at the Tar Heels like someone poking an alligator with a stick. For that day's forecast, it read, *Whether. Today: Carolina will choke, 80%. Thursday: Alumni will cry, 90%.* On the front page was an empty area devoted to mocking Carolina center Eric Montross. *This big, useless white space was placed here to remind you of Eric Montross*, it read.

He wasn't useless that night at the Smith Center. Montross, who was knocked silly twice in the game by blows to the head, scored 12 points and had 9 rebounds as the 9th-ranked Tar Heels ended Duke's dream of a perfect season, 75–73. Laettner also had a dozen points, but he missed a pair of shots that would have sent the game into overtime, and he passed up an open three-pointer in favor of a running two-point try that also missed.

Michael Robbins's lead in the February 6 edition of *The Chronicle* was succinct and sublime: "Is this hell or what?"

No, Duke's version of hell turned real during the first half, when

Hurley broke free on a fast break, went in for a layup, and landed hard on his right foot. Even with the crowd noise, he heard a cracking sound.

As he turned to run back down the floor, he felt like someone was tightening a rope around his foot. Each step produced a jolt of pain.

Hurley didn't say a word. But the look on his face betrayed him.

"Sit down," said Laettner. "You're hurt."

"I'm good," said Hurley, determined to gut it out. "I'm good."

"Bobby, you're hurt. We can see it."

But this was the Carolina game. And this was Hurley, the Jersey kid who was as tough as a steel I beam. He played 37 minutes on one foot, but he couldn't run at full speed and he struggled with his shot.

Hurley knew the foot was broken. He knew it at halftime when the team trainers examined it and asked him how he felt. Fine, fine, said Hurley. It wasn't until after the game, when the foot swelled to the size of a water balloon, that X-rays revealed he had fractured the second metatarsal bone. Recovery time? At least three weeks.

"My man," says Davis. "The best 6-foot white point guard ever . . . very tough."

But . . .

"If he had gone out [of the game], we would have been the only undefeated team."

Says Laettner: "You don't ever blame a team sport on one person. But he had a broken foot. You don't play basketball when you have a broken foot."

Hurley was relegated to street clothes, a walking boot, and cheerleading duties. Krzyzewski moved Grant Hill to point guard and added Lang to the starting lineup. Now all they had to do was travel to the Deaf Dome—LSU's Maravich Assembly Center—for a February 8 game against Shaq.

O'Neal had been waiting for this day. Laettner had outscored him, outrebounded him, and outsmarted him in their first meeting. Now

O'Neal had grown a half-inch taller, had developed a hook shot, and was playing at home.

"February eighth," he had told reporters months earlier. "One-thirty p.m. I got a big X on my calendar."

Duke's arrival was a mega-event in Baton Rouge. The pregame atmosphere was electric and hostile. Lang nearly jumped out of his skin when he noticed that a caged tiger (LSU's Mike the Tiger mascot) was positioned only a few yards behind him in the arena entranceway. And during the game, LSU's student section serenaded Laettner with a chant of "Ho-mo-sex-ual," a crude reference to a mushrooming urban legend involving the Duke center.

In a 1990 interview with Chip Alexander of the *Raleigh News & Observer*, Laettner said, "I have one best friend: my teammate and roommate Brian Davis, and I spend 95 percent of my time with Brian. I don't want anything else; I don't need anything else. . . . All I want to do is be with Brian, play well on the basketball court, and do well in school. That's it: basketball, school, and Brian."

The rumors began to percolate: Laettner and Davis were gay. After all, wasn't it true that they had held hands while walking down a dorm hallway, in full view of some of the Duke football players? (Yes, as a joke.) And wasn't it true that Laettner received mail from gay fans? (Yes. He also led the nation in mail from female fans.)

The two contrarians were at first amused and then annoyed by the portrayals. They had tried to punk the media and fans, but the rumors jumped the containment ditch. Laettner would eventually address the issue with Seth Davis, telling the student newspaper reporter, "I think people have fun talking about it. Rumors can get started with no basis at all. They can gain a lot of strength just by the mere fact that they're rumors. . . . So it's obviously a jealousy thing. It's so pathetic. It's incredible."

Pathetic but useful. When opposing fans taunted Laettner it seemed to relax him. He played all 40 minutes against LSU and scored

22 points with 10 rebounds in the Blue Devils' 77–67 victory. O'Neal scored 25 and had 12 rebounds, but the future No. 1 NBA pick would finish his college career 0–2 against Laettner and Duke.

Grant Hill also played all 40 minutes and played well (16 points, 9 rebounds, 6 assists). Like Rose at Michigan, his size presented instant matchup problems for opposing point guards. It also forced Grant to be more assertive.

Duke won its next three games, but the victories didn't come easily. After a 91–89 win against then lowly Maryland, Krzyzewski chided the Cameron Crazies for sitting on their hands. "We're not a dominant basketball team," he said. "Don't you see that the little guy's not out there? If he's out there, we're a different team."

The little guy—Hurley—was going nuts. His foot was feeling better, but he wasn't allowed to do basketball-related activities. However, he was given clearance to work out on the StairMaster in the Murray Building across the street from Cameron. The former distance runner took out his frustration on the cardiovascular equipment, racking up huge numbers on the step machine, which measured how many "floors" you ran and at what resistance level. Since Hurley couldn't play in games, he created his own competition, leaving a note on the machine for Bilas, who had a reputation for doing marathon sessions on the StairMaster.

I'll beat your number of floors, wrote Hurley.

Bilas saw the note, smiled, then put in a 90-minute workout. "I didn't want that little shit to beat me," says Bilas.

While Hurley rehabbed, Duke lost another game, this time at Wake Forest. A Joel Coliseum record crowd of 14,673 watched as the unranked Demon Deacons stunned the Blue Devils, 72–68.

Duke could have clinched the ACC title that night, but instead scored 1 point in the last 5:19 as Wake overcame a 10-point deficit. The disjointed, error-filled (15 turnovers), and sometimes selfish play angered Krzyzewski.

"There is no question we're not at the peak of our game right now," he told reporters afterward. "It's been a long month. Without Bobby it's a longer month."

In the Associated Press story about the upset, there is no mention of a failed desperation play the Blue Devils ran near the end of regulation. Grant Hill's long baseball pass from the baseline to the opposite free throw line extended came off his fingers wrong and curved toward the sideline. Laettner was pulled out of bounds on the three-quarter-court throw, and that was that.

By the time the team bus returned from Winston-Salem, Krzyzewski had issued his orders for next day's practice: Report to Wallace Wade Stadium at 2 p.m. Be taped up and dressed in practice uniforms.

Wallace Wade is where Duke plays its home football games and where the outdoor track is located.

Oh, shit, thought Clark. *This is going to be World War III.*

Krzyzewski was going to run the Blue Devils to death. He was going to have them run 220s, 440s, 880s until they puked. He would punish them for giving away the Wake Forest game, for not playing defense, for not fighting through adversity. They thought playing at Wake was tough? Wait until they spent the next two hours ralphing in their shoes, gasping for breath after every sprint.

The players assembled in the stadium stands shortly before 2 p.m. Krzyzewski told them to sit down.

Here it comes, thought Clark, who was nearly shaking in fear. He wasn't alone.

But Krzyzewski didn't yell. He spent the next 15 minutes telling his team how good it was. He went from player to player, detailing exactly why each was special and vital to the program. And then he took them across the street to Cameron, where cake and ice cream were waiting for the team in the film room. The players watched about 20 minutes of tape—all the time wondering when their coach was going to order them to the court for a full punishment scrimmage—before

Krzyzewski turned the lights on and said, "All right, guys, see you tomorrow."

Clark looked at his teammates as they made their way to the locker room.

"Uh, what just happened?" he said.

Krzyzewski had taken his players' temperature after the Wake Forest loss and realized they needed some TLC. Laettner had hit a tiny lull in his play. Grant Hill had been thrust into a new position, and the team was still adapting to the change. And the Blue Devils were getting everybody's best shot—and it showed.

This wasn't the first time Krzyzewski had tried theatrics and motivational techniques. Earlier in his Duke coaching career, before a game against a ranked Louisville team, Krzyzewski walked into a darkened Blue Devils locker room holding a single candle. His face illuminated by the small flame, Krzyzewski intoned, "I come to bury Louisville, not to praise them."

The stunt worked great until the flame blew out and nobody could find the door in the pitch-black locker room. Louisville won the game.

Years later, Krzyzewski used the candle shtick again, but this time he held a metal fist in front of him as well. "Individually, we can be broken," he said. "But when we make a fist . . ."

Another time, he channeled his inner Rocky and did a bit from the famous fight movie.

But his favorite tactic, used on his Duke teams season after season, decade after decade, was to invoke his memories of his mother, Emily. "The Purse Story," as it became known, was legendary.

It worked like this: Krzyzewski would come into the locker room, angry about his team's timid play, or lack of toughness, or reluctance to rebound or take charges. And he would tell the Blue Devils the story of his hardworking mom, who scrubbed the floors of the tony Chicago Athletic Club at nights. One evening, after taking the bus back to her neighborhood, a mugger had tried to pull her purse from her arms. But

Emily had refused to let go, clutching the purse with all of her might. The mugger gave up and ran away.

"And she didn't have any money in the purse," Krzyzewski would say. "That's how tough she was." Then he would pause. "But you guys," not bothering to hide the disgust in his voice, "can't even hold on to a rebound."

One Duke player once added under his breath, "Well, if she has any eligibility left, we could use her."

However corny, the methods often worked. Three nights after the cake-and-ice-cream practice, Duke beat Virginia at Cameron to clinch the ACC regular-season title. The Blue Devils next beat UCLA at Pauley Pavilion without Grant Hill, who had an injured ankle, but with Hurley, who had finally been given medical clearance to play, back in the starting lineup. They beat Clemson by a point at Littlejohn. And they beat Carolina on Senior Day at Cameron, prompting Montross to say afterward, "We're definitely looking forward to seeing Duke in the ACC Tournament."

Be careful what you wish for. Duke overpowered the Tar Heels by 20 in the tournament championship. Montross scored just 8 points to Laettner's 25 and was posterized by Thomas Hill on a dunk. Later, when the Blue Devils stopped for a postgame meal, about two dozen fans stood outside the restaurant windows to watch the players eat.

Krzyzewski's team entered the NCAA Tournament ranked No. 1 and the favorite to win a second consecutive national championship. Campbell University coach Billy Lee had it right when he said playing Duke in the first round in Greensboro was like "going into a sword fight with a pocketknife." The Blue Devils won, 82–56.

But during the second-round game against Iowa, the Hurley–Laettner drama reappeared. Up by 24 at halftime, Duke began to get sloppy against the Iowa press. Laettner struggled to find an open teammate, especially Hurley, on an inbounds pass. Then Hurley was late getting a pass to an open Thomas Hill, who got fouled instead of having an easy bucket. As the Blue Devils huddled near the free throw line in front of the Duke bench, Hill said something to Hurley. Laettner joined in. Moments later, Laettner was in Hurley's face, jabbing a finger toward the point guard's chest. Hurley swatted Laettner's hand away.

"Mike," said Brey to Krzyzewski, "call a time-out right now."

The players returned to the Duke sideline. Krzyzewski wanted his players to have an edge to them, but this was too much. A big lead had been reduced to single digits. Krzyzewski was furious.

"Go ahead and lose," he said disgustedly, staring directly at Hurley and Laettner. "You two are gonna let your thing cost us a win. You go ahead and lose. You know what? If you don't want to win, I'm not even going to coach you guys. Where's the key to the locker room?"

And with that, Krzyzewski walked out of the huddle and away from the team.

"We ain't losing, I can tell you that much," muttered Laettner.

Final score: Duke 75, Iowa 62. (And it was a good thing Krzyzewski hadn't followed through on his threat to go to the locker room. He didn't have the key; Williams did.)

Duke advanced to the East Regional semis in Philadelphia. That was the good news. The bad news, at least for Hurley, was the opponent: Seton Hall. That's because the Pirates roster included a 6'2" freshman backup guard who had a long history of brawling with the Duke star.

Dan Hurley had decided to stay close to home and sign with Seton Hall. His father had somehow foreseen the likelihood of a brother vs. brother matchup, telling reporters a year earlier, "I think before Bobby graduates that they could meet in a regional," said Bob Sr. "Or possibly the Final Four."

When the NCAA brackets were released, Dan and Bobby instantly recognized the possibility of a Hurley collision. Both teams were in the East Regional. Both teams were assigned to Greensboro for their opening games. Dan and Bobby had actually sneaked away to a nearby go-kart track during the off day in Greensboro.

But after Seton Hall defeated Missouri to advance to the Sweet 16, the school's sports information director told Dan, "You've got to be ready to deal with some stuff now."

The "stuff" was a media onslaught. Under normal circumstances, one or two reporters might stop by Dan's locker after a game. But when Dan made his way into the Seton Hall locker room after the Mizzou win, a wall of reporters and TV Minicams awaited him.

Holy shit, Dan thought. *Not good.*

Dan felt embarrassed by the attention. He was a freshman backup who had logged some significant minutes, but the team belonged to Bobby's former St. Anthony teammates Terry Dehere and Jerry Walker. Still, a story angle is a story angle, and everyone wanted to know about the upcoming Battle of the Hurleys. Two brothers playing in the City of Brotherly Love. The matchup even attracted the attention of CBS, which dispatched reporter Lesley Visser for a sit-down interview.

The March 24 headline in *The Chronicle* read: *Seton Hall–Duke Will Be Friendly Matchup.* Nothing could have been further from the truth. Yes, Carlesimo and Krzyzewski were good friends. Yes, Carlesimo had coached Bobby the previous summer in the World University Games. Yes, Dehere had played on the same U.S. National team as Laettner, Grant Hill, and Thomas Hill. But there would be nothing friendly about the game itself.

Carlesimo, no dummy, gave Dan some extra minutes in the win against Missouri. He planned to use him even more against Duke, especially against Bobby. He knew how close the two brothers were. The more distracted or conflicted Bobby was by Dan's presence on the court, the better it would be for Seton Hall. To Carlesimo, an emotionally confused Bobby was a good thing.

Bobby's greatest strength was his aggressiveness. Like Laettner, he was constantly in Doberman attack mode. "He was always the guy who slit your throat at the end," says Dan.

But how do you stick your teeth into your kid brother? You don't. The Doberman became a poodle.

In the days leading up to the game, Dan was a nervous wreck. When they spoke on the phone, Bobby told him, "Relax, man." But Dan knew the game plan and Bobby didn't. Seton Hall coaches prepared a meticulous scouting report on each of the Blue Devils players, but Dan didn't need one on Bobby. How many times had he seen his older brother use that signature inside-out dribble with his right hand, the one he learned from watching tapes of Providence's Billy Donovan and Georgia Tech's Mark Price? Bobby would sell the crossover move but then keep it in his right hand and barrel past the lunging defender. Worked almost every time.

By the time tip-off arrived, Dan was so tense that fever sores had broken out on his upper lip. He could feel them as he kneeled at the scorer's table waiting to replace Brian Caver, the starting point guard, early in the game. What should have been a moment to remember— playing in a Sweet 16 NCAA Tournament game as a true freshman— had become a moment to dread.

Bob Sr. and his wife, Chris, were equally torn. "Torturous," says Bob Sr. "For everybody." They were sitting in Duke-supplied seats about 15 rows from the floor. Bobby caught their eyes during warm-ups. Dehere and Walker waved to them, causing other Duke fans to look suspiciously at the Hurleys.

"They played for me," Bob Sr. explained sheepishly.

As Dan took the court, Bobby offered a "What's up? How you doin'?" But the small talk was forced and brief. Dan was a mess and Bobby could barely function.

As Dan loosely guarded Bobby on an early possession, Bobby fell down with the ball near mid-court. "And I couldn't guard a chair," says Dan. "I couldn't guard anybody."

Bobby wasn't much better on defense. Instead of contesting his younger brother's every move—as he had done in every pickup game they had ever played since he was eight—Bobby played passively, almost zombie-like. Bobby wasn't Bobby. "He was brutal," says Dan.

Meanwhile, Laettner tried to mess with Dan. During a pair of Seton Hall free throws, Laettner yelled instructions to a Blue Devils teammate.

"Bring Bobby's little brother over here on a screen so I can deck his ass," said Laettner.

As the free throw went up, Walker, Seton Hall's enforcer, gave Laettner a forearm shiver to the chest. *You want to deck Dan? We'll see about that.*

Duke led by 6 at halftime and eventually ground out an 81–69 victory. When the game ended, Dan and the emotionally exhausted Bobby hugged at mid-court. They shared a sense of disappointment—for Dan, that his team had lost; for Bobby, that his former high school teammates and his brother were hurting—but also a huge sense of relief. Bobby had played 39 minutes and made only 2 of 7 shots. He missed both of his free throw attempts and committed 6 turnovers to 7 assists. Dan had missed all 4 of his shot attempts in 18 minutes of play.

But the Pirates were going home and the Blue Devils were going forward. They were halfway to the 6 tournament wins needed for a championship.

Bobby couldn't wait. In the postgame media sessions, Hurley told reporters, "I'm really looking forward to playing against a team I have no friends on."

That team would be Kentucky.

TEN

March 27, 1992

Three men in black business suits walked solemnly into The Palestra as the Wildcats began what was supposed to be a closed practice. This was odd. Pitino didn't normally allow strangers into practices, especially a practice the day before a regional final against the defending national champions.

The players sneaked quick glances at the three men, each of whom carried a small case and looked as if he were a government agent called to the historic University of Pennsylvania basketball gym to serve extradition papers. Pitino was called over. A few moments later, practice was halted and the players ordered to assemble in front of the suits.

It was time to get measured for Final Four rings.

If there was any doubt in the Wildcats' minds that they were going to beat No. 1 Duke, it vanished at that moment. The players beamed as the fitters sized their ring fingers, and when practice resumed it was as if the UK players had each chugged a half gallon of adrenaline. The practice, held at the same gym where the first-ever NCAA East Regional had been played 53 years earlier, was as crisp as a Marine march formation. "Every player on that team could have performed heart surgery," says Oliver.

The UK game plan was simple: Keep it close. Pitino was convinced that if the Wildcats could stay in Duke's rearview mirror during the first half, settle in, and realize that the Blue Devils weren't invincible, they'd eventually go on a run or two in the second half and win the game. In broad strokes, it was the same game plan Duke had a year earlier against UNLV.

Duke had played at least a half dozen close games during the regular season, winning four, but it hadn't faced a team like Pitino's Wildcats. The Kentucky coach thought the frenetic tempo, the three-pointers, the press (which Pitino figured to release at about the 10-minute mark of the second half), and maybe, just maybe, the pressure of the moment might be too much for Duke to overcome. And with all due respect to Grant Hill and Laettner, Pitino thought UK would have the most talented player on the floor—Mashburn.

Pitino also liked having only one day between games. It meant that the Big Blue Nation, as well as the media that covered the program, would have less contact with his team. Even though Duke's assistants had probably been breaking down UK film for close to a week (just as Sendek, Donovan, and Locke-Mattox [her new last name] had been analyzing Blue Devil film for Kentucky's detailed scouting report), there were more moving parts in Kentucky's system. It was a system played well by very few teams. It would be difficult for Duke's reserves to simulate in their practices.

There was one more UK advantage: human nature. How could the Blue Devils look at the Kentucky roster and not think Duke had a huge talent edge? "If you watch [us] on tape and you start going through your personnel, you realize that Kentucky is not the Who's Who in basketball, except for Mashburn," says Pitino.

That disparity in talent (and, human nature or not, there *was* a disparity) is another reason Pitino wanted to stick the UK press in his back pocket until the second half. If he used it early in the game when Duke's players were fresh, and the Blue Devils poked holes in it and scored easy baskets, it would give Duke confidence and deflate the Wildcats. Then Pitino's team would have some serious problems.

Kentucky was a 7½-point underdog, and nobody outside the commonwealth (and hardly anybody inside of it) thought the spread was unreasonable. If anything, it seemed on the low side. The question wasn't if Duke would beat Kentucky, but by how much?

CBS executive producer Ted Shaker certainly wasn't expecting an upset. He assigned veteran play-by-play man Verne Lundquist, analyst Len Elmore, and sideline reporter Lesley Visser to the Thursday/Saturday regional in Philadelphia. Elmore, a former Maryland star and NBA first-round pick, had made the unusual transition from player to Brooklyn prosecutor to private law practitioner to basketball TV analyst. Lundquist was a pro's pro. His call of Jack Nicklaus's birdie putt on the 71st hole of the Golden Bear's improbable 1986 Masters win ("Maybe . . . *yes, sir!*") was the stuff of sports broadcasting legend.

The network's number-one announcing team of Jim Nantz and Billy Packer was sent to the Friday/Sunday Southeast Regional in Lexington. The Southeast was loaded with ratings magnets and five-star back stories. (Smith and North Carolina . . . the Fab Five and Michigan . . . Player of the Year candidate Jim Jackson and Ohio State . . . the triumphant return of Eddie Sutton and Sean Sutton to Lexington, this time as Oklahoma State coach and point guard, respectively.) Plus, the Southeast Regional final came in the Sunday late-afternoon/early-evening time slot, which fed into the ratings monster *60 Minutes*.

Not that Lundquist was complaining about the assignment. A year earlier, he and Elmore had done the first two rounds of the NCAAs, only to fail to make the CBS cut for the remainder of the tournament. Instead, they were sent to cover the Division II title game in Springfield, Massachusetts. Such was the meritocracy of CBS executive producer Ted Shaker.

Lundquist was happy to have been assigned a regional semi and final, but he didn't think he had been parachuted into hoops heaven.

Sure, having Duke in the regional helped. And in a perfect world, it would be nice if Kentucky could somehow avoid a blowout against the Blue Devils. On name power alone, the game would attract viewers. Keeping the viewers would be another challenge, especially if Duke turned the game into a rout. "It was a nice site," says Lundquist, "but I didn't think it would be anything special."

The *Herald-Leader*'s Tipton gave Kentucky a puncher's chance against Duke. "Because of the three-pointers," he says. "I didn't expect them to win, but I thought it could be more competitive." Longtime *Courier-Journal* sportswriter Rick Bozich felt the same way and said so in a column, suggesting that the Wildcats were capable of an upset. Visser called Detroit Pistons coach Chuck Daly, a former Duke assistant on Vic Bubas's staff in the mid-to-late 1960s, and asked for an assessment. Daly raved about Pitino and Krzyzewski and then said, "This is going to be a much closer game than people think."

But the consensus? "All these doubters in America—nobody gave us a chance to win this game," says Brown.

Ralph Willard, his Western Kentucky team recently eliminated in the NIT, made his way to Philadelphia, where he shared a hotel suite with the Pitinos. In search of divine intervention, Willard and Pitino jogged from the hotel to a place where the patron saint of underdogs resided: the Rocky statue at the Philadelphia Museum of Art. Up the 72 steps they ran, not stopping until they reached the top, where they raised their arms in triumph, just as Sylvester Stallone had done in the movie. "People were looking at us like we were crazy," says Willard.

Not crazy, just desperate. Kentucky was Rocky Balboa. Duke was Apollo Creed.

At a Friday afternoon media session, Farmer was asked about facing the Blue Devils. He was reminded that his Wildcat career had begun four seasons earlier with a 25-point loss to Duke. Now it could end the same way.

"I want to tell everybody," Farmer said, "we have a lot of respect for Duke. But we don't fear them."

Farmer slept well that night, but Woods couldn't quit thinking about the Blue Devils, about how close the Wildcats were to a Final Four. As his roommate, Brown, sawed logs, Woods tossed and turned in bed. Then he channel-surfed. Then he tossed and turned again. In less than 15 hours he was going to start at point guard against the No. 1 team in the country.

Early the next afternoon, Kentucky SID Chris Cameron pulled his rental car into the Spectrum parking lot. The Duke team bus was there, too, surrounded by barricades and screaming girls. It was the Beatles at Shea Stadium.

The Wildcats' arrival at the arena was met with yawns. Thought Cameron: *No one gives us a chance. But you know what? We're still Kentucky.*

And Kentucky's players believed. On the bus ride over from the team hotel, someone asked Feldhaus how he felt about the game. The reserved Feldhaus didn't hesitate. "We can do this," he said.

The Wildcats were confident and also angry. Before they boarded the bus, they had heard one of the TV studio analysts say that Kentucky would be crazy to even consider pressing Duke, that Hurley would cut through it like a finger through cake frosting. The comment was committed to memory.

As the Wildcats changed into their game uniforms, a familiar face entered the locker room. Pitino had invited former UK president Dr. David Roselle to the game as his guest. Roselle had been a casualty of Kentucky politics, forced out at UK by a new governor who made it clear that the university's future funding would be jeopardized if Roselle stayed. Still, Pitino knew that without Roselle he wouldn't have been at Kentucky. And without Pitino, Kentucky wouldn't have been at the Spectrum that day.

Roselle made the hour-long drive north to Philly from the University of Delaware campus, but did so with mixed feelings. He had hired Pitino and he knew most of the coaching staff and players, but he was also a Duke man of sorts, having earned his Ph.D. in mathematics there in 1965.

As he shook hands with the Wildcat players, Roselle reminded Pitino of the school conflict.

"If you cheer for Duke, you'll never get another ticket from me," said Pitino, smiling. Sort of.

Newton and Butters were sitting next to each other at a courtside table. In fact, Butters had brought Newton to Philadelphia on a private plane supplied by a Duke booster.

Just before tip-off, Butters turned to Newton. "Good luck," he said.

"Good luck to you," said Newton.

There was a pause. "Hell," said Butters, "neither one of us means it."

Sitting courtside on press row was Cawood Ledford, whose UK broadcast career would continue as long as the Wildcats kept winning. After 39 years as the "Voice of the Wildcats," the classy Ledford was retiring at tournament's end, whenever that might be. Joining him as usual on the broadcast was Ralph Hacker.

Maybe Ledford knew something. His pregame intro wasn't just optimistic; it was prescient.

Ledford: Duke is attempting to go to the Final Four for the fifth straight time. Duke is favored tonight, but the Cats will make a game of it—and you can count on that.

Kentucky didn't start the game like a team that had been absent from the postseason since 1988. If anything, the Blue Devils, not the Wildcats, looked like the program with postseason stage fright.

When Martinez hit a trey from the top of the key (Martinez? The guy who had made only two threes the entire season?), the Wildcats took a 20–12 lead with 14:18 left in the first half. The bad news: Pelphrey already had 2 fouls and Laettner already had 8 points, 6 of them off dunks or bunny layups.

Less than two and a half minutes later, Duke overtook UK. The Blue

Devils wouldn't trail again in the first half and walked into the locker room with a 50–45 lead.

Pelphrey had 9 points, one for each minute he played. Thank you, 3 personal fouls. Mashburn had 11 points and 4 rebounds, which counterbalanced the 11 points and 5 rebounds Grant Hill had for Duke off the bench. Laettner also had 10 points, a perfect 5 for 5 from the field. The Blue Devils were shooting a Tabasco-hot 72 percent from the field (8 layups and 4 dunks alone) and had almost doubled UK on the boards, 17–9. Kentucky's 2-3 zone was making it easier for Duke to grab rebounds.

But Pitino had his wish. Despite Duke's scorching shooting, the Wildcats were keeping it close. And they were keeping it close without dialing up their press and without Pelphrey on the floor for much of the first half.

"We've just got to keep playing at this pace, stay with our game plan, and we're going to get more confident and we'll have a chance to win the game," Pitino told his team.

Then Duke decided to flex its biceps, turning that 5-point halftime lead into a 12-point advantage after Hurley dropped a three-pointer from the top of the key. Pitino called a time-out with 11:08 left in regulation and UK trailing, 67–55. Pelphrey had 4 fouls, Mashburn 3. Laettner couldn't be stopped (7 for 7 from the field).

The *Courier-Journal*'s Forde had seen enough. He opened his laptop and began writing his game story lead. He would insert the final score of Duke's victory later on.

PHILADELPHIA—Kentucky's dream season collided with the hard reality of Duke's dominance Saturday night. The Wildcats gave it a great run, but Christian Laettner and the Blue Devils were too good too often.

But Forde wasn't in the UK huddle as Pitino decided it was time to switch exclusively to the press. "Now it's our time to win the game," he told the Wildcats during the time-out. "They're ready to get beat. You've taken all their best shots, and they can't put you away."

Brown scored on a layup. Feldhaus stole a pass, gave it to Woods, who fed it to Mashburn for a three. Another Duke turnover became another Mashburn three. An 8–0 burst in 63 seconds had cut the lead to 67–63 with 10:05 left to play.

The game officially embarked on classic status at the 8:06 mark. That's when a 19-year-old basketball pacifist named Aminu Timberlake saw his chest used as a quickie footstool by Laettner.

Timberlake, a No. 2 pencil–thin freshman who prayed before every game, fouled Laettner as the Duke center turned to shoot on the right low post. As Timberlake lay on the ground, Laettner placed his right sneaker heel between the 2 and the 5 on the freshman's jersey. Confusion ensued.

Hacker: Technical foul on Laettner. After he got the blocking call, he turned around and slammed the Kentucky player.

Ledford: So Kentucky's player is going to the bench. Apparently so are Duke right now. And Richie Farmer is back ready to report to the scorer's table. Richie's probably coming in to shoot the free throws. . . . Yeah, he stamped his foot. I don't think he got the player, did he, Ralph?

Hacker: I thought he swung at him. I think he got him.

Suddenly the temperature dial on an already intense game was turned to high.

"Aminu Timberlake was the reason we should have won the game because Laettner should have been thrown out of the game," says Pitino, who often implored the freshman to be tougher. "[Timberlake] was the kid who was stepped on in the game, like Ron Behagen . . . stepped on the kid." (In 1972, University of Minnesota reserve Behagen stomped on the neck and head of an Ohio State player who was lying on the floor in the middle of a melee.) "Same thing. Christian Laettner should have been thrown out of the game because he stepped on Aminu Timberlake."

"People may not talk about it, but star players are treated differently," says Mashburn. "I don't think the officials had the balls to toss

Christian Laettner out of the game. He probably should have been, but I wasn't surprised he wasn't."

The comparison to Behagen is a bit of a stretch, given that Laettner didn't stomp as much as he tapped semi-hard with his foot. Timberlake wasn't removed on a stretcher as the Ohio State player was 20 years earlier (Timberlake smiled and clapped after Laettner was T'd up). Rather than eject Laettner, the officiating crew, led by Tim Higgins, gave UK two free throws.

"I wanted to punch [Laettner] in the face," says Woods. "He stepped on the only guy on our team who wouldn't have gotten up and hit him. If he had done that to anybody else on our team, it would have been a full-fledged brawl."

"There would have been punches thrown, I can promise you that," says Farmer. "He's 6'11", 220—whatever. I would have got up and hit him."

"No way you'd get away with that today," says Pelphrey of Laettner's heel plant. "But we wouldn't be talking about this game if he'd been kicked out. It just wouldn't have been *the* game."

Duke stretched its lead to 10 points with 7:40 remaining in regulation. But Kentucky somehow went on a 12–2 run to tie the game with 5:25 left. Martinez had fouled out earlier on a ticky-tack call. Pelphrey was playing with 4 fouls, Mashburn with 3.

Jennie Pelphrey, who was at the game with her husband, Jack, darted in and out of the deserted Spectrum corridors and restrooms as Kentucky reeled Duke in. She couldn't watch. Instead, she sat inside a bathroom stall and nervously prayed for her son John Leslie and the Wildcats.

The lead volleyed back and forth. During the next 4 minutes and 47 seconds there were nine lead changes or ties. With the score 93–93, Hurley had the ball and a chance to win the game in the final seconds. But his jumper missed.

Overtime.

"As the game moved along, it started to creep into that moment where it felt like there was no crowd there," says Mashburn. "Even though you had two great coaches in Krzyzewski and Pitino, they didn't interfere. It was almost like they were spectators until time-outs were called. . . . It was the flawless pickup game."

Watching spellbound in his Lexington hotel room was CBS's Nantz. He had spent the afternoon at Rupp Arena, where he had attended the Ohio State and Michigan press conferences, then returned to his nearby hotel in time for the second half. As the game kept outdoing itself, Nantz began calling several CBS colleagues who were staying in the same hotel.

"I can't believe we're not there," he said.

A dinner reservation at Bravo Pitino was pushed back. Nantz wasn't budging from his room until the game was finished.

The overtime began at 9:07 p.m. local time. Pelphrey, who kiddingly referred to himself as the Wendy's All-American (there is no such thing—only a McDonald's All-American), hit a three-pointer to give Kentucky the first of four different leads in the 5-minute OT. Hurley tied it, 96–96, with his own three.

Pelphrey made a driving layup. Laettner tied it with two free throws, courtesy of Mashburn's fourth foul. Woods tried a floater that missed, and Laettner got the rebound.

Hacker: If Kentucky can get this ball back without Duke scoring, it could be Kentucky's game.

Ledford: Absolutely.

With just 5 seconds on the shot clock, 37.1 on the big clock, and Pelphrey guarding the sideline inbounds passer Grant Hill, Laettner caught the ball against Mashburn at the mid-left post. He dribbled once, pivoted to his left, split the double-team of Pelphrey and Mashburn, double-clutched, and banked the leaning 8-footer off the glass to give Duke a 100–98 lead.

"I'm running up behind him," says Pelphrey. "I'm going to block his shot. He doesn't see me coming. For whatever reason, he holds the ball, Jamal smacks it out of his hands, he loses it, catches it in a split second, and fires it off the backboard—and it goes in! To me, that was The Shot."

Mashburn made a driving layup and was fouled by Lang. Pitino pumped his right fist, but then caught himself and segued into adjusting the knot in his tie. Mashburn's free throw nudged UK ahead, 101–100. Less than 20 seconds remained.

Hacker: You could not have a more fierce, competitive, or pressure-packed situation for the fans if you were in the championship game of the NCAA right now, Cawood.

Ledford: The N-C-double-A would dream of a game like this in that Final Four.

Then disaster struck for UK. Mashburn picked up his fifth foul while trying to knock the ball from Laettner's hands. "I got all ball on that one," he says.

"I thought we were going to win the game," says Pitino. "I really believed we were going to win the game. Doubt crept in when Mashburn went out of the game."

Kentucky's best player (he had 28 points and 10 rebounds) was gone. Duke's best player was at the line. Laettner made both free throws to give the Blue Devils a 102–101 edge with 14.1 seconds left.

The Wildcats got the ball, but Pitino gestured for a time-out as soon as Woods dribbled past the half-court line.

"Normally I never want to call a time-out," says Pitino. "I never do it. We want to run a play. But we could not get our guys in the play because they were going to go to Mashburn. We were always going to feed it again to Mashburn, and without him we had to run something."

There were 7.8 seconds remaining in overtime and perhaps in their season. How many times in the last three years had he stood in a huddle and seen the same four faces of Pelphrey, Farmer, Feldhaus, and Woods, always so willing and trusting? Damn, he loved these guys. It was only right that all four of them be on the court at this exact moment—though Pitino would have liked Mashburn to be on the court with them.

They would run their usual box play to get the ball inbounds. After that, Pitino told them, Woods would drive the lane, draw a double-team from Duke, and then pass it to one of the UK spot-up shooters, either Pelphrey, Farmer, or Brown. As a last resort, Woods could shoot, but nobody on the UK bench was hoping for that. Feldhaus would be positioned on the baseline and crash the boards for a missed shot.

"Look," said Pitino, "when we take this lead, guys, do not celebrate. They're gonna inbounds it, so do not celebrate. Get back on defense."

Woods, who would turn 22 the next day, didn't consider himself a last resort. "I had dreamed of this situation all my life," he says. "It was an opportunity. I knew the way [Duke] had been playing, that with a ball screen I could get a shot off."

Hacker: Let's set it up for you. The Wildcats—Woods, Pelphrey, Feldhaus, along with Brown and Richie Farmer. The midgets are in there for the Kentucky Wildcats. Here comes Duke.

Ledford: It may be Richie, who's just come off the bench. He's a tough little guy in the clutch. Kentucky has three guards and two forwards. Comes into Woods . . . Woods with Hurley on him . . . Is on the move . . . Here he goes down in the paint . . . His shot up—and gooood! . . . Two seconds. Sean Woods banks it off the glass . . . One-oh-three to One-oh-two. Sean Woods just took it, drove in the paint, tattooed it up on the board and back into the net, and the Cats lead by one.

Laettner had come up the lane to stop Woods's dribble drive after Pelphrey knocked Hurley on his butt with a crushing (and legal) pick near the top of the key. As Woods rounded the corner and into the paint, Oliver thought, *No, no, no . . . Pass it to Farmer . . . Pass it to Brown.* And then Woods's one-handed, 13-foot teardrop over Laettner's outstretched arms caromed off the backboard and through the net.

Yes, yes, yes.

The Spectrum crowd roared in disbelief. Was this really happening?

Cameron, who was keeping the official scorebook at the mid-court scorer's table, couldn't control himself.

"Oh, my god!" he yelled.

Seated next to him was Duke SID Mike Cragg.

"Mike, I'm sorry," said Cameron, embarrassed by the involuntary breach of proper conduct. "I'm so sorry."

"I'm happy for you guys," said Cragg. "You're fine. No big deal."

Pelphrey, always the mother hen, immediately thought of his team-mate Woods, who had taken grief from Pitino and fans this season and previous seasons for his shot selection. *Good for him*, he said to himself. And then he remembered the three men in the black suits.

Wow. We're finally going to get a ring that everybody will have to recognize. No more championships "in their own minds."

Even the understated Lundquist was caught up in the moment.

Lundquist: How did he find the courage to take that kind of shot?

Elmore: You know, it went in, okay. But that was a terrible shot.

But the shot hadn't been an accident. It *looked* lucky, but it wasn't. "That was Woods's shot," says Brown. "Every day in practice he would take that same shot. That was his little move."

Okay, it was a tiny bit lucky. "I wanted to hit the back of the rim," says Woods. "But with the adrenaline, it hit the backboard. But you watch my career at Kentucky; I was good at those high bank shots."

"If the game is over right there," says Farmer, "that goes down as one of the greatest shots of all time in NCAA Tournament history."

Jennie Pelphrey had emerged from her prayer vigil in the bathroom stall in time to see Woods's shot fall through (*Thank you, Lord!*). Now Duke would need its own prayers answered.

Two ticks and a sliver of time is all that separated this patched-together Kentucky team from an upset for the ages, in a game for the ages. The lead, the game, the redemption was all but theirs.

"You know," said Jack Pelphrey to his wife, "we may have to fly to Minneapolis for the Final Four."

ELEVEN

March 28, 1992

Laettner was worried about facing Kentucky. He hadn't actually seen the Wildcats play, but he had heard enough about them during the second half of the season.

There was Mashburn, already projected as an NBA star in the making. There was Mashburn's supporting staff: the three Kentucky-born starters—Pelphrey, Farmer, and Feldhaus—and Woods. Laettner knew a little bit about their story.

"They're the fill-ins for all the kids who got suspended. . . . They're the leftovers," Laettner says. "But they're really good, and they've got this one really good inner-city kid."

And they ran and shot threes until the other team dropped. "I hate the run-and-gun games because it's not Basketball 101," says Laettner. "It's not what I'm best at."

Laettner was concerned that Kentucky's style of play would take him out of the game. Laettner wasn't a sprinter. The two Hills were. Davis was. Hurley was. Lang was. But Laettner was among the slowest players on the team.

Duke loved to run the fast break, but it wasn't designed to play entire games that way. It beat you with defense, with selective running, and with a superior half-court game. Kentucky was the exact opposite. It won by pressing, by scoring off of press-related turnovers, and by shooting lots of three- pointers.

"You cannot impose your will against a team that's just doing all of this *whoosh-whoosh-whoosh* stuff up and down the court, because they don't care," says Laettner. "They just don't care. If they miss, they're just going to come down and shoot the next one. They're playing loosey-goosey, frickin' letting it fly. . . . And I know Pitino. I know his teams are always good."

Hurley had played against Mashburn in high school. Blakeney had seen Farmer play for Clay County at the famed Beach Ball Classic in Myrtle Beach, South Carolina. "He was a bad motherf'er," says Blakeney. "Full-grown mustache at 17 years old. He'd drop 50 on you."

Pitino . . . Mashburn . . . Farmer . . . UK's unconventional offense . . . its nothing-to-lose attitude . . . only one full day to prepare for the Wildcats—it was all enough to grab Duke's attention. But it wasn't necessarily enough to keep it.

"We had respect for them," says Davis. "But we thought we were going to beat them pretty good."

Says Grant Hill: "We thought, *They have one great player. We'll contain him and shut everybody else down.* We were overconfident."

They would play in Philadelphia's Spectrum, an 18,136-seat history book. Philly's own Joe Frazier had fought there. Dorothy Hamill had skated there. So had the Flyers, who weren't against dropping the gloves like Smokin' Joe and leaving some blood and molars on the ice.

Kate Smith had belted out "God Bless America" there. Sinatra, Springsteen, Pavarotti, Hendrix, and U2 all had had gigs there. Elvis Presley had performed there less than a month before his girlfriend found him dead on a bathroom floor at Graceland.

No one would ever confuse the Spectrum with sports' other Sistine Chapels—Fenway Park, Madison Square Garden, Wrigley Field,

Boston Garden, Cameron Indoor Stadium. But it had pedigree and a gritty, no-nonsense charm to it. After all, the place was good enough for Stanley Cups, Final Fours, and NBA and NHL all-star games.

If Duke began the game overconfident, an early 20–12 Kentucky lead forced an instant attitude adjustment. The Wildcats already had four three-pointers—two by Pelphrey, one by Mashburn, and one by Martinez.

Krzyzewski preached patience. Work the ball in low to Laettner. Play tough man-to-man defense. Try to extend UK's perimeter shooting. Pick your spots to run and shoot threes.

Duke tied the game, 20–20, and soon took a 5-point lead. But Kentucky evened it up in 26 seconds with a Woods layup and a Farmer three.

Laettner was right: Pitino's team was good.

"Once we got into it," says Thomas Hill, "Sean Woods was better than Coach Gaudet said he was. John Pelphrey was better than we thought. Woods was giving Bob trouble."

The Blue Devils held a 5-point lead at halftime, and Laettner held a piece of NCAA history. His 10 first-half points gave him 359 NCAA Tournament points, one more than the previous all-time leader, Houston's Elvin Hayes. Not that he cared.

"They're shooting 50 percent [from the field], and they've got that run-and-gun thing, and it's these little white kids from Kentucky, and Mashburn, and I'm worried," says Laettner. "I'm concerned. Pitino's a great frickin' coach. We're a powerhouse, but we're in a pretty tough game."

There were the usual mini-dramatics—nothing serious—between Laettner and Hurley. The Blue Devils had 11 first-half turnovers, which led to 16 UK points. "Bobby wasn't passing the ball like he should have been," says Davis. "Laett got pissed."

But Laettner didn't go full-scale nuclear on Hurley. First of all, Laettner had three turnovers himself, only one fewer than Hurley's four. He also understood how fragile the situation was.

"There's a time to fuck around and be mean," says Laettner. "You can be mean when you're playing Canisius up there at the beginning of the year. But right now, you can't be mean. It's gotta be all love right now. So I didn't jump his ass."

During a mandatory TV time-out with 11:53 left in regulation, officiating crew chief Tim Higgins walked over to his partners Tom Clark and Charles Range. The veteran Higgins had worked the 1990 championship game between UNLV and Duke. Range had officiated the 1991 title game between the Blue Devils and Kansas. Clark was making his NCAA regional final debut.

"I hope this doesn't go down to a last-second shot, because we can't hear the horn," said Higgins.

It was true. The crowd noise, which seemed to swell as the game went on, virtually drowned out the Spectrum horn. The officiating crew already couldn't hear it for time-outs. Just think if there was a late-game situation involving the horn. The crew would be cooked.

But Duke was slowly making that scenario a nonissue. When Hurley sank his second three-pointer of the half, Duke took a 67–55 lead with 11:15 remaining to play. Pitino called a time-out.

"Usually at that point we would close teams out," says Hurley.

Usually. But when play resumed, Kentucky unveiled its press. Pitino junked the 2-3 zone he had been using much of the game, and the Wildcats immediately forced a pair of Duke turnovers.

With 9:43 left in the second half, Mashburn posted up on the left low block, ignored the double team, and sank a short turnaround baseline jumper to cut the Duke lead to 70–65. Laettner had been knocked into the padded base of the basket during the play and decided to exact revenge against the Wildcat he thought responsible for the cheap shot: freshman forward Aminu Timberlake.

Timberlake had a reputation among his own teammates for physical, but never malicious, play. He had popped more than a few jaws in practice.

Laettner waited three Duke possessions to get even with Timberlake.

When the freshman fell to the ground after colliding with (and fouling) Laettner on a shot attempt at the 8:06 mark, the Duke center did a baby grind with his right foot into Timberlake's gut.

CBS's Len Elmore: "That was a pretty darn nasty situation. I don't know if he did it on purpose or not."

CBS's Verne Lundquist, not hiding his disapproval: "Yeah, he did. Pretty obvious."

Laettner instantly received a technical foul. "The refs did the right thing," Laettner says. "They called a tech on me, and that's all it warranted. They should not have kicked me out of the game."

Elmore didn't say it that night, but he knows what he was thinking as he watched the replay. Says Elmore: "My honest opinion of Christian Laettner? I thought he was kind of smarmy in some ways. But his attitude, if he played in my era, I would have knocked him out cold. He had that kind of cockiness. . . . But you give Laettner some credit for that, for the psychological wars that go on. Timberlake was no good from that point on."

The Kentucky fans wanted him tossed. Pitino also thought it warranted an ejection.

"That's his wishful thinking," says Laettner. "Now if it was higher up near the neck or face, hell yeah, I should have been thrown out immediately."

Laettner doesn't deny it was premeditated. In fact, Davis says that Timberlake had elbowed the Duke center earlier in the game, prompting Laettner to say, "I'm going to get this motherfucker."

"Yeah, I did it on purpose," Laettner says. "But I was very much in control. I did it on purpose, but I made sure I didn't do it hard so everyone knew that it wasn't malicious and that I wasn't trying to hurt the kid. But it was just stupid."

It was also a case of mistaken identity. Laettner went after the wrong UK player. It was Feldhaus who had sent Laettner sprawling to the floor with a two-handed shove in the back. But by the time Laettner looked up from the ground, Feldhaus was gone and Timberlake was standing over him as the Wildcats set up their press after Mashburn made the basket.

(There was no replay of the Feldhaus shove. The CBS telecast was semi-prehistoric compared to today's production overload. With rare exceptions, there was no shot clock on the screen and no continuous scoreboard. The TV ads were anything but classics, too: O. J. Simpson as a Hertz spokesperson, Sinbad pitching Reebok shoes, Billy Packer for Oldsmobile.)

Michigan's Rose, whose Wolverines played Ohio State late the next afternoon in the Southeast Regional final in Lexington, watched the game in the team hotel. Rose desperately wanted and fully expected to face Duke for the NCAA championship. When Laettner wasn't ejected, Rose took it as a sign of blatant Duke favoritism.

"See that?" he said to his teammates. "We got to beat more than a team. This is bigger than us. If we just show up and it's even, we're not going to win."

After Laettner sank two free throws and Farmer sank one of the two free throws from the technical foul, Duke led, 75–68. But the Blue Devils couldn't shake UK. They had a 10-point lead with 7:40 remaining, but the Wildcats went on a 12–2 run to tie it, 81–81. Only 5:25 was left on the clock.

"I couldn't figure out what they were doing," says Grant Hill.

Mashburn was virtually unstoppable. He scored 11 points in the first half and was on his way to adding 14 points and 6 rebounds in the second. Davis, Lang, and Grant Hill all took turns trying to guard him.

"I didn't realize how great he was until after the game," says Thomas Hill. "There were times they were afraid to guard that guy. It was like, 'You guard him. No, *you* guard him.'"

It was tied at 81–81, 83–83, 89–89, and 93–93. Hurley had the ball with about 11 seconds left in regulation when he took a handoff from Grant Hill near the Duke bench. He dribbled toward the right side of the lane, and with about four seconds on the clock (and Woods shadowing him), Hurley attempted a running jumper that bounced hard off the back iron. Mashburn got the rebound with 0.8. A failed UK inbounds pass (Laettner was guarding Mashburn as the Kentucky star threw the pass) meant overtime.

"We're pissed," says Davis. "We're literally pissed. We shouldn't be there. Now we're fighting for our lives."

Laettner never touched the ball in the last 31 seconds of regulation. Instead, Hurley took the last shot. He had made huge shots before (the three-pointer against UNLV in the 1991 national semis was part of Duke hoops lore), but never a game-winner.

"I had a pretty good look at it, too, so I was disappointed," says Hurley.

So was Laettner. "I kind of thought maybe he should have passed it to me so I could shoot, but it didn't happen, didn't work out that way," he says. "I was a little disappointed that he didn't throw the ball to me so I could shoot it, but no big deal. . . . I wanted him to hit it. I wanted him to make it."

Davis was less diplomatic. Laettner, he says, should have gotten a chance to shoot or draw a foul. "Bobby should have never shot that ball," he says. "If Laett got the ball, he's such a great free throw shooter, we should win. . . . [Hurley's] thinking about a movie—someone making a movie about him."

The game was perched on a fulcrum, the advantage shifting back and forth by the second.

Pelphrey made a three to give UK a 96–93 lead.

Davis fouled out on a charge with 3:42 to play. "It wasn't a charge," he says, still pleading his case. "It was clearly a block. I swear it was a block."

Hurley missed a three. Grant Hill got the rebound, fed it back to Hurley, who sank the second-chance trey with 2:40 to go—96–96.

Pelphrey hit a difficult driving up-and-under layup with 2:17 left—98–96.

Laettner made two free throws after Mashburn's fourth foul—98–98, with 1:53 remaining.

Woods missed on a leaner drive down the middle at the 1:18 mark. Laettner got the rebound, and Duke called time-out with 54.5 seconds.

As everyone waited for play to resume, Butters, trying to break the tension, turned to his friend Newton and said, "I've got a great idea. Forget the Final Four. Let's make it the Final Five."

"I'll vote for that," said Newton.

"It was my idea," said Butters, "so we get the bye."

Butters prided himself on not just hiding his emotions but locking them in a safe-deposit box. As the Duke AD and a member of the basketball selection committee, he had to be even more careful about keeping a granite face.

"But I never felt what I felt that night," he says. "And I will never feel it again. Neither team deserved to lose."

According to the official play-by-play sheet, here's what happened next: *31.5 Laettner 8' RUNNING JUMP 100–98.*

What an understatement. It was like describing the first moon walk as, *Armstrong SMALL STEP MAN.*

Here's what the play-by-play sheet should have read: *31.5 Laettner 8' OMG! DID HE JUST MAKE THAT FRICKIN' SHOT? 100–98.*

Laettner hit the leaning, eight-foot bank shot with two UK defenders draped on him like bathrobes. "That was luck," says Laettner. "Just throw it up there and sometimes it goes in."

It was more than a running jumper. It foreshadowed things to come.

"Tell you what," says Woods. "That's when I knew it was his night. That was the toughest shot he made all night."

Mashburn drove down the left baseline to the hoop, made the lay-in with 19.6 seconds, and picked up a foul on Lang. Lang had tried to jump out on Pelphrey to stop a possible three-pointer and then had rushed back down to stop Mashburn on the drive. It was a costly foul by

Lang, but it wasn't completely his fault: Duke's help defense had been nonexistent on the play. On the Duke bench, Parks sat between Davis and Blakeney and angrily said, "Why'd he foul?"

Mashburn's free throw completed the three-point play and gave UK a 101–100 lead.

Pitino called time to set his defense and go over time-outs (one apiece), possession arrow (Duke's), and fouls. Grant Hill inbounded it to Hurley, who broke free of the press, then threw a ballsy, two-handed, two-thirds-court-length pass to Laettner. As Laettner drove right toward the basket, Mashburn slapped down on the ball and, according to Tom Clark, the wrist, too.

You didn't need a PA announcement to know Mashburn had fouled out with 14.1 seconds to go. Pitino had rushed onto the court, extended his hand forward, and yelled, "Five!"

Five fouls. Kentucky's best player was gone.

"Thank god," says Laettner, who made both free throws—102–101, Duke.

Kentucky got the ball, moved it over the half-court line, and called timeout with 7.8 seconds. During the break, Krzyzewski reminded the Blue Devils that the possession arrow still favored Duke and told them to immediately call time-out if Kentucky scored (the clock wouldn't stop after a made basket). He had no idea who would take UK's shot. "No, because those guys are on a magic-carpet ride right now," he says. "Any one of them [could shoot]. They all played with their hearts ahead of their talent, and they're veteran college players."

Woods took the inbounds pass, dribbled down the lane, and dropped that Al Michaels "Do you believe in miracles?" shot on the Blue Devils. The moment the shot sailed over Laettner's outstretched hands and dropped through the net, four of the five Blue Devils raised their hands and signaled for a time-out. The group gesture saved Duke precious time. The clock read 2.1 seconds.

Duke had played solid defense on the play. Laettner should have hedged out earlier when Pelphrey set a screen on Hurley, but still, Woods had to parachute a shot over a 6'11" All-American. On a scale of 1 to 10, the degree of difficulty of Woods's shot was a 15.

"He throws that shit up and it goes in," says Davis. "I couldn't believe he made that shot. When have you ever seen a shot like that before? Wasn't like he was Kenny Anderson. He couldn't make it again, I guarantee it. I told Sean that. Told him he couldn't make it in 100 tries."

"Anybody who played pickup ball or anything, if they make a straight-on bank shot, you don't really give them a lot of credit," says Hurley. "You look at them like, 'C'mon, man.' But you have to give him credit for making a huge play at a huge moment. . . . For me, I was coming to realize that this was meant for them and that we were probably done."

Says Krzyzewski: "Christian does a good job of switching and, come on, he banked the damn thing. It's a bank shot. . . . To be quite frank with you, I got angry that shot could beat us. . . . You can't—you shouldn't lose on a bank shot over your 6'11" guy."

Then again, the same 6'11" guy had made a nearly impossible bank shot 24 seconds earlier to put Duke briefly ahead.

"Sometimes the ball goes in when it's not supposed to, like when I banked it against the two guys," says Laettner. "I mean, it shouldn't have gone in, but it went in. [Woods] makes this incredible shot on me and Bobby, and it was my mistake that he got so open and he hits the shot over me."

In the Spectrum stands were Hurley's parents, who had already paid for their flights to Minneapolis and the Final Four. When Woods's shot dropped, Bob Sr. turned to his wife and said, "What are we going to do with those tickets?"

The Blue Devils walked slowly toward the Duke bench as if on a death march. Bilas stood at the edge of that team huddle, his mind fixated on a single, simple thought.

We're screwed.

That's when he heard Krzyzewski tell the Blue Devils, "First of all, we're going to win, okay?"

Bilas, a four-year starter at Duke from 1983–86, had heard the same words when he had played for Krzyzewski—but never under these near-impossible circumstances and never for these stakes. And the truth was, never once had any of Bilas's teams pulled out the miracle win. They had lost every time.

But Bilas knew what Krzyzewski was trying to do. He was trying to project strength and confidence. He was trying to snap the Blue Devils back to reality, even though the final play they were going to run—it didn't have an actual name—had failed miserably against Wake Forest earlier in the season.

Hurley sat on the bench, his face expressionless. "I have to be honest," he says. "There was a big part of me that thought we had lost and our season was over. I knew there were two seconds left and I knew something could happen, but, you know, I didn't see it."

He wasn't alone.

Amaker thought they had lost. So did Grant Hill. "Honestly, I had checked out going back to the huddle," he says. "Literally, I was thinking, *You know what, I guess I'll go to Myrtle Beach next week.*"

Krzyzewski diagrammed the play. Grant Hill would throw the inbounds pass. Lang and Thomas Hill would run the wings and then dart toward the basket, in case of a tipped pass. Hurley would peel off toward mid-court. Laettner would start in the far corner and make his way to the free throw line. The play hadn't worked in late February, but that hadn't stopped Krzyzewski from having his team practice it over and over again in March.

"Grant, can you throw the ball 75 feet?" said Krzyzewski.

"Yeah, I can do that," said Hill, his mood suddenly changing from pessimistic to optimistic.

"Well, don't throw it out of bounds this time, okay?" said Krzyzewski, the hint of a grin on his face.

He turned to Laettner.

"Christian, can you catch the pass?" said Krzyzewski.

"If Grant throws a good pass, I'll catch it," said Laettner.

Laettner was nervous, his hands sweaty. But—and only Laettner would feel this way—it was fun.

"This is why you go to Duke," he says. "You want to be in these situations. You wish you were up 20 to go to the Final Four, but you're not. You're down one. This is why you try to have big nuts your whole life, why you work so hard. . . . [My teammates] know that more than anything my heart is ripping apart because I want to do it so badly for them; they all know that."

As the huddle broke and Laettner walked onto the court, Davis approached him. Said Laettner: "It's done, B. Watch."

Meanwhile, Tom Clark stood alone near the center-court sideline. Perspiration was pouring down from his forehead. He could cup his hands and feel the pools of sweat form in his palms. He was scared.

Moments earlier, Higgins had said to him and Range, "Strap on your equipment, boys. This thing ain't near over."

Great, thought Clark. His first regional final and it had come to this? A one-point game? A last-second situation? The possibility of his whistle deciding which of these two teams advanced to a Final Four? Clark glanced at his partners, wishing he were Higgins or Range. All Higgins would have to do is blow his whistle to start play, hand the ball to the inbounds passer, and begin the 5-second count. That was it. Range had the opposite baseline.

And Clark? He had the worst job in the house. He was responsible for monitoring almost all of the action between the two baselines. In short, he would have to watch nine players in approximately an 85-foot span. If there was a last-second shot, he would have to determine if it had been taken before the final horn—except that nobody could actually hear the horn. And he would have to process all of this information in less than 2.1 seconds.

"My career was on the line," says Clark.

During the long time-out, Clark began running through the most likely scenarios. First of all, Pitino was never going to allow Duke to throw the ball the length of the court. So that was out. Instead, he figured, Duke would get the ball to Hurley around mid-court, and the point guard would attempt a 40- to 45-footer at the buzzer.

Clark began practicing what to do if Duke got a shot off. He would watch the release and then instantly find the shot clock positioned above and slightly behind the Duke backboard. He did it a dozen times, looking at the court and then raising his head to stare at the backboard clock: *Release . . . clock. Release . . . clock. Release . . . clock.*

Meanwhile, the Spectrum was one collective held breath.

Debbie Krzyzewski stood five rows behind the Duke bench, rocking back and forth during the time-out. She reached back to hold her mom's hand. "We're okay," said daughter to mother. "We're okay."

Mickie knew better. She had watched enough games in her life to know it was over. She didn't cry, but she was overcome by sadness and the realization that a Duke team destined for the Final Four wasn't going to get there after all. But then it hit her: the Blue Devils had had a remarkable season. She didn't want her husband or any of the assistant coaches and players to look up and see her like this. So she stood up as a measure of respect for them. She owed them that. "I wasn't going to be a wuss and hide my eyes," says Mickie. "I was going to stand up and take it, show that I was proud."

Bonnie Laettner also had chosen not to be a wuss. In close games she had always retreated to an arena bathroom stall, closed the door, pulled out her St. Joseph Missal (it contained all the Roman Catholic prayers) or, in a pinch, a *Reader's Digest,* and began reading. And to drown out the public address announcer or a radio broadcast piped into the bathroom, she would start flushing the toilet.

But this time she stayed in her seat, her daughter Leanne on one side, Antonio Lang's mother, Betty, on the other. She wore a neck brace (the result of a recent surgery) and a T-shirt that read *The Laettner Legacy*. And she was a wreck.

Dan Hurley sat alone in his Seton Hall dorm room watching the game on a small color TV. *This is the sickest game I've ever seen in my life*, he said to himself. His brother was playing loose and carefree, the opposite of how Bobby had played two days earlier against the Pirates. But what were the chances of Duke scoring now? One in 100? One in 1,000? Then Dan remembered that UMass's Jim McCoy had sunk a desperation shot from beyond half-court in the final seconds of the first half of the Minutemen's regional semifinal game against Kentucky. If UMass could do it . . .

Calvin and Janet Hill were seated four rows behind the Duke bench. Calvin watched Krzyzewski calmly talk to his team. That could mean only one thing: *My god, they've got a play for this situation*, thought Calvin.

In Lexington, Rose's Michigan teammates declared the game done, even with 2.1 seconds on the clock. No, said Rose, Duke would figure out a way to win. Miracle shot . . . phantom foul—one way or another, the Blue Devils were going to win. His teammates scoffed at him.

Tom Clark noticed something: Kentucky didn't have a man guarding Grant Hill on the inbounds pass. Hmmm. That meant Duke might try a longer pass. And that meant Laettner would be the likely target. Kentucky would contest the pass. There could be contact.

Okay, Tom, don't call a foul unless they have to put Laettner in the naval hospital across the street.

Nobody was more surprised by the UK strategy than Grant Hill. In the February 23 game at Joel Coliseum, Wake Forest put 6'9" Derrick Hicks on the ball, and Hill's pass curved toward the sideline. Laettner, guarded by 6'8" Trelonnie Owens, had caught the pass at the foul line extended, but stepped out of bounds before he could attempt a shot.

Now, without someone to pester him, Hill could get comfortable, set his feet, and throw. *This is easy now*, he thought.

Not easy, but easier. He still had to throw it 75 to 80 feet. And the pass had to be high enough so it couldn't be tipped away by Kentucky defenders, but low enough that Laettner could still catch it. The pass would be half of the Duke equation.

Davis was stunned, too—not by Pitino's decision to ignore Grant Hill, but by the position of Pelphrey and Feldhaus. Neither one was fronting Laettner, who hadn't missed a single field goal or free throw the entire game.

Duke radio play-by-play announcer Bob Harris instantly recognized the Blue Devils' formation from the Wake Forest game. *They're going to run the same play, sure as the world,* he thought.

Across the country in Portland, Oregon, second-year Trail Blazers center Alaa Abdelnaby tried to pretend he wasn't watching the Duke–Kentucky game on the Memorial Coliseum scoreboard screen. He was supposed to be warming up for the Blazers' game against the Houston Rockets. "But I can say it now," says Abdelnaby. "I wasn't thinking about the Rockets."

Instead, he was thinking about the Blue Devils. He would take a warm-up shot and then sneak a peek at the video screen. Take another shot, sneak a peek. When Abdelnaby couldn't look (Portland coach Rick Adelman was standing nearby), team trainer Mike Shimensky would flash him hand signals about the overtime score: Kentucky up three . . . tied . . . Kentucky up two . . . tied . . . Duke up two . . . tied . . . Kentucky up one . . . Duke up one . . . Kentucky up one with 2.1 seconds left.

Meanwhile, the crowd at the Memorial Coliseum—the same name as Kentucky's on-campus gym—was going nuts as it watched the overtime in faraway Philly.

Abdelnaby, in the middle of the Blazers' pregame layup drills, couldn't take it anymore. He stopped, stared up at the big screen, and watched as Grant Hill cocked his right arm.

Everyone stopped.

TWELVE

March 28, 1992 (continued)

Pitino did the basketball math in his head. Duke had 2.1 seconds to inbound a pass, then have someone catch it and then shoot it or have someone catch it and then tip it to someone else for a shot. The clock wouldn't start until the inbounds pass was touched by a player. A miracle was possible.

Pitino and his staff quickly decided not to put a man on the inbounds passer, who they figured would be the 6'8" Grant Hill. They were concerned that Krzyzewski might try one of Dean Smith's favorite desperation plays: have the passer run the baseline, which would force the defender to run with him, and then set a player in the defender's path and hope to draw a foul when the defender slammed into him.

The Wildcats also didn't have much height. Mashburn and Martinez had fouled out, and Pitino wasn't about to insert one of his 6'9" freshmen (Timberlake or Andre Riddick) into such a crucial situation. Anyway, Grant Hill was tall enough to throw over a defender, and he had the option of running the baseline to get free.

There wasn't any question about Grant Hill's target: It would be Laettner. If Pitino were Krzyzewski, that's who he'd throw it to.

Pitino instructed Feldhaus and Pelphrey to form a human sandwich around the 6'11" Laettner. The 6'7" Feldhaus in front, the 6'7" Pelphrey in back. Had he not fouled out, it would have been Mashburn who fronted the Duke center.

Farmer would shadow Thomas Hill. Woods would be on Lang. Brown would guard Hurley. Five defenders for four Duke threats.

Brown had been beaten in the Mississippi state high school tournament two consecutive years by last-second shots, and again in the semifinals of the national junior college tournament. The basketball gods owed him.

All we got to do is take care of our defense, get one stop, and we're going to the Final Four, he told himself.

Oliver glanced at the clock and then at the dispirited Duke players as they sat on the Blue Devil bench. *We got this thing*, thought Oliver.

He wasn't alone. "I knew we were going to the Final Four," says Woods. "No doubt in my mind."

With two players bracketing Laettner, Pitino thought the Duke star would have no choice but to tip the ball to another Blue Devil.

"Don't leave your man on the sidelines and run to Laettner," Pitino told Farmer, Brown, and Woods. "Stay at home. He's probably going to tip it."

Then, just as the huddle broke, Pitino grabbed Pelphrey and Feldhaus.

"The guy hasn't missed a shot," he told them. "Whatever you do, don't foul him. Make them make a play."

"And that," says Pitino now, "was my mistake."

I t was the most famous pass in Duke sports history, including football. Time—and heartbeats—stopped.

"Grant throws that ball," says referee Tom Clark. "The ball is in flight. When I tell you your whole life passes in front of you, I'm not kidding."

Harris began his call on the Duke radio network of the final play.

Bobby Hurley up the floor with Laettner. . . . They throw it the length of the floor . . .

Clark made his way down the sideline as the final play unfolded. He looked for a foul as Laettner reached up to catch the pass with two hands. There was none—Pelphrey and Feldhaus didn't contest the pass.

Laettner catches . . . comes down . . . dribble . . .

Laettner had decided during the time-out that he had time for one dribble and one fake. Clark watched to make sure Laettner didn't shuffle his feet during his dribble and pivot. There was no traveling.

However, there was panic on the Duke bench as Laettner dribbled the ball once. Says Marty Clark: "I think we all sort of shared the exact same sentiment: *What the fuck you doing, man? You're putting it on the deck? That's real smart.*"

Laettner turned toward the basket. Pelphrey backed away. Feldhaus, at the last moment, made a tepid attempt to challenge the shot. Too late—the ball was out of Laettner's hands. Tom Clark saw the release and then stared at the clock: 0.2 seconds. The shot fell straight through.

Shoots . . . Scoooooooooooorrrrrrrrrrrres! Christian Laettner has hit the bucket at the buzzer. The Blue Devils win it, 104–103. Look out Minneapolis, here come the Blue Devils!

Tom Clark looked immediately at the scorer's table. "Was it good or not?" someone asked. Clark waved it good.

The Spectrum became a human exclamation point. Pandemonium. Bedlam. Cheers. Tears.

Lang pumped his fists and fell to the ground in joy, his arms and legs splayed like he'd been electrocuted. "When he shot the ball, everything went silent," he says. "I didn't hear anything. When it went in, you just heard the net."

Laettner sprinted toward the opposite end of the court while his teammates, led by Hurley and Davis, chased after him. "When he caught the ball, time stood still," says Davis. "God slowed it down. . . .

You knew there were angels present. Nothing feels like that. You can't replicate that feeling, because it's so pure. It's from above."

Says Laettner: "It was just utter frickin' pandemonium. I'm just running around like an idiot. Everyone is chasing me down, and we end up creating a pile right in front of Kentucky's bench—we didn't mean for it to happen. They wanted to kill us, and we're hugging each other, crying, and screaming. . . . God, it was so much fun."

Thomas Hill stood with his hands interlocked behind his head, his face contorted in utter disbelief as he stared into the crowd.

Krzyzewski slammed a towel down in celebration.

Amaker raised his arms in triumph, thinking, *There's no way we're not going to win it all.*

Gaudet, who turned 50 that day, slapped his hands and then leaned back in his metal folding chair with a satisfied smile, like the Senate president in the final scene of *Mr. Smith Goes to Washington.* He couldn't jump, because he was scheduled to undergo double hernia surgery the next day.

Duke's Cragg could jump—and did. "Oh, my god!" he yelled. Then he turned to Kentucky's Cameron and said, "I'm sorry, Chris. I didn't mean to do that." Cameron shook his hand and congratulated him on the victory.

Lundquist and Elmore said nothing. There had been Lundquist's perfect nine-word call—"There's the pass to Laettner . . . puts it up . . . *yesssss!!!*"—followed by 75 seconds of delicious silence (or in the business, a "lay out").

Moments earlier in the CBS production truck, producer Craig Silver had screamed, "He made it! Oh, my god!" as Laettner's shot fell through. Silver, who had turned 33 a day earlier, quickly composed himself and, with the help of director Mike Arnold, coordinated the series of reaction shots from CBS's handheld and isolation cameras. None of the reactions was more iconic than Thomas Hill's.

"It hit me all at once," says Hill. "When the shot goes in, I look at the crowd, then I'm laughing and then it's, *Oh, my god. . . .* It was incredible. I remember the smell of the gym. I remember everything. The ushers. The crowd."

Thomas Hill didn't join the Duke dog pile in front of the UK bench. Instead, he hugged a playful Gaudet. "Hey, Thomas," joked Gaudet, "snap out of it. We got another overtime."

A Duke team manager rushed onto the court and stuffed the game ball under his shirt for safekeeping. Pitino and Krzyzewski exchanged handshakes.

Debbie Krzyzewski fell back into her seat, buried her head in her hands, and started crying. Her younger sister Jamie, who had been in tears since Woods's shot, now switched to tears of joy. When Debbie, Jamie, and Mickie finally reached the court, Mike Krzyzewski put his arms around them and said, "I called it."

Butters said to Newton: "We have just seen the greatest basketball game that has ever been played."

What would become Ledford's final UK play-by-play call of his distinguished career had begun so matter-of-factly—"One-oh-three to one-oh-two. All right, Laettner way back at that end. So is Hurley."—and ended so quickly with a voice of sadness and resignation.

Ledford: So Kentucky—here comes the loooong pass and Laettner's got it . . . Puts down a dribble . . . Turns with a jumper . . . Gooood! . . . And Duke wins it, 104 to 103. That is why they're number one. . . . Well, heartbreak for Kentucky, a team that fought its heart out. But give Duke credit. It did what it had to do. And Kentucky could not come up with the ball on the long pass downcourt. And Duke goes to the Final Four, 104 to 103 in overtime. Be right back. This is the UK basketball network.

"Oh, my god, it seemed like the ball—it looked like the Hindenburg, just floating," says Oliver. "Not just that, but it seemed like it was 20 minutes before he shot it. Just think about that. Just think if he wouldn't have made that shot."

Just think if the pass had curved a foot or two away from Laettner. Just think if the pass had been tipped. Just think if the shot had caught a little too much of the rim and bounced harmlessly away.

But the shot had swished through, and the shock waves rippled across the Spectrum court.

Farmer crumpled to the floor in front of the Duke bench. All he had ever known was basketball. And now, in 2.1 seconds, his career was finished. Farmer staggered up and put his hands to his knees. The first person to console him was Krzyzewski.

"Listen, you guys are not losers," said Krzyzewski, as he hugged Farmer. "The scoreboard may say that you lost, but you guys are the classiest bunch of kids that I've seen play this game in a long time."

The gesture still amazes Farmer. "You ask a lot of people in [Kentucky] and they'll tell you they don't like Duke, they don't like Coach K, they don't like anything to do with Duke because that game brings back so many bad memories for so many people," he says. "But I will never forget what he said."

Woods also fell to the floor. Duke fans stepped over him as they stormed the court. When Woods got up, he ran—nowhere in particular, he just ran—and slammed into *Cats' Pause* editor Oscar Combs, who was making his way across the court. Woods grabbed Combs and began crying.

"Hey, it's okay," said Combs, as he walked Woods back toward the UK locker room. "It's okay."

But Combs knew better. "You go from one second being the hero of your life, to a second later, it's all gone," Combs says.

Brown stared at the scoreboard, betrayed by those basketball gods. *No, it didn't happen to me again. Are you serious?*

Forde frantically inserted Laettner's miracle shot into his story, changed the "Kentucky Wins" lead to "Kentucky Loses" and immediately filed it to his editors in time for the first edition. His press-row seat had given him the perfect angle to watch Laettner's shot. As it left the Duke star's hands, Forde had thought, *Oh, that's good.* And it was.

Rena Vicini, a UK assistant SID, stood behind the Wildcats bench, still gesturing wildly and uselessly that Laettner's shot had come after the final buzzer. Junior Braddy did the same from the bench.

Jack Pelphrey's first words after Laettner's game winner: "I guess not." As in, Jack and Jennie weren't going to Minneapolis after all.

Back in his 170-year-old home in the horse farm country just outside Lexington, Bill Curry stared blankly at the TV screen. He knew what his friend Pitino and those players were going through.

"I think three times in my life my knees have buckled—I'm talking about when nobody touches you," says Curry. "Once was when I was coaching at Alabama and we missed a field goal to lose to LSU, 19 to 18. The second time was when what's-his-name made that shot. The third time was when [then ESPN broadcast partner] Dave Barnett told me Johnny Unitas [a former Curry teammate] had died."

CBS line producer Craig Silver ordered four consecutive replays of the final shot: one from an overhead sideline angle, one from the baseline, one reaction shot of the Duke bench, and one reaction shot of the Kentucky bench. Pitino's final instruction—"Whatever you do, don't foul him"—had been followed in exacting detail.

Instead of risking contact and an official's whistle, Feldhaus and Pelphrey had drifted behind Laettner as the ball was thrown. Laettner, like a football defensive back going for an interception, caught the pass at its highest point and, more important, caught it almost uncontested near the free throw line. As Laettner came down with the ball, Feldhaus stood almost motionless with his arms upraised. Pelphrey, fanned out to Laettner's left, acted as if the Duke All-American was radioactive and actually moved away.

"Paralyzed," says Mashburn. "That's what they looked like."

"Where I was," says Woods, "I could have ran and knocked the ball down. But I'm thinking, *These guys are right there.*"

As the clock read 1.2 seconds, Laettner, his back to the basket, took a single dribble to his right and then pivoted left toward Pelphrey, who kept waiting for the final horn. Pelphrey had backed off, allowing Laettner to square up and have a full view of the basket. With 0.3 seconds remaining, Laettner released the jumper. Feldhaus had cautiously tried to contest the shot with his left hand, but then pulled his hand back, still worried about fouling. Pelphrey never left his feet.

"When I turned, [the shot] was definitely on line," says Feldhaus. "Just like every other shot he hit that game."

And when it went through? (Feldhaus pauses to compose himself.) "Couldn't believe it," he says through misty eyes.

The mind can do strange things. As Laettner celebrated, Pelphrey stood stupefied by what had just happened. When Grant Hill had thrown the pass, Pelphrey was positive he had intercepted it. "Christian Laettner took it out of my hand," he says.

But when he later saw a replay, Pelphrey's memory didn't match reality. "I didn't have my hands on it," he says. "I didn't come close to catching it."

Boston Globe columnist Bob Ryan, considered a basketball Yoda by his sportswriting colleagues, immediately recognized that he had just witnessed something more than a close call for mighty Duke. He had witnessed hoops history.

Ryan scrawled a note on the back of the roster sheet he used to keep his play-by-play notes. As he walked by Ledford, Ryan held up the note.

Best Game Ever?

Ledford, still wearing his headset, nodded yes.

There had been NCAA Tournament upsets (North Carolina State over Houston in 1983), landmark moments (Texas Western over Kentucky in 1966), dynasties established (UCLA's 7 consecutive championships,

10 out of 12), but nothing as compelling as this. Ryan would write a follow-up column proclaiming it the best college basketball game he had ever seen.

"And nothing's surpassed it since," says Ryan. "If the game stopped with Woods's basket—and did not include Laettner's basket—I would have said the same thing."

Of course, none of that mattered to Kentucky's players as they slowly made their way off the Spectrum court. They had come so agonizingly close to victory, and now they just wanted to get away from the crash scene, get away from the joyous Dookies as they prepared to cut down the nets. So they walked silently and zombie-like toward their painted cinderblock locker room. Their faces were a combination of shock and exhaustion, but mostly shock.

As the Kentucky players staggered away, CBS sideline reporter Leslie Visser rushed toward Krzyzewski for a postgame interview. Moments earlier, she had glanced at her arms. Goose bumps. Red Smith, the Pulitzer Prize–winning sportswriter for the *New York Times*, had once given her a piece of advice. "Whenever you're at an event, make a memory," he had said.

Those goose bumps were now Visser's memory.

Higgins, Range, and Clark ran off the court, down a hallway, and into their dressing room. Once inside, Higgins plopped down on a couch, folded his arms, and casually asked, "Was it good?"

"Yeah," said Clark, "two-tenths of a second."

"Okay," said Higgins, smiling.

An officiating observer knocked on the door.

"Tom, was it good?"

"Two-tenths of a second," he said.

"You know they're going to be checking," said the observer. "But I thought it was good, too."

It was. Video replays confirmed that Clark got it right.

Two-tenths of a second. Perhaps the difference between a moment's hesitation and four Duke players instantly calling a time-out after Woods's shot.

In Lexington, Rose turned to his Michigan teammates and said, "I told you! I told you!"

Nantz turned off his hotel room TV and met a handful of CBS crew members in the lobby. "We didn't need a lot of time and reflection to realize it had been one of the classic games in basketball," he says.

In Portland, Abdelnaby sprinted through the layup line, high-fived fans, and jumped on the backs of his Portland teammates. "The place went insane when he made the shot," says Abdelnaby. (And Portland won its game, too.)

After reciting the final score and sending viewers back to the CBS studio show in New York, there was nothing left for Lundquist to do but to marinate himself in the moment. Lundquist and Elmore removed their headsets but stayed in their courtside seats for nearly 20 seconds, neither man saying a word to the other.

"It almost took your breath away," says Lundquist of the game.

About five minutes later, Lundquist spotted Krzyzewski standing on the court.

"Mike, congratulations," he said. "That was a thriller."

Said Krzyzewski: "I just knew if we could get it into the son of a bitch's hands, he could make the shot."

The SOB had only wanted a chance to take the last shot. If it went in, wonderful. If it didn't, then such were the whims of the basketball gods. He could live with whatever outcome.

"I said, *That's a good look . . . it's got a chance,*" says Laettner. "I landed and it frickin' went in. And when it went in, it was the most spiritual experience I've had in my entire life. . . . God was good. God was great, but I didn't know he was that good."

Bob Ryan approached Elmore. "Lenny, until tonight the greatest college basketball game was supposed to be Maryland–North Carolina

State," said Ryan of the 1974 ACC Championship Game, won in overtime, 103–100, by NC State. "Was this one better?"

Elmore, who played in that 1974 game, thought about it for a few moments and finally said, "Yes, this was more meaningful."

The Wildcats had to walk down the same hallway where the officials' dressing room was located. Tom Clark looked out a small window on the door and saw them coming. Pelphrey was sobbing.

As the UK locker room door was pulled shut, the finality of the moment hit them. Oliver smashed two chairs in anger. Then, with one hand, he squeezed an unopened can of Coke so hard that it exploded. Carmel-colored soda droplets dripped from his white dress shirt.

Oliver replayed the entire game in his mind and tried to find something, anything that the Wildcats could have done better. "I came up with nothing," he says. "Fuck, we did everything. That was the greatest game ever."

Three years earlier, when the NCAA had seriously considered shutting down the rogue UK program, *Sports Illustrated* had pounced on the controversy. The magazine's headline still froze the hearts of Wildcats fans: "Kentucky's Shame."

Now Pitino, who had been offered the UK job the same week that the *SI* cover hit the newsstands, stood in the middle of the locker room. He could hear two sounds: the muffled Duke celebration from the court and the crying of several of his Wildcat players slouched in front of their lockers.

Pitino held something in his hand. It was that same *SI* cover of 1989, and he brandished it as if he were a Baptist minister waving a Bible.

He had brought the magazine to Philadelphia just in case the Wildcats lost. For years he had kept it, despised it, and used it for motivation. Now it was time to be rid of it.

His voice breaking, his eyes red, Pitino told his team, "What you've accomplished in just a very short period of time is to take this program from its nadir to the highest point."

Kentucky's shame had become Kentucky's pride. They had lost a game, but they had won back a program's reputation and done so honorably. That, said Pitino, composing himself, was more important than reaching any Final Four.

"You can't let your basketball career be defined by 2.1 seconds," he told the Wildcats. "When you come out of that shower, I don't want any more tears."

Except that the more Pitino talked, the more *he* cried. He had been at Kentucky for only three seasons, but Pelphrey, Feldhaus, Farmer, and Woods—true UK blue bloods—had been there from the beginning. They had seen the stunning fall from grace of Sutton, the revelation of clumsily handled payments to a recruit, academic cheating, the TV camera crews parked outside their dorm rooms, the first losing Kentucky season in 62 years, the firing of hoops legend Hagan, the NCAA investigation, the program's neutering by harsh penalties, the hiring of Newton, the dance with Carlesimo, and the hiring of Pitino.

And through it all, Pelphrey, Feldhaus, Farmer, and Woods had chosen to stay. That's why Pitino cried—not because of the loss to Duke, but because he had seen what those four players endured. And now he had coached them for the last time. For a man who preached sacrifice and dedication, Pitino understood better than anyone what those four players' presence had meant to Big Blue basketball.

"But at that point, there was nothing he could tell us that could stop the pain," says Woods. "For us seniors, we only had that one year."

Meanwhile, outside the locker room, CBS's Visser pleaded with Kentucky officials to open the door. So did the anxious newspaper reporters, whose deadlines were approaching at warp speed.

As the NCAA-mandated "cooling-off period" came and went, the reporters began to demand immediate access to the locker room.

"Over my dead body," said Cameron, who wasn't going to allow the media inside without Pitino's okay.

"That can be arranged!" shouted a sportswriter.

When the door was finally opened, reporters streamed in and made a beeline for Pelphrey's locker. He wasn't there. Instead, he was 15 feet away, leaning against a bathroom stall and sobbing. He stayed there several minutes before composing himself and walking to the middle of the locker room, where a handful of reporters waited.

"[Laettner] hit a great shot," said Pelphrey. "I don't think there's any way to explain that. Words can't describe it. A great player made a great shot."

Someone asked if he could describe Kentucky's season.

"I'd like to," said Pelphrey, as his eyes welled with tears, "but I can't . . . talk."

And then he walked back into the bathroom and repeated to himself, "I can't talk . . . I can't talk."

Pitino was still so shaken at the postgame news conference that he mistakenly said that Hill had inbounded the ball from the sideline rather than the baseline. He was an emotional wreck.

"I was truly dazed," Pitino says. "It was like getting hit by a truck."

Newton waited until Pitino had finished his news conference and postgame radio show before approaching the UK coach. He put his arm around Pitino and said, "Rick, I know how disappointed you are. The chance to get to a Final Four is a coach's dream, and they're few and far between. But this could be—just could be—a blessing in disguise. It could be the best thing for our program and our fans in the future. Our fans are fanatics. I'm not sure this team was good enough to make a deep run in the Final Four."

Pitino was incredulous. "Are you crazy?" he said.

"I don't think so," said Newton.

"I think you have to be. You've got to take these chances when you get them."

Willard had sat two rows behind the Kentucky bench. Afterward, he tried to console Pitino. But Pitino kept asking, "Why didn't I put a guy on the ball?"

"Hey, it's over," Willard told his friend. "I wouldn't have put a guy on the ball either. I would have sandwiched Laettner. You did the right thing."

But Pitino wouldn't stop second-guessing himself. Willard gave up and returned to the hotel.

"I've never, ever seen him beat himself up so unmercifully like he did that game," Willard says. "But if you stay in the profession long enough, you're going to get your heart taken out. . . . You had to think the odds were overwhelmingly in your favor and that that game is over. Something would have to happen perfectly for Duke to win that game. And it did."

"Hell, I wouldn't have put someone on the ball either," says Newton. "To think of covering the ball made no sense to me. What it took was a perfect pass, a perfect catch, a perfect turn, and a perfect shot. You could do that 75 times without anybody guarding you and not hit the damn thing."

Forde rushed from the Kentucky locker room to the media work room to write a completely new version of his first-edition story for the front page of the *Courier-Journal*. It had been the most stressful deadline night of his career. His colleague Bozich noticed Forde staring at the empty computer screen.

"Look," said Bozich, "it was the best game I've ever seen. Do your best."

Tipton, too, was overwhelmed by the last-second chain of events. "That's the only game I've ever covered that I didn't want to write about," he says. "I felt totally inadequate to write it. I just wanted to go someplace and drink beer and talk about it."

At courtside, the great Ledford was saying his farewells to the Big Blue Nation. (CBS had wanted to acknowledge his career during the second half, but they couldn't find a dead spot to do it. The game had been too good.) He drew on the words of John Greenleaf Whittier, applying the poet's writings to the 1992 UK team, which had become one of his favorites.

Ledford: "The saddest words of tongue or pen are these: What might have been. Kentucky almost pulled it off."

And then he delivered what he thought would be the final words of his illustrious radio career. He wasn't expecting a guest.

Ledford: Most of all, my heartfelt thanks to you for your support, your loyalty, and your friendship over these 39 years. Perhaps Adolph Rupp said it best. I'd like to borrow his words for my good-bye that he used in his good-bye speech, and the words are these: "For those of you who have gone down the glory road with me, my eternal thanks."... From Philadelphia, this is Cawood Ledford saying good-bye—Well, here's coach Mike Krzyzewski. Great game, Mike. Apparently he's going to sit in with us for a minute.... And Coach, congratulations. It was a great, great game.

Krzyzewski: Thanks, Cawood. I wanted to seek you guys out because all the Kentucky fans would be listening. And just to say how much empathy we have as a staff and team for the Kentucky kids. They were absolutely sensational. It was one of the best college games—maybe the best I've ever been associated with. So many kids from both sides made great plays and made coaches look good. I feel bad for them. I hope you believe that.

Ledford: I do.

Krzyzewski: Because Richie Farmer, Jamal Mashburn, Pelphrey, Gimel Martinez, those kids we've gotten to know over the years. They're great kids. And C. M. Newton and I are as close as anybody can be. I feel bad for him, along with our exultation, so to speak. I just want to congratulate them on a truly fantastic year. I hope we represent this region now well when we go to the Final Four.

Ledford: Coach K...

Krzyzewski: And thank you for a great career for you.

Ledford: Thank you kindly.

When Krzyzewski and the Blue Devils finally returned to their locker room, Davis scribbled a trivia question on a whiteboard.

Who's the first black guy to go to four Final Fours?

Answer: The Duke recruiting afterthought—just in case anyone had forgotten.

Krzyzewski gathered the team together and asked them to press the Pause button on their celebration. "Let's just think for a minute or two about the Kentucky kids," he said.

Typical Krzyzewski. He believed in basketball karma, that the game was bigger than any coach or player.

"We all knew we were thrust into a moment that the multitudes never get a chance to be in, and as a result of being in that moment, if we handled it all right, all of us would be glorified with it," says Krzyzewski. "Kentucky was [glorified], and should be. I love that, and I don't see that very often in sport. I will always ultimately respect Rick Pitino because he handled this in a way—if he doesn't handle this right, then the kids don't get what they should get from this, you know what I mean? I just think he was superb in this. If I could take one person and say this is why this became even bigger, it would have been Rick and how he handled all this.

"There's a lot of good stuff there for a basketball person. Not just how the game was, but how people acted, how the kids acted. There wasn't anybody popping their jerseys. You saw our guys hugging their guys. . . . When you win a game like that—and in that way—if you don't show some humility and empathy during that time, then you're a bum. You're just a bum. The basketball gods should just say, 'You'll never have another moment like that. If you don't know how to handle that one, you're never gonna have another one.'"

Later that evening, after waiting for the traffic to thin out around Broad Street and Pattison Avenue, Higgins met up with his wife and a friend for the drive home to New Jersey. Higgins was an old-school ref. It was all about getting the call right, not about who was playing or what they were playing for. Season opener or Final Four, Higgins treated each the same.

But as he pulled out of the Spectrum parking lot, Higgins had to admit that this night and this game felt different. He turned to his wife and said, "I think you just watched the greatest game ever played."

It was an evening of bitter and sweet. Roselle drove back to Delaware that night strangely fulfilled by the game. Three years earlier, he had stood in front of Pelphrey, Woods, Farmer, and Feldhaus and vowed that one day they would be proud to say they were University of Kentucky Wildcats.

As it turned out, that day was March 28, 1992. And Roselle had been there to witness it.

"I think it was one of the most well-spent late afternoons and evenings ever for me," Roselle says. "It was just a wonderful experience to see those kids. Sean Woods made that shot, and all things being normal, we would have that game."

We?

"Yes, I was rooting for [UK]," he says. "I always do what Pitino tells me to do."

The writers and broadcasters eventually made their way back to the media hotel and to its hospitality lounge. "Usually you get in there after a game and it starts thinning out after an hour and a half," says Combs. "But nobody left that night. We stayed up until 3 or 4 a.m., really not believing what we'd just seen. We may never live to see another game like this."

The mood was more somber when the Wildcats finally returned to their downtown Philadelphia hotel, the historic but somewhat dark and gloomy Warwick. As the players entered the marble-floored lobby, they were met by their parents, friends, and assorted Kentucky fans. It was a basketball wake. Everywhere you looked someone was crying. Cameron took the elevator up to his room, sat down on the bed, and wept. It was the first (and last) time in his career that he cried after a game.

A short time later, Cameron returned to the hotel lobby. The scene was the same: Pelphrey, Feldhaus, and Farmer encircled by well-meaning but tearful fans. Cameron looked at Vicini and said, "We've got to get them out of here."

So they grabbed the three players by the arms and pulled them away from the lobby, through the hotel kitchen, and out a back door. They made the short walk from the team hotel to the media hotel, where Vicini was staying. Once in Vicini's room, Cameron and Vicini raided the minibar.

"Your eligibility is up, you're adults," he told Pelphrey, Feldhaus, and Farmer, as they pulled out tiny bottles of bourbon, scotch, vodka, and gin.

And then the five of them drank the night away. The toasts were always the same.

To Kentucky. And to the ones who stayed.

THIRTEEN

April 4, 1992

I f Bobby Hurley dreaded the game against Seton Hall and his brother Dan, then Krzyzewski now faced a similar predicament in the Final Four: Not brother vs. brother, but pupil vs. mentor/close friend/ former boss/legend.

Duke's opponent in the national semifinals at the Metrodome in Minneapolis would be the Indiana Hoosiers. Bob Knight's Indiana Hoosiers.

Five years earlier, in the Midwest Regional semifinals in Cincinnati, Krzyzewski and Knight had coached against each other for the first time. The two men tried to downplay the meeting that March 1987 day, with Knight facetiously asking, "Where's Mike gonna play?" and Krzyzewski reminding the media that he coached against the other team, not the other coach.

But as the interview sessions continued, the defense mechanisms of each coach began to let down. Knight allowed that he and Krzyzewski were "extremely close as a player, as a coach." And then he offered a quintessential Knight compliment: "They're extremely well coached. I taught [him], they ought to be."

In return, Krzyzewski paid homage to the IU coach, telling reporters, "Knight and I are about as close friends as you can get."

When Indiana beat Duke in that Midwest Regional semifinal, Knight said afterward, "I'm pleased for our players, but I personally didn't enjoy the game at all. . . . I'm very proud and admiring of what [Krzyzewski has] accomplished. . . . I'd rather not meet him as an opponent." Knight's Hoosiers went on to win the 1987 Final Four, giving Knight his third national championship.

By 1992, the tectonic plates of college basketball had shifted, and with them the circumstances surrounding Krzyzewski and Knight. Krzyzewski remained a devout Knight disciple and friend. He was always quick to credit Knight for creating and shaping his life and career. But by any measurement, Krzyzewski was no longer subordinate to Knight. He was becoming an equal, thanks to a national championship in 1991 and, with this latest run, a mind-boggling five consecutive Final Four appearances and six out of the previous seven. Only UCLA's John Wooden had put together a longer streak (a never-will-happen-again nine in a row). Knight had never reached the Final Four in consecutive seasons.

"I honestly don't think that over the time that Mike has been a coach, that I've really had much influence on Mike," said Knight the day before the national semis. "I think that Mike has put his own program together. . . . I think what he's done has been done through his own efforts and I think would have been done regardless if he would have played for me or not."

Knight's program had struggled in the postseason recently. The Hoosiers were eliminated in the first round of the NCAAs in 1988 and 1990, and made it no further than the regional semifinals in 1989 and 1991. But this latest IU team, with Calbert Cheaney, Greg Graham, Alan Henderson, and Eric Anderson, was more than capable of winning a national title. Knight could look at the other side of the Final Four bracket and see Bob Huggins's Cincinnati Bearcats, a team IU had beaten by 21 points earlier in the season; and Michigan, against whom

IU had split its two games, winning by 15 and losing by 8. If Knight could somehow squeeze past Duke, he liked his chances.

But first he had to deal with a controversy involving, of all things, a leather bullwhip.

During an open practice at the West Regional in Albuquerque, New Mexico, Knight had walked onto the court carrying a bullwhip. Purchased by his players and presented to him by his son, Pat Knight, it was a gag gift, playing off his reputation for being hard on his players. Everything was fine until Knight pretended to use the whip on the backside of a bent-over Cheaney, who is black. National outrage ensued.

Knight refused to apologize, saying that his gesture was clearly a joke. To those who found his actions inappropriate, Knight said, "Those are kind of sad people." Cheaney himself had said, "It was all in fun."

Joke or no joke, the incident infuriated at least one Duke player. And still does.

"He's a racist, a fucking racist," says Davis. "Bringing out a whip. He should have been fired. If he was a black coach, he'd've been fired. I couldn't believe he did that. If John Thompson did that to a white kid, he'd've been fired."

Laettner didn't have time to worry about Knight's controversies; it was the IU team that worried him. He had always respected and admired Knight, dating back to the days when Knight had recruited him, and he knew the IU coach would have six long days to prepare and install a game plan. The Hoosiers played lockdown defense, were tough and unselfish, and ran a motion offense—in short, a mirror image of the Blue Devils. Even though the pace of the game would be more deliberate and to Laettner's liking—no more Pitino track meet—Knight would come up with an innovative wrinkle or two.

The Duke center also knew that a post-Kentucky letdown was almost inevitable. The high of hitting the game-winning shot against Kentucky, of hitting *every* shot he took against Kentucky, was beginning to fade. After all, how can you do better than perfection? You can't, which is why it was almost predictable that Laettner would need his teammates' help in the Final Four.

Laettner, who was averaging 22 points per game, had been right about Knight: The Indiana coach devised a plan to limit the Duke center's effectiveness by double- and sometimes triple-teaming Laettner in the low post with a combination of Henderson, Anderson, and Matt Nover. A flustered Laettner responded by missing some chippies early in the game and then disappearing for the rest of the first half. He converted only 1 of 6 field goal attempts in the first 20 minutes. The Hoosiers led by as many as 12 points before Bobby Hurley came to the rescue.

Hurley recognized early in the game that Laettner was going to have trouble scoring, so he began launching surgical air strikes from behind the three-point arc. He hit 4 of 5 threes in the first half, whittling the margin to 42–37 at halftime. It was only the third time all season Duke had trailed at the half.

In the Duke locker room, Krzyzewski told the Blue Devils that only Hurley—who had outscored the other four starters, 16–15—had played at a championship level; everyone else, especially Laettner, would be smart to follow Hurley's lead. Even Hurley told Laettner to step up his game. "And I just had to sit there and take it from everybody because I wasn't doing so well at that point," says Laettner. "So not to make excuses, but I was getting double- and triple-teamed, playing really weak, and I had a lot of turnovers. Coach K was in my ass a little, and Bobby kind of backed him up and got in my ass a little bit. I'm a good enough teammate and not enough of an asshole to not take it."

Laettner played better in the second half (though he would finish with only 8 points—breaking his streak of 46 consecutive double-figure games—and 10 rebounds), but the game clearly belonged to Hurley, whose 26 points equaled his career high, with important help from the last man off Duke's bench that night, Marty Clark. After the Duke lineup had been reduced by two—Davis injured his ankle with 8:17 remaining to play, and Grant Hill (14 points scored) fouled out with 1:44—Clark made his entrance into the game and into Blue Devils hoops history.

Perhaps it was coincidence, nothing more, but when Krzyzewski looked down the bench to replace Grant Hill in the lineup, Clark was the only Duke reserve leaning forward in his seat. The other two substitution possibilities—Blakeney and Ast—were sitting straight up, partially hidden by the other reserves. Krzyzewski went with the leaner.

Clark sank 5 vital free throws in the final 87 seconds of the game (Duke made 14 of 16 in the last minute). Without those free throws, the game would have belonged to the Hoosiers and *their* last player off the bench, Todd Leary, who made 3 three-pointers in 25 seconds down the stretch. The final margin was 3 points, 81–78.

Indiana fans will argue that Duke was aided by a sixth man: game official Ted Valentine, part of an officiating crew that whistled the Hoosiers for 33 fouls leading to 42 Duke free throw attempts and 28 points. In the second half alone, Duke shot 34 free throws compared to IU's 8.

Krzyzewski's players knew how much the win meant to their coach. He acted as if the game were against Indiana, but Knight *was* Indiana. More important, Knight was the man to whom he owed so much. No other coach's opinion—and approval—meant more to him than Knight's.

But unlike their first coaching encounter in 1987, when Knight had showered Krzyzewski with heartfelt praise, the postgame love this time was noticeably one-sided. As the final horn sounded, Krzyzewski walked down the sideline to shake hands with his mentor. This would not be easy, just as it had not been easy for Krzyzewski after the loss in 1987. But friendship would trump disappointment, and respect would overpower the sting of defeat, right? In the mid-week teleconference Krzyzewski had said of Knight: "He's had a big impact on who I am and what I've become in coaching. We'll be good friends after the game, too."

But when Krzyzewski reached Knight on the sideline, the reception was Greenland cold. Krzyzewski stuck his hand out and received a fly-by, wet-fish handshake from Knight. There was no warm embrace, no hand to the shoulder, no lingering conversation. And just to rub it in, Knight made a beeline down the Duke bench to hug Colonel Tom Rogers, a West Point grad and career officer who had worked on Knight's Army staff and later came to Duke as a special assistant to Butters.

Krzyzewski had just been dissed, and for a moment the Duke coach wore the bewildered look of a child asking *What'd I do?* before moving on to shake hands with the other Indiana assistants and players. The "We'll be good friends after the game" theory was in ruins.

Afterward, Knight, along with several IU players, went to the postgame interview room at the Metrodome. Krzyzewski and key Duke players would immediately follow Knight's session. Knight, who was sometimes more agreeable after losses than after victories, complimented Hurley's play, discussed his own team's inability to score in the second half, and answered a variety of other questions before leaving the dais. Standing behind the blue cloth curtain in the holding area were Krzyzewski and his players. Surely Knight would pause and speak to him as they traded places.

Instead, Knight blew past Krzyzewski. For those behind the curtain—Mickie Krzyzewski, those Duke players, members of the Duke support staff—Knight's behavior was shocking. "What pissed us off is that Coach K loved him," says Davis. "That's all he talked about was Coach Knight. Mickie Krzyzewski is the nicest woman. Coach K is the greatest coach. They did not deserve that. He's not perfect, but he did not deserve that. . . . That proved Bobby was jealous of Coach K."

Says Laettner: "I thought it was messed up."

A reporter asked Krzyzewski about the "cool" postgame handshake, but the Duke coach quickly extinguished the flammable properties of the question. "I think he was fine," he said of Knight. "It was a tough loss. I don't know what a cool handshake is. He said, 'Congratulations and good luck.' That's about what I would expect him to say."

But Krzyzewski, a veteran of Knight's ever-changing moods, knew Knight was anything but fine. In his pocket was a note written by

Knight and delivered to Krzyzewski not long after the final buzzer had sounded. The gist of Knight's message: Krzyzewski had let him down.

The note's contents staggered Krzyzewski. So did Knight's postgame treatment of him. It was a long ride back to the Duke team hotel in suburban Bloomington.

"I saw it and I didn't understand it," says Mickie of the brush-off. "When we got on the team bus, Mike was very, very affected by it and didn't understand it either. It was sad. It was really sad. Mike was hurt by that."

A previously robust friendship was suddenly in need of a tourniquet. But instead of blaming Knight, Krzyzewski began questioning his own actions.

Had I somehow broken some sort of coaching protocol during the game?

Had I not shown enough respect?

How could I have made it better for Knight?

In the end, Krzyzewski decided he had done nothing to trigger Knight's reaction. He would later learn that a *Sports Illustrated* story, written by Curry Kirkpatrick and published the week of the Final Four, had apparently been the Molotov cocktail that blew up their relationship. One paragraph read, "In 1987 Indiana beat Duke in the Midwest Regional semifinals, a crucible that a friend of Krzyzewski's describes as the 'divorce' between the two coaches, because Krzyzewski wanted so badly to eliminate the notion that he was nothing without Knight's patronage. Since then Coach K has taken every opportunity to outline their many differences while still staying on Knight's good side—wherever that is—undoubtedly a stickier task than teaching dozens of trophy makers how to spell his name."

The "divorce" . . . nothing without Knight's patronage . . . outline their many differences. In what Mickie describes delicately as a "misunderstanding," Knight apparently thought Krzyzewski wanted to distance himself from the IU coach. Given Krzyzewski's long history of crediting Knight for, well, almost everything, it's difficult to understand why

Knight would connect all those dots. His gripe, it appears, should have been with Krzyzewski's unnamed friend rather than with Krzyzewski. But loyalty was Knight's currency of choice, and in his mind Krzyzewski had violated that bond.

Cold cuts and fruit were served in Krzyzewski's hotel suite at the Radisson South after the game. But Krzyzewski was in no real mood to celebrate. The incident with Knight had taken the joy out of the victory.

(The cold war between the two men would last for the next nine years. It wasn't until May 2001, when Krzyzewski was elected to the Basketball Hall of Fame, that a détente took place. Krzyzewski needed a Hall of Fame member as an official inductor for the October ceremony. He knew there was only one person he could ask: Knight.

"How are you going to do that?" Mickie said.

"I'm going to call him," Krzyzewski said.

He called, Knight accepted the invitation, and, says Mickie, "[Knight] was spectacular." But make no mistake: Had Krzyzewski not reached out, the cold war would have continued. "In the journey of my dad's life," says Debbie Krzyzewski Savarino, "I think [the incident] changed the way he . . . I think it made my dad's approach to his relationship with Coach Knight much healthier.")

With less than 48 hours between the semifinal win against Indiana and Monday night's championship game against Michigan, who had beaten Cincinnati, 76–72, Krzyzewski didn't have time to obsess over the Knight situation. His video staff had arrived in Minneapolis with an extensive library of game tape of Indiana, but even before the Duke–IU matchup, his assistants began breaking down tape of Michigan and Cincinnati. Now that the Hoosiers were gone, Krzyzewski settled into his hotel room and began poring over video of the Wolverines.

The team Duke had beaten in overtime four months earlier at Ann Arbor was vastly different from the one it would face at the Metrodome. The Wolverines' starting lineup had changed, from three freshmen starters (Webber, Rose, and Howard) in December to all five (adding

Jackson and King). Their rotation had changed. But their carefree arrogance remained the same. If anything, Michigan's historic, audacious run to the national championship game had empowered the young Wolverines even more. You needed a chamois to soak up the excess confidence the Fab Five oozed. "We had no fear, man," says Howard.

In the Michigan locker room after the victory against Cincinnati, someone wrote "Payback" on the white greaseboard. They had wished hard for this rematch since losing to the Blue Devils in December.

This wasn't only about beating the defending national champions, or becoming national champions themselves. It was about planting a flag on college basketball's conservative landscape and claiming the future. "We felt like it was our turn," says Rose, who had become Michigan's soul and voice. King adds, "It was like, *This is where we're supposed to be. We're on the stage now. We're here. We're not selling woof tickets. We're backing it up.*"

Woof tickets—all bark, no bite. But Michigan had front teeth and molars and the will to use them. They were there to beat the precious Dookies. Didn't matter that U of M's starting lineup was all freshmen. Didn't matter if they didn't follow hoops etiquette. You don't like it? Deal with it.

Back in December, Michigan was a curiosity piece. The Wolverines were talented—you had to be blind not to see their skills, especially those of the freakishly coordinated Webber. But please, they were built around five freshmen. Nobody except those five freshmen expected them to get this far—just one victory away from a national title, a trophy presentation, and centerpiece status in CBS's schlocky but popular "One Shining Moment" postgame montage.

A basketball and even cultural revolution was taking place, with the Fab Five storming the palace gates. There had been impact freshmen before—Quinn Buckner and later Isiah Thomas at Indiana, Earvin Johnson at Michigan State, Bernard King at Tennessee, Patrick Ewing at Georgetown, Sam Perkins and later Michael Jordan at North Carolina,

Wayman Tisdale at Oklahoma, Derrick Coleman at Syracuse, Chris Jackson at LSU, and Pervis Ellison at Louisville—but they almost always had senior leadership to hold their hands. And even rarer was when a freshman, such as Ellison or Jordan, led a team to a national championship.

This was a genuine paradigm shift. The Fab Five was rewriting the rules on the fly. Their audacity and talent made all things possible, including an upset of Duke.

Rose looked at the two rosters and couldn't think of one trade he'd make—not Laettner for Webber, not Grant Hill for Howard, not Hurley for him. No way would Rose take any of the Dookies over his teammates. That's because the Fab Five was superglued together. It wasn't just five freshmen but, says Rose, "a brotherhood, a fellowship. The Fab Five was a worldwide moniker."

But Fisher made sure his players knew they were not universally loved. The Michigan coach would post on the locker room wall some of the letters he received at his office ("Racist things," says Rose. "Hateful things. Evil things."). Fisher was bringing the brotherhood closer, tightening the circle. The message was clear: There were those in the outside world who were intimidated and even repulsed by the Fab Five. To those people, Duke was safe, wholesome, more white. The Fab Five was—how best to put it?—more threatening.

"They were the anti–Fab Five," says Rose of Duke. "If the Fab Five was considered thugs and killers, [the Blue Devils] were clean-cut and calculating. In the '60s, people [in the black community] would have probably called them [Uncle] Toms. That's not a fair judgment for 17-, 18-year-old kids, but that was the perception when they played Vegas, and it was heightened when they played us. . . . They were the wholesome kids. It was okay to be like Brian Davis, Grant Hill, and Thomas Hill. It was not okay to be like Jalen Rose. . . . We're just some thugs who happen to be in the championship game with baggy shorts and black socks."

Says Duke's Blakeney: "I don't know what White America thinks, but Black America thinks that Duke players are soft. . . . We're kind of known as the Huxtable kind of kids."

The racial undertones were impossible to ignore. The Michigan players had watched the Kentucky–Duke game and seen Laettner escape ejection after stepping on Timberlake's chest. To them, it was evidence, like fingerprints on a gun handle, that CBS, the college basketball establishment, the majority of basketball fans, and even the refs wanted Duke—America's Sweetheart—to win. It wasn't a conspiracy, per se, but players like Rose thought that the favored Blue Devils would get the benefit of the doubt on every close call.

Was it an inferiority complex? Sort of. Michigan *was* the underdog. But the Wolverines were building their own passionate, eclectic following: Michigan alums and students, of course; the first wave of anti-Dookies; and young blacks and whites, often urban, who saw the Fab Five as a cultural phenomenon and an alternative to conventional basketball programs. The Fab Five, who had rooted for the Rebels against Duke a year earlier, represented something different, almost defiant. "We felt like the whole world was kissing up to [Duke] already, so why should we pucker up?" says Rose.

As much as the Fab Five wanted a rematch with the Blue Devils, Duke's players were eager to face Michigan again. They had sensed—accurately—that while the Wolverines respected them, they didn't respect them *that* much.

Hurley in particular was counting the minutes until tip-off. If he could have picked any team to play in the championship game, it would have been Michigan. It annoyed his basketball-purist sensibilities that the Fab Five had received so much attention but hadn't *won* anything yet. They hadn't won the first game against Duke. They hadn't won the Big Ten Conference title (the Wolverines tied for third). They had chirped—they were good at chirping, all but sure they were going to beat the Blue Devils—but Hurley had heard lots of chirpers in Jersey, at Five-Star, in the ACC. Vegas had earned the right to chirp because they had won when it mattered. But not Michigan. Not yet.

Duke's players had seen video highlights of the Wolverines' Friday practice session. The sessions, open to the public the day before the semifinal games, are usually nothing more than glorified shootarounds. The real work takes place in private practices, often in off-site gyms. The Blue Devils noticed that several of the Michigan players wore their jerseys inside out. The Wolverines were in a playful mood, and they practiced that way in the public session. They weren't the first team to treat the open practice as if it were an exhibition.

Duke wasn't playful. Jerseys weren't worn inside out. Krzyzewski wasn't about to reveal any state secrets in an open session, but every minute of his practices had a purpose. Krzyzewski knew he had a special team, a team on the brink of doing something historic. It had talent, experience, and ego—the holy trinity of championships. If not for Hurley's foot injury, the Blue Devils would have likely entered the NCAA Tournament with an unbeaten record. But even with those two regular-season losses, this '92 team was unlike any other Krzyzewski had ever coached. The Blue Devils had *it*. Then again, so did UNLV a year earlier, and look what happened to the Runnin' Rebels. One minute they were favorites for the rare repeat; the next minute they were victims of one of the great upsets. Krzyzewski didn't want to be a victim. He wanted to dispose of the Fab Five and their baggy shorts and have his team take its place among the best ever.

There were three major concerns, though: Laettner, Davis, and Michigan.

Laettner's performance against Indiana in the semi raised a red flag to the Duke coaching staff. It had nothing to do with his effort—Laettner always played hard—but the cumulative effect of the regular season and postseason had taken its toll on him. He had won every meaningful player-of-the-year award and had carried Duke when nobody else could. His box score against Kentucky was an instant classic. How many players had hit a last-second, game-winning shot to send their team to a Final Four? Laettner had done it twice.

But by the time Duke advanced to the title game, Laettner was emotionally drained. Krzyzewski and his coaching staff could see it. The other Blue Devils could see it. Even Laettner, who was the master of mind games, realized he was suffering from a Kentucky hangover. It was understandable. It also was a problem.

Meanwhile, Davis had limped off the court late in the Indiana game with an ankle injury. The results of an MRI were announced the next day: a high ankle sprain. It was a lie. "They called it a sprain, but I broke it," says Davis. "I didn't tell anybody, either."

Davis and trainer Dave Engelhardt spent every waking moment treating the ankle. Krzyzewski had told the media that Davis's "sprain" would likely keep the senior forward on the bench Monday night. Made sense, since Davis was still on crutches, barely able to walk.

Of course, anger can have restorative powers, too. Davis despised the Fab Five. The thought of missing the national title game gnawed at him, but the thought of missing the national championship game *and* missing another shot at Michigan fueled him. "The Fab Five were the biggest jackasses in college basketball," he says. "The only Fab Five was the Jackson family."

Check that—Davis thought Webber was cool. "But the rest of them?" he says. "Please."

The third issue for Krzyzewski was Michigan's talent. Not only that, but with each of their five wins in the tournament the Wolverines were growing more confident, more self-assured, and more vocal—if that was possible.

Laettner saw a Michigan team with unapologetic swagger. They were so young and loosey-goosey he worried they might be immune to the pressures of Monday night's championship. Arrogance and ignorance— sometimes a winning combination. Plus, the Wolverines could draw strength from that overtime loss in Ann Arbor, when they could have—perhaps should have—beaten Duke.

For his part, Webber told reporters that he didn't appreciate getting second billing in the December 14 Duke–Michigan game: "I had so much resentment. People kept asking me what am I going to do with Christian Laettner. I wanted them to be asking him what he was going to do with me."

Michigan's verbal swagger intensified in the pregame warm-ups. During the layup drills, several of Michigan's black players began to yell racially themed insults at Duke's black players.

"They were calling us Uncle Toms before a national championship game," Davis says. "They're talking shit: 'Uncle Tom' . . . 'House' (as in House Negro—slaves who worked in the home rather than in the fields). . . . They thought they were so street. We're like, 'Fuck you. We'll see you in a few minutes.'"

"Field niggers. House niggers. Uncle Toms," says Mark Williams, Duke's African-American senior manager. "They were very aggressive and negative."

"I do not remember that," says King. "I won't say that it didn't happen. We're talking about the game within the game. There's a lot of things said during the game. Really, all you're doing at that point is trying to touch buttons and nerves and get people talking about things. To me, that stuff is fun. I grew up that way. You roll with it. You have fun with it."

Says Rose: "I'm not going to say it didn't happen, but I don't remember it happening. I wouldn't be surprised if we did it. I wouldn't be surprised if I was one of them who did it. If they remembered it, it happened. But if I can get in your head, that's going to affect you. And if it's Good versus Evil, then we might as well take it all the way there."

It wasn't the first time Duke's black players had heard such taunts. Thomas Hill would return home to Texas during the summer and be subjected to the same name-calling. "The black guys that go to Duke—

I could write a book on the whole subject," he says. "If you're worried about somebody being an Uncle Tom, then you're not focused."

Michigan's insults both angered and amused the Duke players. Many of the Blue Devils had remembered a different Webber during his recruiting visit to Durham. To see him take on this other persona at Michigan—part 8 Mile Road and part antiestablishment—was surprising to those who knew him, including Grant Hill.

"I think that's something he struggled with," says Grant Hill. "We're not as close—when we got in the NBA we didn't stay as close—but I'd see the things he'd say or do, and that's not Chris. He's very intelligent, very well spoken, but, you know, that's another big issue: There's something wrong when you feel as an African-American you have to dumb down. I know I'm as guilty as anybody for feeling like, in wanting acceptance, I have to talk or act a certain way in order to feel accepted by my own people. It's stupid. It's foolish. It's wrong. It's ignorant. But certainly I've gone through it, and I'm sure others have as well."

Says Thomas Hill: "Webber [is] not what he portrayed himself as at Michigan. That's hilarious. That's what's so funny to us. We kind of laughed at those dudes because we kind of knew who they were."

Davis didn't laugh; he seethed. To call him a "Tom" or a "House" was to stick an ice pick in his heart. He hadn't attended a private high school. There were no Mercedeses where he grew up in Atlantic City and D.C. Davis was the first person in his family to set foot in a college classroom. He had never had a white friend until he arrived at Duke and met Laettner. "He made me redefine what I thought about white people," says Davis.

Davis wanted to crush Michigan and the Fab Five. Humiliate them. Embarrass them. He had never heard an opposing team talk as much trash as Michigan had talked. During layup drills. In the tunnel before the game.

The Wolverines *were* in the heads of the Duke players. Davis was angry. Hurley thought the Wolverines talked too much. Thomas Hill relished the idea of shutting down (and shutting up) the mouthy Wolverines. Meanwhile, Grant Hill, who would start in place of Davis and his broken ankle, and Lang were their usual composed selves. And Laettner was . . . well, nobody knew exactly what to expect from him in his record 23rd NCAA Tournament game, nearly the equivalent of another full season playing for Duke.

As Laettner took the floor against the Wolverines, Krzyzewski and his staff could only hope that their star center had recovered from his uneven Indiana game. Against Michigan they couldn't afford another 8-point Laettner performance.

As it turned out, Laettner's play in the first half wasn't as gruesome as the Indiana game; it was worse. He had as many turnovers (7) as points and rebounds combined. Someone had kidnapped Laettner and replaced him with a stiff. The guy who couldn't miss a shot against Kentucky had difficulty making them against Indiana and now Michigan. He was 1 of 6 from the field in the first half of the IU game, 2 of 8 in the first half of the U of M game. Duke had trailed the Hoosiers by 5 at halftime, and now trailed the Wolverines by 1, 31–30. The two Hills and Hurley were keeping Duke in the game.

This time Hurley didn't wait for Krzyzewski to call out Laettner in the Duke locker room. He carpet-bombed Laettner with four-letter words and told him, "You're not here. What are you doing? We need you to win this game."

Thomas Hill assisted in the session. Davis watched in amazement.

"It was the first time and only time Bobby took a leadership stance—where it was audible," Davis says. "That was a big spark. He was fired up, pissed off."

Again, Laettner sat there and took it. And again, Hurley, Krzyzewski, and the rest of the team spent equal time building up Laettner's confidence before the Blue Devils returned to the court.

"By the time we got to Michigan," says Krzyzewski of Laettner, "I thought he was emotionally drained. And in the first half against Michigan, Laettner threw the ball more to Michigan than he did to Duke. Laettner was horrible and I got on him. But the guy who got on him the most was Hurley. And it had an impact. This was the reversal. I took Christian out three different times in the first half, from 'Are you okay?' to blasting him, but it took that little number 11 [Hurley] to get that impact. In other words, it wasn't me who got him out of it; it was Bobby."

Laettner responded with a layup (assist from Hurley) and then a three-pointer (assist from Hurley) in the first 45 seconds of the second half.

With less than seven minutes left in the game, Duke held a 48–45 lead. And then, says Rose, "Grant Hill dunked. I remember looking around and we all had four fouls. That's when they kicked it in."

Says Howard: "Duke was Duke."

Duke outscored Michigan 23–6 in the final 6:51 and won 71–51. The Blue Devils were surgical and merciless. Had it been up to Davis, who gutted out 10 minutes of play on a broken ankle, Duke would have tried to make it a 31-point margin—one point more than the Blue Devils' losing margin to UNLV in the 1990 title game. "We tried to blow them up," says Davis.

Laettner finished with 19 points and 7 rebounds. Thomas Hill, the only Duke player to score in double figures in all six tournament games, had 16 points. Hurley, voted the Final Four Most Outstanding Player, had 9 points and 7 assists. But it was Grant Hill, with his 18 points, 10 rebounds, 5 assists, 3 steals, and 2 blocks, who was the difference in the game. Laettner was the best player in the country, but Grant Hill was the best player on the court that night.

For most of his life, conflicted by his race, his standing, and his family's celebrity, he had tried to simply fit in. Now he stuck out, way out, thanks to a basketball résumé that included his Rock Chalk Tomahawk slam against Kansas an April earlier, a perfect last-second pass to Laettner against Kentucky in the regional, and a signature, defining performance against Michigan. When there was no margin for error, Grant Hill had aced two championship finals and a regional final. Best of all, nobody talked about his 1991 haircut anymore.

The Wolverines forgot how to score and forgot how to defend—not a good combination. And something else happened: Despite their arrogance, brashness, confidence—whatever you want to call it—they had nothing left when the throbbing pressure of a long season and a championship game began to envelop them late in the second half. Trash-talking hadn't worked. The payback theme hadn't worked. Webber and Rose, both weighed down by foul trouble, hadn't worked. Duke knew the feeling. It had been in a similar situation against Vegas in 1990 and it had collapsed, too.

"I can't explain that game," says King. "I can't put my finger on it. After the game I felt so—I was so *tired*. All of the emotions kind of ran out. I'd never felt that way before."

That's because Michigan had never lost that way before. The defeat explained the postgame tears in the Wolverines' locker room. Said Webber: "There will never be another freshman class that will do that again." And 20 years later, he's still right.

Like Pelphrey, Rose didn't watch a replay of his loss to Duke—and still hasn't. The way he figures it, who wants to see their team get T-boned at the Final Four intersection? Rose actually remembers more details of the Duke–Kentucky game than he does of Michigan's game against the Dookies. Selective memory.

"Number one, we got beat by a better team," says Rose. "I think we had to be emotionally fatigued."

Everyone was. Reaching a national championship game with five freshmen starters was almost incomprehensible. But winning consecutive national titles, withstanding the pressures of a season-long No. 1 ranking, and dealing with unprecedented media and fan attention were even more impressive. Duke's players returned to Durham for a celebratory rally at Cameron Indoor and then, at last, shut down their engines. "We were exhausted," says Davis.

Somewhere that evening of April 6, 1992, Bob Knight saw the final score and grunted his approval. He was deeply upset with Krzyzewski for what he at the time considered a personal betrayal, but some habits are difficult to break. Earlier in the day he had called his longtime friend Bob Hammel, sports editor of the Bloomington, Indiana, *Herald-Times*. He told Hammel he was pulling hard for Krzyzewski.

No matter what, Knight always rooted for his guys.

FOURTEEN

April 7, 1992

The day after the loss to Duke, the Wildcats had boarded their charter plane wondering if they had let down their coach, one another, and their fans. They had been 2.1 seconds from restoring Kentucky basketball to its rightful place—the Final Four—and somehow it had slipped through their hands.

They weren't ashamed—they had done their best and were beaten by the best—but the Big Blue Nation doesn't take defeat well. UK fans would surely pick apart the loss like turkey from a Thanksgiving bone. A seemingly safe one-point lead had become an excruciating one-point loss. They had failed.

And then the plane landed at Blue Grass Airport, and several players noticed a gathering of thousands of UK fans lining the fences near the private terminal. The players peered out the windows in amazement. *Don't they know we lost the game?*

The fans cheered. Waved signs. Applauded.

The Wildcats walked off the plane and directly onto a charter bus for the six-and-a-half-mile drive back to campus. And there they were again: more UK fans lining almost the entire route into Lexington.

"It was like the president was in town," says Oliver. "I don't think people understand what that game meant to the people who lived in Kentucky."

The players' jaws dropped. They thought they had lost a game when, in fact, they had won over a state. Even Louisville fans had to grudgingly admit that the Wildcats played inspired basketball against No. 1 Duke.

Oliver drove home and was greeted by his two-year-old daughter, Ashley. *At last,* Oliver thought, *unconditional love.*

Instead . . . "Daddy, you lost game?" she said.

"Yeah, we lost game," said Daddy.

Chris Cameron, as part of his host-school duties, had had to go directly to Rupp Arena to help work the Southeast Regional final between Ohio State and Michigan. Nobody in Lexington cared about that matchup. All anyone talked about that day was Duke vs. Kentucky.

Cameron saw Newton at Rupp later that day.

"I don't think I'll ever get over this," he told Newton.

"You will," Newton said, "but it will take a long time."

A week later, as Newton, Cameron, Pitino, and the Wildcats assembled in early April at a packed Rupp Arena for the annual basketball awards ceremony, there was a growing sense of pride within the program. The memory of the loss still hurt deeply, but there was no denying the game's national impact. The *New York Times* reported that President George H. W. Bush had left the White House the morning after the game for a brisk walk around nearby Lafayette Park and had asked reporters, "Did you see the ending of the Duke game?"

About an hour before the awards ceremony began, Pelphrey was asked to report to courtside for a radio interview. There was a contest to name the 1992 team, and Pelphrey was supposed to go on the air and help narrow down the list of candidates. So he walked out to the court, never bothering to look around, took a seat, put on a headset, and chatted on the air about nicknames.

Kentucky liked naming its teams. The 1948 national champion

Wildcats were "The Fabulous Five," predating Michigan's Fab Five by 43 years. The 1958 national champion Wildcats were "The Fiddlin' Five." UK's 1966 national runners-up were "Rupp's Runts." But what to call a team that not only didn't win a national title, but didn't win a regional?

Radio contest or no contest, Newton and Pitino had already decided on a name. A Ledford comment had been the inspiration. The UK broadcaster told Pitino that it had been an "unforgettable" season—and the word had stuck with the coach.

Meanwhile, Newton had secretly arranged for a surprise addition to the awards program. Only a handful of UK insiders were aware of what was about to happen.

As the team assembled on the floor, Pelphrey figured Mashburn would get most of the awards (and deservedly so). There would be some speeches, some tears, some applause, and that would be that. Pelphrey's UK career would be officially finished.

But after the team awards were handed out (Mashburn was indeed named UK's Most Valuable Player), Newton reached for the microphone and began talking about the ultimate honor at Kentucky. Pelphrey turned and glanced up over his shoulder. *Oh, my gosh!*

Nobody, including Pelphrey, had thought earlier to look at the rafters. Why would they? Kentucky had never retired the jerseys of players who failed to win a championship or compile record-setting personal statistics.

He nudged Feldhaus, who was standing next to him, and said in a hushed voice, "Deron, you're not going to believe this."

"What is it?" said Feldhaus.

"They're going to retire our jerseys. Turn around and look."

Moments later, Newton unveiled the jersey numbers of Pelphrey, Feldhaus, Farmer, and Woods—"The Unforgettables."

"We retire these jerseys in honor of four young men who have been the heart and soul of our basketball program the past three years," said

Newton to the crowd. "Three years ago our basketball program was devastated. Today it is back on top, due largely to four young men who persevered, who weathered the hard times and brought the good times back to Kentucky basketball. Their contributions to UK basketball cannot be measured in statistics or record books."

Newton's gesture made sense because of the complicated nature of Kentucky's unlikely basketball renaissance. Pelphrey, Feldhaus, Woods, and Farmer were immortalized not because of their athletic prowess but because they were loyal when Kentucky's program hung in limbo. Wildcats fans never forget loyalty, hard work, and humility.

The retired jerseys came with a warning label. Says Newton: "I told them, 'If you don't finish your degrees and graduate, the jerseys come down.'"

Degrees were earned. The jerseys—No. 11, Woods; No. 12, Feldhaus; No. 32, Farmer; and No. 34, Pelphrey—remained.

"As ridiculous as the honor is, we always hoped we could just *go* there [to UK]. We let ourselves dream," says Pelphrey.

Oliver couldn't help himself that day. He got misty-eyed. He had tried to break those players. Run them off. But they wouldn't leave. Instead, they broke *him*. He became a believer.

"You go back to the first day we went there and saw those guys," Oliver says. "They beat the odds. Those are guys nobody wanted.

"That [Duke] game—it was their proudest moment. You ask people to name their favorite team, and I'll tell you what they're going to say. They're going to say the Unforgettables. I wish I was one of those guys for one day. In the state of Kentucky, they're gods. You know what, though? They're good boys."

FIFTEEN

2010

Krzyzewski doesn't have much spare time. His meeting with the Duke assistant coaches ran late. A player's personal issue requires his attention. And he has a flight to catch.

"I can give you maybe 45 minutes," he says, not unkindly, as he glances at his watch.

A staff member slips in a DVD of the Duke–Kentucky game. Moments later, the 70-inch SMART Board screen glows to life. Krzyzewski rewinds his memory to 1992 and fast-forwards the DVD to overtime.

First stop: Pelphrey hits a three-pointer to give Kentucky the first of three leads in OT. Krzyzewski freezes the screen as the ball snaps the net.

"A lot of times these guys will be judged by the last play—what Pelphrey may not have done," Krzyzewski says. "But okay, the first shot of overtime [Krzyzewski rewinds the DVD and replays Pelphrey's trey from the top of the circle]—pretty f'in' good. Pretty good. Those four kids around Mashburn were pretty damn good. I'm glad that Kentucky celebrated them so much and didn't take that one play and say, 'If you would have played in front [of Laettner]' and all that kind of stuff."

Krzyzewski leans forward in his chair. He's thinking like a coach, not like someone taking a pleasant video stroll down March Madness lane. He's that guy again, the 45-year-old Krzyzewski of 1992.

Every possession is analyzed. Every situation is explained. Back and forth with the clicker.

"That three-pointer, now there's a lot of pressure on us because this is really a two-possession game," he says. "A three-point shot is really a two-possession lead unless you hit a three-point shot."

Duke commits a charging foul. Krzyzewski pauses the DVD to see which Kentucky player sacrificed his body.

"Okay, Pelphrey hit a three and just took a charge," he says. "I'm not his cousin or anything. I'm not trying to vindicate him, but he did a *lot* of good things."

Krzyzewski nods as Thomas Hill hedges out and plays great help defense as Woods tries unsuccessfully to find a soft spot in the Duke defense. He marvels at Hurley's fearlessness as the point guard misses a three, gets the ball back, and, without hesitation, sinks a trey.

"Talk about big shots," he says.

Pelphrey works his way in front of the basket, fakes out Grant Hill, and lays the ball in over Laettner and Lang.

"See what I'm saying?" says Krzyzewski. "The son of a bitch was the hero, but ends up not being the hero. You know what I mean?"

Krzyzewski has a thin, fond smile on his face as the OT continues. He knows the outcome, but that isn't why he's smiling. He smiles because of the effort of the players, all of them—his and Kentucky's. He can feel it again now. The intensity and purity of the moments. Crowd noise? Krzyzewski says he didn't hear a thing during those final minutes of overtime.

"It was a game where so many kids played great," he says. "Every play in this overtime has been a good play."

Laettner splits a double team and banks the leaner off the backboard for a score.

"Look at that f'in' shot," says Krzyzewski.

Mashburn scores and gets fouled. Krzyzewski pauses and rewinds. Even after all these years he's annoyed that the Blue Devils were slow with their help defense.

Hurley completes a ballsy two-handed pass to Laettner with the game in the balance. Laettner catches it and drives to the basket; Mashburn fouls him and fouls out. All because Hurley took a chance.

"Look at that little shit," Krzyzewski says, laughing. "We're down by one with 19 [seconds] left and he throws it two-thirds of the court. Just watch how he throws it. I would not say he's scared. I mean, how many ways do I love him? Hurley's pass to Laettner—those guys are etched together in time."

Duke trails by one with 2.1 seconds left to play. Grant Hill is alone on the baseline.

"Probably putting a guy on the ball is something I might have done," says Krzyzewski, "but I can see not doing it. Because they didn't have their big guy [Mashburn] in, so they're worried about Laettner down there . . . so trying to double-team is a good strategy. They [Pelphrey and Feldhaus] just ended up being on the sides of him."

Laettner hits the shot for the ages. Lundquist delivers his "Yessssss!" Farmer crumples in front of the Duke bench. Krzyzewski rushes over to embrace him. It was Weber High all over again—Krzyzewski always the first to shake hands with the opposing team.

"I couldn't . . . it's almost like I couldn't stand to see that kid like that," he says.

Almost an hour has come and gone since Krzyzewski began dissecting the overtime. He has to get to the airport. He pauses the DVD as the final score is flashed on the screen.

"Yeah, I get chills thinking about it," Krzyzewski says. "It is just such a cool thing. And how lucky that we were part of that."

Duke: coached by the son of parents whose first language was Polish; its star center from a family of humble means; its point guard from high school basketball royalty; its most gifted player a child of privilege but also of perspective; its small forward virtually ignored by Duke recruiters; its other guard fueled by anger, resentment, and an inferiority complex. The center and the point guard share a like-hate relationship. America has a love-hate thing with the Blue Devils. They get everybody's best punches. And yet it works. And a hard, protective shell of mutual respect forms over the team. They succeed because of and in spite of themselves.

"I'm not saying it would beat everybody in the history of the game," says Krzyzewski, "but that team was one of the greatest teams to ever play college basketball."

And then there is Kentucky: coached by a Yankee workaholic obsessed with the pursuit of perfection; its star recruit willing to take an unprecedented gamble on a program on life support; its roster score-sheet thin; its three original Kentuckians long on UK allegiance but short on talent; its other original member married, for better or worse, to Big Blue. They're too busy fearing Pitino and his strength coach to notice how long a long shot they really are. And yet it works. They succeed because of and in spite of themselves.

"I'll love those guys until the day I leave this world," says Brown, who, in a touch of irony, later became coach of the Dillard University Bleu Devils in New Orleans.

Love. Sounds corny, but it is the tie that binds those teams and those teammates. Laettner still watches replays of the Duke–Kentucky game, but not for the reasons you think. He watches to see how high Marty Clark jumps after The Shot swishes through. He watches to see the joy on the walk-on Ron Burt's face. He watches to see Cherokee Parks's expression change like a stoplight, from high anxiety to exultation.

"They put up with me for the whole year and I was hard on them, but we're all going for the same cause, you know what I mean?" says Laettner. "So much blood, sweat, and tears. So much commitment and devotion. It's such a good feeling, and I literally tear up and am filled with joy and emotion when I see their reactions."

Says Davis: "You feel it to this day. Every March it's that good ol' lovin' feeling."

Laettner has nothing from that game except memories, which isn't such a bad thing. But he wishes he had that ball, that net, and those sneakers.

He was the Asshole then, but there is something conciliatory about his tone now. He did what he thought he had to do back then. He was young; they all were.

Laettner stays in touch with his former teammates, some more than others. In 2009, Hurley and Laettner were among almost two dozen former Blue Devils who returned to Duke as coaches for the K Academy, Krzyzewski's annual basketball fantasy camp. After a few drinks at an evening social function, Laettner and Hurley couldn't help it: They exchanged heartfelt guy hugs.

"Man, we really did it, Laett," said Hurley.

"Bobby, I know. You don't got to tell me. I know."

And so it went the rest of the night.

As Krzyzewski says, Hurley and Laettner are forever linked. They are friends—not like Laettner and Davis, or Laettner and Clark—but they are closer than they were. The scar tissue is almost gone.

"We shared something that is incredible, and as the years go by we're realizing more and more that it was something good," says Laettner. "He realized how important I was to him, and I have always realized how important he was to me—from Day One. That's why I was so hard on him."

Laettner's No. 32 jersey was retired in 1992. Hurley, who named his oldest daughter Cameron ("I'm over the top on that," he says) and still has the scissors the Blue Devils used to snip the nets in '92, saw his No. 11 jersey retired in 1993. Grant Hill's No. 33 jersey joined them in 1994. And even though their career numbers weren't as impressive, you could argue that Davis and Thomas Hill deserve to have their jersey numbers hanging from those same Cameron Indoor rafters. They were part of Duke's unforgettables.

Kentucky's scar tissue remains thick in places, too. Other than the usual array of unavoidable highlights, Pelphrey has never watched a replay.

"I know the ending to that game," he says. "I think with the players and the coach, it's so hard to get certain snapshots out of your head. Only time helps heal it. There's something very traumatic about that game for me. I have no desire to bring those things up."

After his UK career was complete, Pelphrey played professionally in Spain and France. "Trying to get away from it," he says—"it" being Laettner's shot.

When he returned home, his first coaching job was as an assistant on Sutton's Oklahoma State staff. Symmetry. And little by little, 104–103 isn't as debilitating as it once was.

"I'm comfortable with the outcome now," says Pelphrey. "I don't believe anymore that my life would have been better if we'd won and gone to the Final Four."

Oliver, who was best man at Pelphrey's wedding, is no different. No game-tape nostalgia tours for him. Too painful.

"Cannot do it," he says. "Cannot and will not. If it's on, I will act as if I'm from outer space. Now, if I'm in Heaven and my dad is up there and he wants to watch it, then we'll watch it. But I won't watch it down here."

Oliver left Kentucky in 1992 for the NFL, but returned to UK in 2010. He adores everything about being back in Lexington. Everything except March.

"I hate the NCAA Tournament, that time of year," he says. "To be 2.1 seconds away—that feeling comes back in my stomach. You've got to relive that, man. Every year I've got to watch The Shot. I'm afraid of needles, but I'd rather take 10 shots than watch that guy take that shot every year. There's no escaping it. I'm going to have to watch that shot until they put me in the ground."

Martinez has seen the game again. He can't help it. His friends text him whenever it's on ESPN.

"You were on Classic," they'll write.

Gimel's response: "Did we win this time?"

Woods has seen it. So has Feldhaus, but not for nearly 20 years.

On Christmas Day of 2009, the Wazzo Sports Network, based in London, Kentucky, showed the game as part of a UK basketball classics package. And yes, Kentucky, there is a Santa Claus. Wazzo's version of the game ended with Woods's floater and the Wildcats ahead.

Studio host and network vice president Jeff Sheppard, who won two national championships at UK and was voted the Most Outstanding Player of the 1998 Final Four, told viewers that day, "We're not watching that [Laettner] shot again." And they didn't. Instead, Sheppard introduced the next classic game: Kentucky's 86–84 victory in the 1998 South Regional final. Against Duke.

Merry Christmas.

The Shot became a part of popular culture. Chris Farley and *Saturday Night Live* did a sketch on it. Laettner and Pitino years later filmed a lighthearted Vitaminwater commercial playing off The Shot.

In the summer of 1992, a horse by the name of Laettner Be Gone ran at the Red Mile, Lexington's harness track. Sheppard has heard countless stories from UK followers who wept when Laettner's shot swished through. Others sat motionless for hours after the Wildcats' loss, too depressed to move. Others kicked over couches and chairs in anger. Lamps didn't do well either.

"He is the most hated opponent in the history of Kentucky basketball," said Sheppard. Coaches around the country have studied those final 2.1 seconds like generals at the War College. To put a man on the ball, or not put a man on the ball . . . that is the eternal basketball question.

"I would tell you that for all of us in coaching, if we're in that situation, we will put a guy on the ball," says Kentucky's Calipari. "We will now, because I saw what happened. You know what I'm saying? My whole point will be—and I don't care how small my guy is—you won't throw the perfect pass if we're all over you screaming and going nuts. If that's me, I'm putting a guy on the ball because of that play. And even if my guys all fouled out, I'm putting a guy on the ball. I'll put the manager on the ball. Somebody's going on the ball. And that's not to be mean or down on what [Pitino] did."

Says Pitino: "People make too much of it."

True story: At a coaching clinic seven months after the game, Pitino stood on the court discussing length-of-the-floor late-game situations. As about 500 coaches watched, Pitino put 3 seconds on the clock, put a defender on the inbound passer, and then blew the whistle. It was the Duke scenario all over again.

The player made the pass. The other player caught it, shot, and . . . sank the shot at the buzzer. Pitino turned to the coaches and said, "I *knew* I wasn't supposed to put a guy on the ball!"

In the years that followed, Pitino took two UK teams to the national title game, defeating Syracuse in 1996 and losing to Arizona in '97. After that loss, he left Lexington to return to the NBA, as coach and team president of the Boston Celtics. That didn't go over well in Big Blue Nation, a feeling that got worse when he came back to the college game as head coach of Louisville in 2001.

Among those who are willing to rush to his defense is a player Pitino tried to break into a thousand little twangy pieces: Richie Farmer. "I think people, especially UK fans, need to appreciate Coach Pitino for what he did for this program," says Farmer. "We were at an all-time low probably for the program, and I think he was the exact right person for that job at that time. . . . We went from 13–19, being on probation, being here with eight scholarship players to three years later taking the No. 1 team in the country down to a shot that they don't hit one out of a hundred times, maybe more than that."

Time doesn't heal all wounds. In some cases it hides them, nothing more.

"Would I like to play them again?" says Oliver. "Fuuuck. I'd like to play them right now."

About a half dozen years ago, Bilas and Woods found themselves sitting next to each other at a University of North Carolina practice. Bilas was there with ESPN. Woods was there as an assistant coach at High Point University.

Small talk was exchanged, followed by moments of awkward silence. The memories of March 28, 1992, bubbled just below the surface.

Bilas finally asked the question.

"Do you think about it?" he said.

Woods turned to him.

"Only every day."

AFTERWORD

April 2012

Michael Kidd-Gilchrist and Marquis Teague weren't even born when Duke beat Kentucky on March 28, 1992. Anthony Davis had just turned one year old a few weeks earlier. Doron Lamb was four months old. Terrence Jones was almost three months old.

But nearly 20 years to the day of The Shot, this UK starting lineup of three freshmen and two sophomores not only won a national championship, but helped Big Blue Nation put a tiny bit more distance between the past and the present. And by tiny bit, I mean that perhaps fewer Kentucky fans will wear their "I Still Hate Laettner" T-shirts.

I covered the Wildcats from the start of their 2011–12 NCAA tournament run to the end. From the rounds of 64 and 32 in Louisville, to the Sweet 16 and Elite Eight in Atlanta and to the Final Four in New Orleans. Never once did I think there was a team in the entire field better than UK. Not even close.

Krzyzewski's Duke team was in the field. But in a 20-year role reversal, this time Kentucky was the overwhelming favorite to win it all as the overall No. 1 seed, and Duke was a flawed No. 2 seed.

The NCAA selection committee did what it could to put everyone in a time capsule and turn the dial back to 1992. It placed the Wildcats in the same corner of the bracket as the Blue Devils, meaning that if the basketball gods cooperated, UK and Duke would meet in the South Regional final. And just for fun, it even included Pitino and his No. 4-seeded Louisville team in the West Regional bracket. The winner of the South would play the winner of the West in a Final Four semi.

The potential symmetry of it all was almost overwhelming. A Duke-Kentucky rematch on the 20-year anniversary of UK's most heartbreaking loss? A possible coaching collision between Pitino and Calipari—but this time with Calipari as UK's coach—on that same 20-year time line as the March 26, 1992, Kentucky-UMass game?

No fan base supports its team more, and no fan base worries more than that of Kentucky's. The mere thought of facing Duke in the regional final must have thrilled *and* terrified Big Blue Nation. The same holds true for facing Pitino and despised in-state rival U of L.

If UK won . . . a sense of retribution, even revenge against Duke. But if it lost . . . there would be no way to quantify the basketball pain.

Instead, the unthinkable happened: Duke, which entered the postseason as the all-time leader in NCAA Tournament winning percentage, lost its opening round game to No. 15 seed Lehigh, 75–70. Kentucky fans howled with delight.

The Lehigh upset deprived the tournament of a UK-Duke 20-year class reunion—that is, if the Blue Devils could have even made it that far. They would have had to have to beaten Xavier in the next round and then survived the über-athletic Baylor Bears in the Sweet 16. Considering the inconsistent play of Duke—and a late-season injury to starter Ryan Kelly—it was a 50/50 proposition. Lehigh made it a 0/100 possibility.

Meanwhile, Kentucky continued its scorched-court policy, flicking away Western Kentucky by 15, Iowa State by 16, Indiana by 12, and Baylor by 12. But even as UK won, Wildcat fans still held their now-legendary grudge against Duke.

It usually happened during pregame warm-ups, or during halftime, or during a time-out. The arena or stadium big screen would show a pre-programmed trivia question or highlight involving a Duke player. And wherever Kentucky was playing during the tournament—Louisville's

Yum! Center, Atlanta's Georgia Dome, New Orleans' Mercedes-Benz Superdome—UK fans would instantly boo and hiss at the sight of Grant Hill, Hurley, or worst of all, Laettner. And you needed ear protection when the big screen showed a replay of The Shot.

Duke didn't reach the Final Four in 2012, but Pitino did. His Louisville team squeezed its way past Davidson, New Mexico, West No. 1 seed Michigan State, and then Florida, which was coached by Pitino's former UK assistant, Donovan. So the tournament didn't get Duke-Kentucky, but it got perhaps the next best thing: Pitino vs. Kentucky and Calipari.

Pitino and Calipari, anything but friends, played nice during the news conferences leading up to the Final Four semi, but the Commonwealth was a mess. A 71-year-old U of L fan punched a 68-year-old Kentucky fan at a Georgetown, Kentucky, dialysis clinic. They were arguing over who would win the game.

The Louisville fan won the fight, but Kentucky won the game, beating Pitino's Cardinals by eight points. Louisville had its chances, but it didn't have UK's talent. Nobody did.

The Kentucky roster was built around Davis, a 6'11" freshman center whose defensive skills transformed the team. He blocked shots. He altered shots. His mere presence convinced some opposing players to not even *attempt* shots. He demoralized anyone who wandered into the lane.

Kidd-Gilchrist, another freshman, played every second of every minute as if his scholarship depended on effort expended. He had come to UK from St. Patrick High School in Elizabeth, New Jersey, a survivor of personal tragedy and hardship. And, in a six-degrees-of-separation thing, Kidd-Gilchrist had lost the state championship to Hurley's old man and old school: Bob Hurley Sr. and St. Anthony.

Teague, the freshman point guard, came to Kentucky from Indianapolis. He overcame his early- and mid-season jitters and developed into a deceivingly efficient player.

Jones, the sophomore power forward, could dominate a game when sufficiently interested. At times during the tournament, he did exactly that. And Lamb, the sophomore guard, provided UK with double-digit scoring.

There were others—senior guard Darius Miller, in particular—who made a profound difference on those Wildcats. But when you remember this national championship team, you will always recall how frighteningly young and talented it was—and how it was together for only a single, brilliant season.

Only several weeks after Kentucky defeated Kansas in the title game, all five UK starters declared themselves eligible for the NBA draft. Davis scored exactly one field goal in the win against the Jayhawks, but it was his other work (16 rebounds, 5 assists, 6 blocks, 3 steals) that earned him the Final Four Most Outstanding Player honors. Unibrow was the only choice for the award.

Anyway, there are one and dones, and then there are one and dones who actually do something. Davis, Kidd-Gilchrist, and Teague did something; they helped Kentucky win its first national title since 1998.

I'm not sure some Kentucky followers will ever forgive Laettner for that turnaround jumper at the buzzer. I introduced myself and handed a copy of the hardcover version of this book to actress and UK alum/superfan Ashley Judd during halftime of one of the NCAA tournament games. She took it as if it were radioactive, as if she needed a hazmat suit and tongs to handle it. She dropped the book in her oversize purse, said something about her desk being "closed for the year," and then walked away.

I have two theories about her reaction: she thought it was a TV or movie script, or she could see the book cover through the thin plastic bag—the book cover featuring Laettner and The Shot.

Twenty years—and counting—have passed since that game, that season, that Duke championship team and those UK Unforgettables. Krzyzewski, Pitino, and Calipari were all part of that NCAA East Regional in late March of 1992. And they remain a part of college basketball today.

A new banner celebrating UK's 2011–12 national title now hangs from the rafters of Rupp Arena. But no matter how many championships Kentucky and Duke win in the future, those two programs will forever be linked by a long ago night at the Spectrum in Philadelphia.

As it should be.

—Gene Wojciechowski

ACKNOWLEDGMENTS

Had it not been for little John David Spatola, this book would have never been written. Or more correctly, it would have never been written by me. It would have been authored, and wonderfully so, I'm sure, by Jamie Spatola, the youngest daughter of Duke coach Mike Krzyzewski.

But Chris and Jamie Spatola had a newborn son about the same time Jamie completed work on a similar Duke–Kentucky proposal. Something had to give, and John David won out. Meanwhile, I became the father of a bouncing baby book project. The joys of adoption, eh?

I covered the 1992 college basketball season and NCAA Tournament for the *Los Angeles Times*. In my 30 years as a sportswriter, the Duke–Kentucky East Regional final remains the best game I have ever seen in person . . . in anything. It's the best game a lot of people have ever seen. I know this because they offer, without prompting, every detail of where they were and how they reacted when Christian Laettner beat the clock—and Kentucky—with The Shot.

If nothing else, there has been no college hoops game like it. I have DVD and VHS copies and watch it before the start of every March Madness. And I still find myself inching toward the edge of my seat.

It was the kind of game where the people who played in it, who coached it, who watched it were, in varying degrees, forever changed by it. It was a game, yes, but it was also a rarity. It was a time when you could root for both teams.

The game has almost attained drinking age now, but I always thought it deserved its own 20th anniversary party. Luckily, so did those associated with the game and with those two proud programs, Duke and Kentucky.

My favorite Laettner book moment came at a Mediterranean restaurant near his home in the Jacksonville, Florida, area. As he waited for his dish of hummus to arrive, I made my pitch for extended interview time. Said Laettner: "I can talk about myself all day."

And he could. And did. The more he talked, the more it became evident that he has two loves in his life: his family and Duke basketball. Not only did Laettner give me lots of quality time, perspective, and candor, he also helped arrange other interviews with family and Duke teammates. And who texts a writer to see if they need any more help with the project? Laettner did. He was the book's MVP.

The Krzyzewski family also gets varsity letters. Mike Krzyzewski squeezed me into his cramped schedule during two separate visits to Durham, including one during his 2010 championship season. He, wife Mickie, and daughters Debbie and Jamie were incredibly generous with their time and their insights. Duke basketball is the ultimate mom-and-pop shop, and I mean that in a good way. Family means something there.

Speaking of family, the Hurleys went far beyond the call of duty. My thanks to Bob Sr., Bobby, and Dan. Bobby watched a DVD of the game with me and provided play-by-play analysis (as did Krzyzewski). He also showed me a modest trophy case in his house that contains priceless Duke memorabilia, as well as a baseball he's had since he was 11. It still has his handwriting on it: *April 18, 1982. Home run was over the right center field fence*. That's Hurley—never afraid to swing for the fences.

The Laettner family—George, Bonnie, and Chris—were extremely gracious and helpful, even during the many follow-up interviews. The same holds true for Grant Hill. On a rare NBA off day, Mr. Nice Guy drove to my hotel in Scottsdale, Arizona, plopped down on a couch, and answered questions for hours, even though I had asked for only 45 minutes. My apologies to his wife, Tamia—Grant was too polite to say he had to go. And my thanks to his parents, Calvin and Janet, for their interview time.

Brian Davis's nickname is "The Mayor." It's true; he should run for office. I didn't want the interview to end.

Equally candid and remarkably giving of their time were his teammates Thomas Hill, Antonio Lang, Kenny Blakeney, and Marty Clark. My many thanks also to former Duke assistant coaches Pete Gaudet, Mike Brey, and Tommy Amaker, as well as former managers Mark Williams and Ashok Varadhan. Staff members Sonny Falcone, Dave Engelhardt (now retired), and Mike Cragg also provided invaluable detail (Cragg, for years, has provided invaluable friendship, too). And former athletic director Tom Butters, who rightfully has a building named after him at Duke, gave me an oral history lesson on the Krzyzewski era.

Longtime Duke play-by-play man Bob Harris couldn't have been more helpful. And Krzyzewski's best friend, Dennis Mlynski, escorted me on the Coach K Way-Back machine, as did Mike Siemplenski.

Former Duke players Jay Bilas (an ESPN colleague who could make a living just off his imitation of Krzyzewski), Kenny Dennard, and Alaa Abdelnaby, in particular, gave me considerable interview time. Jason Williams and Ricky Price also offered quality Krzyzewski-related input. And special thanks to Duke assistants Steve Wojciechowski (who gave up a promising ABC Afternoon Movies production career for coaching) and Chris Collins for their many insights. I'd want my son to play for either one of them.

Also of considerable assistance were Duke's Jon Jackson, Matt Plizga, Art Chase, Kevin Cullen, and Ben Blevins. And the staff of Duke's Rare Book, Manuscript, and Special Collections Library found box after box of research material for me during my campus visits.

Rick Pitino was no less cooperative or giving of his time during my trips to Louisville. He agreed to two separate interviews and discussed every facet of the Kentucky rebuilding project. I can't thank him enough for his hospitality and kindness. Or Louisville SID Kenny Klein, who helped arrange them.

The Unforgettables—Richie Farmer, Deron Feldhaus, John Pelphrey, and Sean Woods—were unforgettably gracious with their time and recollections. The memories of those seasons and that game still create strong emotions for them. They were kind enough to share those feelings and memories with me. And yes, I could understand every word of Farmer's eastern Kentucky accent.

Jamal Mashburn gave me not one but two sit-down interview sessions. He won't say it, but others will: without him, there might not have been the Unforgettables. What a gentleman.

I owe very large thank-you notes to the other UK players I spoke with: Dale Brown, Gimel Martinez, and Travis Ford. Pitino's coaching staff at the time—Herb Sendek, Billy Donovan, Tubby Smith, Ralph Willard, and Bernadette Mattox—happily and enthusiastically agreed to interview requests. And for the record, good luck finding a better coaching staff than the ones Pitino assembled during those early years at Kentucky.

If there is a nicer man than C. M. Newton, I'd like to meet him. He answered every question, and then some. But I'd expect nothing less from a fellow Fort Lauderdale High School Flying L (coincidence: Lauderdale High's fight song music is the same as Kentucky's).

Dr. David Roselle was gracious with his time and quick with his e-mail follow-ups. He, Newton, and Pitino provided the infrastructure to help rescue UK basketball during some very dark days.

Pelphrey's mom, Jennie, and his brother, Jerry, represented the family well in interviews. Jennie was a sweetheart.

Bill Curry, one of my favorite people on the planet, still astounds me with his ability to tell a story. And he told stories galore about Pitino's kindnesses to him.

Jerry Tipton and Oscar Combs were on the UK front lines back then, and they shared their many experiences.

Eddie Sutton, who found post-UK success and contentment at Oklahoma State, gave me quality time when he didn't have to. Helluva coach.

I'm convinced that if you cut open a vein on Rock Oliver's forearm, it would bleed blue. He and Duke's Davis reminded me of each other: so full of passion and compassion for their programs.

And a very special thanks to Chris Cameron, the former UK sports information director. I didn't bother him less than 10,000 times during the project. And each time his response was the same: He never tires talking about those UK players, those coaches, and those times.

Current Kentucky coach John Calipari, who still marvels at the effort and performance of that 1992 UK team, shoehorned me into his in-season schedule. And DeWayne Peevy and John Hayden of the UK media relations staff were generous with their assistance, as were the kind people of the Big Blue Sports Network. And thanks, too, to former UK player Jeff Sheppard.

Three of Michigan's famous Fab Five offered their considerable time and perspective. Juwan Howard even interrupted a trip to the movies to call and talk. Jimmy King was outstanding. And Jalen Rose, another ESPN'er, never shied away from any question. The book is better because of their candor.

The 1992 CBS mafia—Verne Lundquist, Lesley Visser, Len Elmore, Jim Nantz, Craig Silver, and Robin Brendle—held my hand as I asked a series of Broadcasting 101 questions. What I like best about them (other than their obvious expertise) is that they seem genuinely appreciative of having been able to witness that season and—in the case of Lundquist, Elmore, Visser, and Silver—the Duke–Kentucky game in person.

Also adding thick layers of expertise were the great Bob Ryan, Dick Vitale, Bob Hammel, Rick Majerus, Jerry Tarkanian, Dick Weiss, and P. J. Carlesimo.

I thank game officials Tim Higgins and Tom Clark for their multiple interview sessions. And I remain appreciative of the help provided to me by Howard Garfinkel, Ike Richman of Comcast-Spectacor, and Wake Forest's Mike Lepore.

I owe much to Steve Wulf and Gary Hoenig, who championed the proposal cause. It's hard to go wrong when a writer as gifted as Wulf is your first-edit safety net.

This book wouldn't have been written without baby Spatola, but it wouldn't have been published without John Skipper. Even more impressive: He's a Tar Heel and he *still* green-lighted a Duke book. Anyway, he made miracles happen. He does that a lot.

John Walsh's fingerprints can be found on pages of this book—and that's always a good thing. The same can be said of Penguin Group president and publisher extraordinaire David Rosenthal. I'd never won the Lotto—until he signed onto the project and paired me with editor Jeff Neuman. If you asked Neuman to edit the back of a cereal box, he could make it sound literate. He made this book better. Much better.

ESPN.com editor in chief Rob King and executive editor Patrick Stiegman were their usual supportive selves. Ditto for senior editor Michael Knisley.

My friend first and agent second, Janet Pawson, steered me in the appropriate directions. She has impeccable instincts, but better yet, a laugh to die for. I still don't know how I got so lucky. And ditto for Michelle Hall, also of Headline Media.

Rick Reilly, Bill Plaschke, and Pat Forde are like those smart kids in math class who can solve any equation. I would call and draw the problem on the board, and they would figure out the answer in, oh, two minutes. Without them, I'd still be on chapter one.

A salute also to Ivan Maisel, John Marvel, Phil Rogers, Mike Downey, Rick Morrissey, Mark Kazlowski, and Beth Cecil.

My brother, Joe, didn't do much on the project except transcribe the better part of 82 interviews (most of them ungodly in length), offer handfuls of wise advice, laugh at all the right places, and talk me off high ledges. Sometimes I wonder who's really the older brother.

T. L. Mann, as always, was his strong, silent self. And daughters Lara and Taylor were incandescently wonderful during a long year of writing.

Books are hard to write. The only thing harder to do is to live with someone writing the book. That would be my wife, Cheryl, who still knocks me silly with her eyes, her smile, her South Side Chicago accent, and the sacrifices she makes during these projects. I keep waiting for her to plunge a knitting needle into my back, but instead she says things like, "I really want to watch the OT of that Duke–Kentucky game." Better yet, she sounds like she means it. Cheryl isn't my better half; she's the better seven-eighths.

In early 2011, a wrecking ball began turning the Spectrum into a pile of indistinguishable rubble. It was demolished to make room for a "retail, restaurant and entertainment district" called Philly Live. Sigh.

I was there in late 2009 when Pearl Jam played the final gig at the place, a four-night farewell that began October 27 with "Corduroy" and ended October 31 with "Yellow Ledbetter." Now *that* was a proper good-bye.

I walked the entire concourse that night, just for old times' sake. On one of the arena suite doors was a photograph of Laettner during the '92 Duke–Kentucky game. And before Eddie Vedder and the fellas took the stage, a commemorative video of the Spectrum's finest moments was shown on the arena big screens. Grant Hill's pass to Laettner made the cut.

Not long before the wrecking ball performed its grim duty, the public was allowed one final look inside. For $25, you could take part in the "If You Can Carry It, You Can Keep It" festivities. In short, a cut-rate estate sale.

Forget chairs, signage, toilet seats . . . whatever. I know what I would have grabbed and carried.

You got it: the Laettner photo.

NOTES

Unless otherwise specified, the material in this book is the result of my own interviews (listed in the Acknowledgments), research, and coverage of past college basketball events, such as the 1992 NCAA Tournament.

If the word "says" is used in conjunction with a quote, the words come from my interviews for the book, giving the speaker's thoughts and reflections today, which may or may not benefit from the passage of time. Statements made twenty years ago are indicated with some version of the past tense (e.g., "said").

When quotes were given in a group-interview setting, such as post-game press conferences or media days, I did not attribute those remarks to a specific publication. In those cases, "told reporters" is the operative attribution.

Facts and figures, such as scoring averages, records, schedules, etc., were found in an assortment of resource material, most often in the NCAA database or school media guides.

The remainder of the exclusive material is noted below.

CHAPTER ONE

10 *always has been*: Academy of Achievement interview, May 22, 1997. Achievement.org.
13 *spat on the second-place trophy in disgust*: "Blue Angel," *Sports Illustrated*, March 16, 1992.
14 *other than helping my mom and me*: John Feinstein, *A Season on the Brink* (New York: Macmillan, 1986), p. 104.

15 *"He's the only winner they have over there"*: "Floundering Duke Hosts Terps Today," *Washington Post*, February 16, 1980.

21 *"from something like that"*: "Battle for Tobacco Road: Duke vs. Carolina," *HBO Sports*, February 2009.

CHAPTER TWO

28 *"there are going to be some tough times"*: Associated Press, April 28, 1989.

35 *could come at any minute*: "P. J.'s Heart in New Jersey," *Newsday*, April 30, 1989.

38 *as many as two seasons*: "Dodging a Bullet," *Sports Illustrated*, May 29, 1989.

42 *"It didn't happen in Hawaii as far as I'm concerned"*: "Leaning This Way Or . . ." *Newsday*, May 24, 1989.

42 *"throughout his entire head coaching career"*: Associated Press, May 23, 1989.

43 *"That's yesterday's news"*: "Kentucky Enters Era of Optimism," *USA Today*, June 2, 1989.

CHAPTER THREE

62 *"I've won and lost a few myself"*: "Duke's Laettner Arrival," *Washington Post*, March 27, 1989.

63 *"We're not going to have Quin and Danny and John anymore"*: "Duke Succeeds Despite Stress and Injury," *New York Times*, March 31, 1989.

63 *win a national championship as Blue Devils*: "Hometown Title Is Snyder's Goal," *Miami Herald*, April 2, 1989.

63 *"But I'm not going to let it possess me"*: "Duke Succeeds Despite Stress and Injury," *New York Times*, March 31, 1989.

64 *"But we did"*: "Teary End to Ferry Ride," *Newsday*, April 2, 1989.

CHAPTER FOUR

67 *"it's certainly not good for our league"*: Associated Press, May 19, 1989.

69 *the answer was zero*: "Pitino Makes Preparations at Kentucky," *St. Louis Post-Dispatch*, September 3, 1989.

88 *"the Rick Pitino era begins"*: "Hey, Rick, Happy New Year!" *Newsday*, October 16, 1989.

96 *"Do you want me to call a time-out for you?"*: "Kansas 150, Kentucky 95: 1989 Rout of Wildcats Unforgettable in Jayhawks Hoops Lore," *Lawrence Journal-World*, January 1, 2005.

CHAPTER FIVE

108 *"now you'll never see me play"*: "On Defense at St. Anthony's," *USA Today*, October 6, 2002.

114 *UNLV coach Jerry Tarkanian*: "What Fight?" *Orange County Register*, December 8, 1989.

118 *"fake enthusiasm"*: *Raleigh News & Observer*, March 5, 1991.

120 *"if they didn't do so much talking"*: "Runaway!" *Sports Illustrated*, April 9, 1990.

CHAPTER SIX

134 *"we won the championship"*: Associated Press, March 2, 1991.

134 *"They've got Kentucky back on top"*: *1991–92 University of Kentucky Basketball Guide*, p. 118.

CHAPTER SEVEN

141 *Little Grant did headstands there*: "The Son Is Shining," *Sports Illustrated*, February 1, 1993.

155 *floor burns on his bloodied knees*: *Eastern Basketball*, March 1991.

158 *"I like the toughness of my team"*: *Charlotte Observer*, March 4, 1991.

158 *"whiny faces out there today"*: *Greensboro News & Record*, March 11, 1991.

159 *innocent chalkboard*: "Indy Qualifying," *Sports Illustrated*, March 25, 1991.

160 *"and they're going home"*: Ibid.

161 *on about 400,000 pieces of mail*: Associated Press, April 4, 1991.

161 *"So what the hell are we doing here?"*: "Yes!" *Sports Illustrated*, April 8, 1991.

165 *"We've got one more game; don't forget that"*: "Vegas Another Team to Win One in a Row," *The National*, April 1, 1991.

166 *"You think you're too big right now"*: *New York Post*, April 3, 1991.

167 *"We finally got it for you, baby!"*: *Greensboro News & Record*, April 3, 1991.

168 *"When will we do it again?"*: "Yes!" *Sports Illustrated*, April 8, 1991.

CHAPTER EIGHT

178 *"We are not"*: Associated Press, November 23, 1991.

CHAPTER NINE

192 *said recruiting guru Bob Gibbons*: *Raleigh News & Observer*, October 23, 1990.

192 *could barely recall the ceremony*: *UCLA Bruin Sports Extra*, March 1992.

194 *"That's just him"*: "Laettner Teaches the Art of Replacing Himself," *Los Angeles Times*, November 14, 1991.

194 *"every day in practice"*: Ibid.

194 *Whatever, dude*: *The Chronicle*, November 26, 1991.

195 *walk-on since 1987*: *The Chronicle*, October 17, 1991.

196 *"is that we didn't die"*: *The Chronicle*, December 6, 1991.

203 *U of M defensive rotation*: "Mouths in the Middle: Now It's Time to Motor," *Seattle Post-Intelligencer*, April 6, 1992.

203 *"that was excellent"*: *The Chronicle*, January 31, 1992.

206 *"I got a big X on my calendar"*: *United Press International*, November 23, 1991.

207 *"we're a different team"*: *The Chronicle*, February 21, 1992.

CHAPTER THIRTEEN

267 *"spell his name"*: "Boys to Men," *Sports Illustrated*, April 6, 1992.

274 *"going to do with me"*: "Win or Lose, Webber to Have Fun," *USA Today,* April 6, 1992.

CHAPTER FOURTEEN

281 *"ending of the Duke game?"*: "Kentucky and Duke: As Good As It Gets," *New York Times*, March 30, 1992.

283 *"in statistics or record books"*: *1992–93 University of Kentucky Basketball Guide*, p. 164.

CHAPTER FIFTEEN

290 *Lexington's harness track*: "The Shot Heard Round the World," *Sports Illustrated*, December 28, 1992.

INDEX